THE LITERATURE OF LABOUR

By the same author

Marxistische Literaturkritik in England (ed.)
Caudwell im Kontext
The Socialist Novel in Britain (ed.)

THE LITERATURE OF LABOUR

Two Hundred Years of Working-Class Writing

H. Gustav Klaus
Reader in English and Acting Professor
University of Osnabrück

ST. MARTIN'S PRESS   New York

ISBN 0-312-48805

Library of Congress Cataloging in Publication Data

Klaus, H. Gustav, 1944–
  The literature of labour.

  Bibliography: p.
  Includes index.
  1. English literature—History and criticism.
2. Labouring class writings, English—History and
criticism.   3. Labour and labouring classes in literature.
4. Labour and labouring classes—Great Britain—History.
I. Title.
PR120.L33K55   1985   820'.9'3520623   84–17711
ISBN 0-312-48805-X

Dedicated
to two members of my family
who fought and suffered for their socialist convictions

Heinrich Prinz
who was imprisoned under Bismarck's anti-socialist laws

and

Johanna Kirchner (1889–1944)
who was beheaded by Hitler's executioner

CONTENTS

PREFACE

The Literature of Labour owes its title to a branch of social
history which by now can boast an enviable record of research
and conference activities but remains virtually ignored by
literary scholars. If one of the stimulating insights of this
discipline over recent years has been the recognition that
labour history is more than just the history of the labour
movement, the implication for the study of the literature of
labour is that it cannot content itself with considering only
the solid achievements of this tradition nor, another error,
concentrating exclusively on periods of social disturbance
and revolutionary manifestations. Nothing less than a reconstruction of the origins and growth, the breakdowns and
weaknesses of this literature is the task of this still new field
of research.

Yet, in another sense, its object of study resembles that of
the old labour history; for just as the organisers and organised of the working-class movement were always a minority,
so working-class writers and even readers never numbered
very many. What is more, often the fighter and the writer
(whether as pamphleteer or poet, autobiographer or novelist) were one. But right from the beginning we also
encounter the a-political author who remains aloof from, or
even hostile to, the labour movement. And the study of the
literature of labour cannot afford to brush their efforts aside.
Nor can it leave out the massive contribution of writers not
born into the working class, but bringing a seriousness of
concern, an acceptance of the subjectivity of the working
class and of its objective role in the historical process, to
their presentation of proletarian themes.

The historian of this literature must, then, examine the
forgotten volume of poetry by the obscure artisan and the
often-quoted memoir of the well-known radical, the anonymous militant pamphlet and the 'quiet' novel of working-
class life. For this project neither the condescension of the

scholar trained in the 'great tradition' nor the triumphalist superior attitude of some latter-day socialists will be helpful.

The literature of labour as a global term thus covers plebeian, working-class, proto-socialist and socialist literature, as they emerge and unfold alongside the making and re-making of the working class. The 'two hundred years' of the subtitle are meant to challenge lazy notions about the existence and history of this kind of writing. Since the present book opens with an examination of the impact of Stephen Duck's *The Thresher's Labour* (1730) on other plebeian authors, another fifty years might easily have been added, were the last examples of working-class writing considered here not taken from the 1930s but from contemporary literary practice.

Even among the nucleus of critics in Britain, who have lately taken an interest in this literature, there still seems to be a tacit understanding that it is only the works of this century, and of the 1930s in particular, that matter. Very few studies have reached back beyond the First World War—the only exception being the towering position accorded to *The Ragged Trousered Philanthropists*, though this work is typically regarded as an isolated phenomenon rather than the crest of a wave of socialist novel-writing that rose in the 1900s.

However, to assert that the literature of labour has its origins in the eighteenth century and that there is a considerable amount of memorable and still powerful or moving work of an older stamp waiting to be examined or even re-issued, is not the same as saying that we are dealing with a tradition of unbroken continuity. While it is true that, certainly from the 1820s onward, no decade is without its significant contribution to this kind of literature, such literary efforts sprang in most cases from isolated initiatives and were seldom connected with previous literary endeavours by working people, even if the breakthrough of a 'poet of the poor' could inspire his fellow workmen and women long after his death.

The only sustained attempt in the nineteenth century to construct a tradition of 'democratic' poetry and connect it with an ongoing literary production is to be found in the columns of the Chartist press. The fact that no comparable popular progressive lineage of novel-writing seemed available, together with a general distrust of fiction especially prevalent in Owenite circles, may be one reason for the long abstention of Chartist writers from the novel. When they eventually moved into this field, they wavered between a melodramatic and a historical mode, the latter eventually gaining the upper hand (see chapter 3). And yet a thoroughgoing search and investigation of the buried prose of the period 1790–1840 might still reveal a dotted line of radical fiction, starting with the Jacobin novelists and Woodhouse's quite different 'Novel in Verse' (see chapter 1), including the utopian works examined in chapter 2 and linking up with the early Chartist tales of William James Linton and Thomas Doubleday—though to see it in this perspective may concede too much to generic fixations.

The essays collected here have been written on different occasions for different purposes. The method of presentation varies accordingly, from expository and historiographical to argumentative and evaluative. Though arranged in chronological order, they lay no claim to cover the ground evenly or systematically. The second half of the nineteenth century is particularly thinly represented. This reflects to some extent the general state of research into the subject. Of no period is our knowledge of working-class and socialist writing more deficient.

In their differing procedures these essays ought, then, best be read as options within a field of possibilities open to the student of the subject. At the same time, they might also be taken as paradigmatic forays into unknown territory: the account of coalminers' writing, for example, may serve as a call to investigate the literature of other industries; the excursion into a neglected area of utopian fantasy as an appeal to study other modes of writing (historical fiction, political verse, and so on).

Methodologically, none of this is new, except perhaps for the inherent belief that the literature of labour deserves and repays the same kind of painstaking and dedicated study that scholars have reserved for the mainstream tradition. The range and variety of the material and hence the need for detailed enquiry cannot be emphasised too strongly.

A reviewer of the preceding collaborative volume *The*

Socialist Novel in Britain asked whether the underlying
intention behind the recovery and consideration of such
'obscure' literary areas, texts and problems is addition to the
established literary canon or its replacement by a different
lineage. I would put the issue in somewhat different terms.
The necessary reassessment of English literature as a whole
cannot be carried out without substantial knowledge of the
traditions and movements that have been erased from the
map of literary history. Within this total national heritage
the literature of labour represents a distinctive current
which, through its connection with the formation and history
of the working class, requires particular attention, not only
because in it we find articulated the ideas, values and feelings of the largest class in society, but also because a future
transformation of society along socialist lines is bound to
revalue the uses made of literacy by its pioneers. In this
sense, obviously, any selective tradition posing as a canon
which excludes large areas of recorded human experience
and communication on account of class-bound assumptions
about Culture and Literature cannot go unchallenged.

But the real issue seems to me to lie elsewhere, in the
relationship between the dominant tradition (part of which
may have been received into the canon) and the (manifest
or latent) countervailing tendencies with which the major
working-class compositions are imbued. It is in exploring the
nature of this complex, interpenetrating and yet, 'in the last
instance', dominant relational process that we get to the
heart of the literary culture of a period. Without the inclusion of alternative or opposing literary practices, in so far as
they exist in any significant strength at any given historical
moment, no account of the wider writing-reading relations
of a period is complete or adequate.

Just as the concept of literature needs to be as all-
embracing as possible so as to include the rich areas of pamphleteering and memoir-writing (see chapter 4), we need a
wide perspective of sympathetic working-class representation as we move into the twentieth century. The last chapter,
dealing with the documentary wave of the 1930s and 1940s,
is not exclusively or primarily concerned with literature. To
give the new media their proper due—film, photography and

broadcasting, which figure prominently here, were then still comparatively new—is not to join the chorus of the end-of-the-book prophets. I for one would conjecture that the activity of book-reading will retain its usefulness and, more relevantly, its aesthetic attraction alongside the new forms of reception made available by the electronic media. Instead of lamenting the decline of the book culture, scholars with an interest in cultural artefacts should respond imaginatively to the growing differentiation and specificity of aesthetic expressions which these technological innovations effect.

Several people read and commented on one or other of the chapters in this book. I owe personal thanks to Andy Croft, Ulla Jasper, John Rignall, Kiernan Ryan and Ian Watson for pointing out awkward or misleading statements and formulations to me and thus forcing me to re-write certain passages with, hopefully, greater clarity.

I have also profited from questions asked by colleagues and students who heard earlier versions of some of the chapters delivered as papers: at the Sociology of Literature Conference in Essex, at Aalborg and Roskilde Universitetscenters, at the English Institutes of Odense and Copenhagen Universities, at the Technical University of Hannover and, last but not least, my own institution, the University of Osnabrück.

The usual acknowledgements are due to the following publications in which portions of this book appeared in different form or in another language: 'Plebeian Poets in Eighteenth-Century England', *Zeitschrift für Anglistik und Amerikanistik* (Leipzig), vol. 31 (1983); 'Harold Heslop: Miner Novelist', *Anglo-American Studies* (Salamanca), vol. 2 (1982); 'Socialist Novels of 1936', *1936: The Sociology of Literature,* vol. 2: Practices of Literature and Politics (Essex, 1979); 'Let the People Speak for Themselves', *Gulliver* (West Berlin), vols. 4 and 6 (1978–9). For the present edition all the articles have been revised and updated.

H. Gustav Klaus

1 PLEBEIAN POETS IN EIGHTEENTH-CENTURY ENGLAND

In Carl Philipp Moritz's *Travels Chiefly on Foot, through Several Parts of England in 1782*, the young German writer and teacher often seems to be impressed by the high standard of education among the lower classes of society:

> My landlady, who is only a tailor's widow, reads her Milton and tells me that she first won her late husband's affection by her excellent recitation of Milton. This single case would prove nothing, had not I myself met several people from the lower classes who all knew their national authors and some of whom had read their works. . . . In Germany there has been no poet since Gellert who has had a name among the common people.[1]

Moritz's observation is quite commonplace in contemporary travel literature on England. As early as 1758 Samuel Johnson had noted that 'All foreigners remark that the knowledge of the common people of England is greater than that of any other vulgar.'[2]

However, almost without exception these commentators took only one aspect of literacy into consideration—the receptivity of the labouring poor. But, in fact, the really remarkable thing about their desire for education is that they were no longer prepared to remain mere passive observers of the literary life but aspired to take an active, creative part in it. By turning their hand to literary creation of their own, a considerable number of artisans and agricultural labourers (both men and women) showed that they intended to move beyond the orally transmitted popular forms like the song or ballad, which had up to that time been the sole vehicles of literary expression for the common people.

The literary public of the eighteenth century reacted to the aspirations of these authors partly with astonishment, partly with amusement. A 'suitable' name was quickly found for the phenomenon which gave expression to its deviation from the prevailing norm: 'uneducated poets'—not versed in classical ideals, which were considered the essential background to a literary career. The patronising condescension apparent in this label is also characteristic of the critical treatment of these poets during the following two hundred years, in so far as they were afforded any attention at all.

It is only in our time that Unwin and Ashraf have referred instead to peasant or rural poets.[3] Although these are unbiased terms, they are not quite accurate, as many of the writers of verse were artisans and urban dwellers. The term suggested here, plebeian poets, is an attempt to encompass the whole spectrum, and includes poets from all strata of the lower classes, both before the Industrial Revolution and during the period of transition.

The question of terminology is, however, the least of the problems to be overcome in dealing with the work of these poets. As they have largely been omitted from the literary histories and anthologies of verse, it is first of all necessary to give substantial contours to our object of study. This is done here by concentrating on the works of the English (rather than the Scottish or Irish) representatives of this tradition.[4] Their contribution is of enough consequence to justify this limitation.

The two waves of plebeian poetry

Any consideration of eighteenth-century plebeian poetry must begin by acknowledging the enormous influence which Stephen Duck yielded over his literate fellow-workmen. It is interesting that this poet should have had something of a revival over the last decade or so,[5] but by and large this renewed interest in *The Thresher's Labour* comes from a rereading of the pastoral tradition, in which Duck is offered as an obstinate counter-example, a spokesman of the 'anti-pastoral'.[6] While such an approach makes sense up to a point, it remains inadequate as long as it does not take into account the dawning of a plebeian literature, which found its first exponent in Duck. The literary breakthrough of this poet inspired at least four other contemporary craftsmen and labourers (Banks, Collier, Frizzle, Tatersal)—not to mention those inspired later—and these are only those who made their voices heard, i.e. whose work was also published. The real number is almost certain to have been far greater. A combination of fortunate circumstances—attracting the attention of a local scholar, finding a patron and so on—was necessary before any lines written during or, more likely, after work could find their way to the printing presses. This may also account for the time-lag between the first immediate response to Duck (Banks, 1730) and the last one to emerge in the 1730s (Collier, 1739).[7] Mary Collier, moreover, actually claims that for a long time she had resisted any suggestion to publish what she had composed for her own pleasure, and for recitation to friends and workmates.[8]

Not all were so modest. The poor thresher's unprecedented rise doubtless served as an incentive for his successors. Until his twenty-fifth year, Duck (1705–1756) had worked as a farmhand in Charlton, Wiltshire, his weekly wages amounting, according to the title page of one of the first pirated editions of his poetry, to no more than 4s. 6d. This information is not altogether reliable, just as 1705 may not be the true year of his birth.[9] There can, however, be no doubt that farm labourers' wages in Wiltshire, and in the west of England as a whole, were among the lowest in the country.[10] Overnight, the versifying thresher was discovered, celebrated as a genius, summoned to Court by the Queen and provided with a small house, complete with an annuity. He, who had been craving for an education, was now offered the standard 'diet' of the age: classical languages, learned treatises, polite literature. Professionally, the outcome was that he became a clergyman; artistically, a disciplined poet, regularly producing dull, stylised verse, modelled on contemporary neo-classical poetry.

Those labourers who followed Duck's career with fascination could not anticipate these consequences. Nor could they foresee that many years later the author would drown himself in a river; whether in a fit of mental derangement or not is still in question. In any case, his fate seems to indicate that the transition from rags to riches, from farmhand to preacher, from plebeian to scholarly poet, was not without its stresses and strains. The case of Duck, with its combination of literary success and social advancement, aroused the emotions of the educated classes of the eighteenth century just as much as those of the literate labourers and artisans.

The reactions of the upper classes will be dealt with later. Of major interest here are the literary references to Duck by his plebeian fellow-writers, present in significant profusion. Their leitmotif is evoked in the motto which introduces Robert Tatersal's volume of poetry *The Bricklayer's Miscellany*:

> Since Rustick Threshers entertain the Muse
> Why may not Bricklayers too their Subjects chuse?[11]

In other words, what a thresher can do, a skilled bricklayer can do just as well. The arrogance manifest here has its roots in the structure of the working population, which in the first half of the eighteenth century can be divided into three classes of differing status:[12] the highly skilled and relatively well-paid craftsmen and artisans, including printers, tailors, watchmakers and skilled workers in the building trade; next, the still apprenticed but lesser-paid textile trades, glaziers, leather-dressers and the like; and finally, at the lower end, labourers of all descriptions, amongst them transport workers, farmhands and miners. As members of the latter group were not considered to follow a recognised trade, but were, indeed, hired on a short-term basis or, as in the case of the miners, bound by yearly contracts, they were by contemporary standards not in possession of their birthright as 'freeborn Englishmen'.[13]

Therefore Tatersal's 'model' was two steps lower down the social ladder than he himself. In keeping with this, the bricklayer boasts in another passage of the highly skilled nature of his trade:

> And Why not *Bricklayers* exercise their Quill,
> Whose Art surmounts a Country Thresher's still:
> A *Flail*, a *Trowel*, Weapons very good,
> If fitly us'd and rightly understood;

> But close engag'd, beware the *useless Flail*
> The Trowel then can terribly prevail:
> If *Threshers, Millers,* entertain the Muse,
> Why may not *Bricklayers* too their Subjects chuse?[14]

The miller alluded to here is a John Frizzle from Enniskillen
in Ireland, who in the meantime had published some verses
in *The Gentleman's Magazine* and had addressed them to
Duck:

> O *Stephen, Stephen* if thy gentler Ear
> Can yet a rustick Verse unruffled hear,
> Receive these Lines, but look for not much Skill,
> Nor yet for Smoothness, from a Water-Mill.
> I near the Hopper stand with dusty Coat,
> And, if my Mouth be open, dusty Throat.
> The Stones, the Wheels, the Water make a Din,
> Hogs grunt without, or squeeks a Rat within
> To mediate sweet Verse is this a Place?
> . . . .
> And can I write? ah! make my Case your own,
> A Miller Poet let a Thrasher own.[15]

To Duck, who was meanwhile settling down to life at Court
and anxiously trying to live up to the expectations of his
patrons, those following his example and seeking his favour
must have been more of an embarrassment than anything
else.

There is certainly evidence that many were envious of
Duck, favoured by the Muses and protected by the Queen as
he was. However, it is misleading to speak, as Davies does,
of a 'sordid greediness' or, like Kovačević, to impute that the
actions of the writers were governed by opportunism.[16] No
doubt an important aspect of their writing, though hardly
the only motive, was to give vent to the desperate wish,
hopeless though it seemed to be, that they, too, might rise
above their station in life, a life of drudgery under degrad-
ing, underpaid conditions. This ambition is expressed most
frankly in Tatersal's poem 'The Author's Wish', which con-
cluded his first volume of poetry:

> Had I a Competence to suit my Will,
> One hundred Pounds should my Request fulfil;

> Could I each Year this Stipend once receive,
> Describe my Muse the Manner how to live;
> Exempt from Cares I'd learn to be content,
> And ne'er regret what Heav'n to me hath sent.[17]

Then he visualises the house, the furniture, a wife and the garden, and imagines the leisure hours spent fishing, riding and reading, not forgetting his creature comforts. But all this has little to do with ill-will and greediness. Tatersal's basic attitude is one of natural materialism, finding fulfilment in this life. The end of his daydream goes like this—and here we have, in fact, the key to understanding not only this poem, but others also:

> Ye Gods cou'd I so kind a Fate enjoy,
> No more these Hands the *Trowel* shou'd employ,
> *Mortar* and *Bricks*, no longer wou'd I chuse
> But cleanse those *Limy* Badges from my Muse.[18]

The land of milk and honey portrayed here is meant as an imaginary counterpart to the daily drudgery which the writer describes so strikingly elsewhere.

Whereas Duck and the consequences of his success form one wave of plebeian poetry in the eighteenth century (the 1730s), the second phase, occurring in the last quarter of the century, is not governed by any single figure or publication date. From the 1770s onwards a number of authors emerge, obviously independently of each other, and in the following decade there are many (Bryant, Woodhouse, Yearsley) who were not merely the literary one-day wonders characteristic of the interim period. At the same time, several differences are apparent in this new movement. Apart from Duck, the poets of the first phase were only able to publish one or two volumes of poetry, whereas now Bloomfield, Woodhouse and Yearsley managed to produce an impressive number of works. A further difference is that for the first time they turned to other literary forms. Ann Yearsley wrote a historical drama and a four-volume novel in the Gothic genre. James Woodhouse left an autobiographical 'novel in verse'.[19] It testifies to a greater confidence in their artistic abilities that these authors became more prolific and more various in their literary efforts. Up till then only Duck had—thanks to his position as the Queen's protégé—been successful, but now several poets (Bloomfield, Woodhouse, Yearsley) tried, if not actually to live from their writing, at least to create an existence for themselves other than a proletarian one which hindered any intensive pursuit of a literary career. To avoid any misunderstanding it is important to stress that these literary laurels brought no prosperity. After a brief period of fame, Yearsley and Bloomfield lived in modest circumstances; and Woodhouse ended his days as an impoverished bookseller. However, the determination with which these authors pursued their vocation is an expression of strengthened self-confidence and most certainly proof that envy and opportunism were not the most decisive factors in making them turn their hands to writing.

Social determinants of plebeian poetry

It is noteworthy that of the ten writers considered here two are female. The ratio of women to men among the aristocratic and bourgeois writers of the period is not any higher.[20] As for occupations, the list is headed by cobblers (Bloomfield, Bennet, Lucas, Woodhouse), but agricultural workers of one kind or another figure as frequently (Bloomfield, Collier, Duck, Woodhouse, Yearsley), although most of these were only temporarily employed on the land. Apart from Tatersal, there was one other writer who worked as a bricklayer from time to time. There is one pipemaker (Bryant) and one silk-weaver (Banks). This shows that literary talent seems to have been evenly distributed among the different sections of the working population.

Some regional peculiarities are conspicuous. More than half of the plebeian poets came from the rural areas of the west of England (Bennet, Collier, Duck, Lucas, Woodhouse, Yearsley), one from Suffolk (Bloomfield), and three from London and its immediate surroundings (Banks, Bryant, Tatersal). To make the geographical position clearer: not one came from an area north of the line from Birmingham to Norwich. Woodhouse's Rowley (Regis) in Worcestershire

was the point furthest from London. It would certainly, however, be incorrect to conclude from this that illiteracy was
more widespread among the craftsmen of the north. In spite
of our fragmentary knowledge of the extent of literacy
among the lower classes, this assumption can only be considered valid for the seventeenth, but no longer for the eighteenth century.[21] Evidently, however, the further away from
the south they lived, the less likely it was that the common
people would find ways of taking an active part in literary
life.

Not all regions seem to have been able to profit to the
same extent from the non-renewal of the Licensing Act of
1695, which was a decisive precondition for the growth of
the reading public, even though parliament did not justify
this move on the grounds of the freedom of the press but
gave economic reasons for the lifting of restrictions in the
printing and newspaper trade. It is true that there were now
printing-presses in the provincial towns, whereas during the
period of censorship these had been concentrated in London
and the two university cities, and for the purpose of more
effective control had been kept very limited in number.[22] It is
equally true that newspapers and periodicals were now being
published in all the bigger towns. And yet evidence seems to
suggest that the south of England, and the potential plebeian
poets residing there, benefited most from the upsurge of
literary life. In any case, the volumes of poetry written by
our authors were not all published in London, but in Bristol
(Yearsley), Birmingham (Woodhouse), Oxford (Bennet),
Salisbury (Lucas) and Winchester (Collier).

But how did the poems of a cobbler or farm-labourer
reach the hands of a publisher? In most cases the poetic
talent was discovered by a local scholar—frequently a country parson—who took the poet under his wing. This protec-
tor—whose interest itself reflected the wider public interest
in literature and who was again more often found in the
south—did not act as an open-handed benefactor but was
rather a kind of bridge between the author and the publishing trade. He found prospective customers for the literary
product, who agreed in advance to purchase a copy and thus
supplied the necessary financial guarantees for the printer-

publisher. This method known as subscription, has been characterised by Arnold Hauser as the historical link between old-type patronage and production for an anonymous market:

Patronage is replaced by the publishing houses; subscription, which has most aptly been described as collective patronage, forms the transition between the two. Patronage is a purely aristocratic form of relationship between writer and public; subscription loosens the ties but still preserves certain aspects of the personal nature of this relationship.[23]

Most of the poetry volumes under review thus contain a list of subscribers, often with as many as two hundred names. (The frequency with which certain names reappear would be worth an analysis in itself.) The case of Duck, who had found a direct benefactor in Queen Caroline, was then exceptional; subscription was the rule. Even though subsequently some members of the aristocracy and gentry still gave their personal support to poets from among the common people—Shenstone and Mrs Montagu offered Woodhouse a post, Hannah More and later the Earl of Bristol became the patrons of Ann Yearsley, and the Duke of Grafton helped Bloomfield out—historically speaking patronage as such was in decline from the third decade of the eighteenth century onwards.[24] On the other hand, publication for an audience completely unknown to the author—an impersonal relationship corresponding to the principle of commodity exchange—was first to become general practice in the Romantic period, and was then to give rise to the well-known reactions of dissatisfaction and annoyance of the Romantic artist. The period in which the plebeian poets emerged lies in between and thus constitutes a unique situation. By the first half of the nineteenth century the situation would have changed for prospective working-class writers, some of whom would then be able to publish their work in the journals of the labour movement.

A final factor of some importance for the evolution of plebeian poetry was the considerable degree of literacy among working people—as was illustrated by the introductory quotation. According to recent estimates, the literacy rate amongst the labouring classes alone (excluding urban artisans) remained at the time fairly constant between 35 and 40 per cent, except for a drop in the third quarter of the century.[25] It is, of course, tempting to associate the two waves of plebeian poetry with the two major literacy campaigns of the eighteenth century, the first wave in emulation of Duck with the charity school movement at the beginning of the century, the second with the rapid development of Sunday schools from the 1780s onwards.

In the charity schools the children of the poor were instructed in reading, writing and arithmetic as well as trained to be humble and submissive. Under the guardianship of the Society for Promoting Christian Knowledge many such schools were founded, although here again there was a greater concentration in the south of England and in the cities, particularly London.[26] There is no way to measure the success of these schools. But an interesting side-effect is that loud laments could be heard from certain sections of the ruling class, bewailing the fact that the production process was losing valuable labour power. At least two of our poets—Duck and Woodhouse—attended charity schools for some time.[27] We know, however, that it was years later in private study that both of them developed what literary skills and knowledge they possessed. In the case of the two woman poets, Mary Collier and Ann Yearsley, there is no evidence that they ever enjoyed any formal education.[28]. Both were taught to read and write at home, in the family. It would therefore be rash to conclude that there is a close connection between the religiously and philanthropically motivated instruction of the working people from above and their own attempts at literary articulation.

This is also true of the second phase of the literacy campaigns, which took place under the banner of the evangelical revival. According to the founder of the Sunday school movement, the guiding principle of his educational institutions was 'establishing notices of duty, and practical habits of order and decorum, at an early stage'.[29] The aim was clearly, by training in punctuality and diligence, by drumming parts of the catechism and suitable quotations from the Bible into the heads of the poor, to contain pauperism, which was gradually getting the upper hand. Purely quantitatively the results of the Sunday schools look impressive: in 1797 there were nearly 70,000 pupils in more than 1,000 schools.[30] It is, however, part of the dialectic of such mass instruction that it is not possible to judge its qualitative effects exactly. As the anonymous threatening letters to the rich and mighty show, for example,[31] at least some of the beneficiaries of this education were in a position to lead their newly-acquired abilities of articulation into quite different channels from those ever imagined by the fathers of the charity and Sunday schools.

Main themes of plebeian poetry

Two central concerns need to be singled out for discussion: the portrayal of work and the proclamation of a literature with laws of its own.

Possibly Duck's greatest merit is his intuitive recognition that work is a theme worthy of literary treatment. *The Thresher's Labour*, written while he was still a casual labourer in Wiltshire, offers a vision of man's relationship with nature which goes beyond a mere celebration of the latter's blessings. Nor does the poem content itself with presenting those tilling the soil purely as agile and cheerful fellows in the background, but actually focuses on their working conditions:

> Divested of our Cloaths, with Flail in Hand,
> At proper Distance, Front to Front we stand:
> And first the Threshal's gently swung, to prove,
> Whether with just Exactness it will move:
> That once secure, we swiftly whirl them round,
> From the strong Planks our Crab-tree Staves rebound,
> And echoing Barns return the rattling Sound.
> Now in the Air our knotty Weapons fly,
> And now with equal Force descend from high;
> Down one, one up, so well they keep the time.
> .   .   .   .
> But when the scorching Sun is mounted high,
> And no kind Barns with friendly Shade are nigh;
> Our weary Scythes entangle in the Grass,
> While Streams of Sweat run trickling down apace.[32]

His complaint about the monotony of agricultural labour serves to remind us that boring, routine work did not come into being with the advent of the factory:

> Week after Week, we this dull Task pursue,
> Unless when winn'wing Days produce a new;
> A new, indeed, but frequently a worse![33]

Read again through twentieth-century eyes, it sounds like a modern evocation of work on the production line, when the author deplores that the farmhands have no respite from their labour; they cannot forget it in their leisure time, at night or even in their dreams:

> Nor, when asleep, are we secure from Pain;
> We then perform our labours o'er again;
> Our mimic Fancy ever restless seems;
> And what we act awake, she acts in Dreams.
> Hard Fate! our Labours ev'n in Sleep don't cease;[34]

Never before had there been such a truthful description of workaday routine in verse. But Duck does not confine himself to a depiction of his own situation and—remarkably enough—that of his workmates; he also provides a frank and unembellished portrait of the capitalist landlord:

> The Threshal yields but to the Master's Curse.
> He counts the Bushels, counts how much a Day;
> He swears we've idled half our Time away:
> 'Why, look ye, Rogues, d'ye think that this will do?'
> 'Your Neighbours thrash as much again as you'.[35]

The climax comes at the end when the harvest festival, which generations of pastoral poets had celebrated as the reconciliation of master and servants before God, is exposed as a great delusion:

> Our Master, joyful, at the pleasing Sight,
> Invites us all to feast with him at Night.
> A Table plentifully spread we find,
> And Jugs of humming Ale to chear the Mind;
> Which he, too gen'rous, pushes round so fast,

> We think no Toils to come, nor mind the past
> But the next morning soon reveals the Cheat,
> When the same Toils we must again repeat;
> To the same Barns must back again return.[36]

Though it has nowhere been granted such a status, *The Thresher's Labour* is a landmark in the history of English poetry. I know of nothing else written in the first half of the eighteenth century which comes anywhere near its realistic representation of everyday working life and the relationship between capitalist (landlord) and (agricultural) labourer. Never before had a poetic speaker renounced the 'I' perspective in favour of the solidary 'we' and thus made himself the mouthpiece of all those on whose shoulders the rural order rested. The work from the mainstream tradition which comes closest to such a portrayal is James Thomson's cycle on the seasons, which appeared at about the same time. But worlds separate the unadorned presentation of agricultural labour in Duck's poem and the view expressed by Thomson:

> Now swarms the village o'er the jovial mead—
> The rustic youth, brown with meridian toil,
> Healthful and strong; full as the summer rose
> Blown by prevailing suns, the ruddy maid
> Half naked, swelling on the sight, and all
> Her kindled graces burning o'er her cheek.
> Even stooping age is here; and infant hands
> Trial the long rake, or, with the fragrant load
> O'ercharged, amid the kind oppression roll.
> . . . .
> while heard from dale to dale,
> Waking the breeze, resounds the blended voice
> Of happy labour, love, and social glee.[37]

Thomson admits that the work is hard, but refuses to look too closely, and toil is transfigured into 'happy labour'. Even such a brief comparison illustrates what a radical break had been made with the pastoral tradition, a break triggered by Duck's example, but by no means limited to his poem.

The popularity of *The Thresher's Labour* with his immediate successors is proof enough that Duck had exploited a thoroughly proletarian theme in this poem.

Without exception succeeding writers present poetic images of their respective working conditions, and while none achieves the intensity, the tangibility and the range of their predecessor, they complete and enrich Duck's tableau. In comparison with the latter's deadly serious and bitter account, Tatersal, for example, presents a decidedly lively and bluntly humorous view of the behaviour of the brick-layers during their morning and lunch breaks:

> And now precipitant away we steer,
> To eat our Viands, and to get some Beer;
> Where midst the Clamour, Noise, and smoky Din
> Of Dust, Tobacco, Chaws, and drinking *Gin*,
> The short Half-hour we merrily do spin
> When for Desert some with their Sun-burnt Fists,
> Cram in a Chaw of Half an Ounce at least,
> And then to sweep the Passage clean within,
> Wash down their Throats a Quartern full of *Gin*.[38]

To Mary Collier (1690–176?), who took offence at Duck's unflattering passages on the work of the 'prattling Females, arm'd with Rake and Prong', we are indebted for one of the first, if not the very earliest, literary commentaries, in which the triple burden of working women—wage-labour, housework and the rearing of children—is clearly recognised and resented:

> When Ev'ning does approach, we homeward hie
> And our domestick Toils incessantly ply:
> Against your coming Home prepare to get
> Our Work all done, Our House in order set:
> *Bacon* and *Dumpling* in the pot we boil,
> Our Beds we make, our Swine we feed the while;
> Then wait at Door to see you coming Home,
> And set the Table out against you come;
>   .   .   .   .
> Our Children put to Bed, with greatest Care
> We all Things for your coming home prepare:
> You sup, and go to Bed without Delay,
> And rest yourselves till the ensuing Day;
> While we, alas! but little Sleep can have,
> Because our froward Children cry and rave;[39]

In her courageous reply to Duck, who quite obviously did not include the female agricultural workers in his 'we', Collier tentatively approaches another form of solidarity: a sisterhood of the poor, of working women.[40]

In the second wave of plebeian poetry the theme of work was no longer of such significance, although in *The Life and Lucubrations of Crispinus Scriblerus,* Woodhouse does give a detailed account of his various duties as steward on Elizabeth Montagu's estate. Similarly Bloomfield illustrates the errands and duties of *The Farmer's Boy* in his poem of that title. However, the experiences are robbed of much of their immediacy by the tendency of these poets—as, for example, Ann Yearsley—to make the poetic expression of their own experiences more abstract and distant by using the third person singular: the speaker is no longer a participant, but has become an onlooker.[41] Accordingly, this figure remains more isolated instead of channelling his or her individual experience into a feeling of solidarity like Duck and Collier. Yearsley and Bloomfield were doubtless aware of the representative character of their experiences, as can be seen from their letters.[42] However, the poetic resources at their disposal proved to be an obstacle to a more direct, concrete and realistic message.

Apart from the theme of work, the second significant subject of plebeian verse is the discussion of those views which denied the poor the right to create their own literature. This defence of the right of agricultural labourers and craftsmen to their own literature, which occurs more frequently in the second wave of poetry, seems to be a reaction to the rejection they experienced after the initial curiosity of the public in their work had been satisfied and their literature had lost its novelty value.

These literary works were the object of carping and malicious criticism from the very beginning. Even Duck aroused the envy not only of his social equals. But it was his successors who were subjected to the full impact of sneering hostility. The *Grub-Street Journal* of 1731 passed judgement of John Banks:

The poor Weaver has been tempted to neglect his business, by Stephen Duck's good fortune . . . the best way to encourage the weaver would be . . . to wear the manufactures of Great Britain; and the most suitable encouragement to the thresher would be to give him a small farm in the country; laying both under an absolute restraint never more to write a line of verse.[43]

Others who went along with the prevailing opinion did not judge the literary efforts of the poor quite so harshly, although the knowledge that poetry was as infectious as smallpox (according to Richard West in 1737)[44] did make them rather uneasy. *The Monthly Review* of 1778 deemed it presumptuous that any tailor, cobbler or weaver should have the impudence to compose rhymes and feel them worthy of public attention.[45] Even the greatest minds of the century were not above jumping on this bandwagon. 'They had better furnish the man with good implements for his trade, than raise subscriptions for his poems', was Dr Johnson's comment on Woodhouse. 'He may make an excellent shoemaker, but can never make a good poet.'[46] And it was in the same spirit that the ageing Walpole indulged in a fit of malice when, referring to Ann Yearsley, he remarked: 'Am I in the wrong for thinking that these parish Saphos had better be bound 'prentices to mantua-makers, than be appointed chambermaids to Mesdemoiselles the Muses!'[47]

Of all the plebeian poets John Lucas was the most eloquent in his response to these criticisms. In a simulated dialogue with a well-meaning friend, which functions as an 'apology' for his only volume of poetry, he takes up the admonition that a shoemaker should stay at his last:

> Philo, forbear, nor waste your time
> In reading, or composing rhyme;
> Think on the low, the abject sphere
> You are ordain'd to act in here,
> Nor hope to raise on wings of fame
> From dark obscurity your name.
> But granting this, that you succeed,
> Does any gain from it proceed?
> Will fame content the hungry Muse,
> Or give the naked wretch some cloaths?[48]

The author counters these rebukes with his determination to surmount the dark powers of ignorance and error in spite of

fear of poverty and occasional doubts about his poetic
talent:

> Wisdom's my wish, my soul's desire,
> To her I ardently aspire.
> However low or mean the sphere
> By Providence assign'd me here.[49]

In this way the author refutes several objections, including
the opinion that a lack of education is an insurmountable
handicap for a self-taught poet. He makes it unequivocally
plain that wisdom does not depend on a classical education
and that poetic talent is not a monopoly of the educated
classes. Any amount of knowledge remains a dead letter
unless it is inspired by a 'spark of true celestial fire'.

His poem 'The Author to his Muse' demonstrates clearly
that Lucas tackles his poetry from a quite different standpoint than the learned critics approach it. He admits his lack
of formal schooling without any trace of inferiority:

> For me, I cannot boast the rules
> Which learned masters teach in schools;
> The useful rules of grammar clear,
> Alas! they never reach'd my ear,
> Yielding instruction how to write
> Correctly, elegant, polite.[50]

Correctly, elegant and polite—this triad of terms sums up
the taste and principles adhered to by the Augustan poets.
At the same time, however, the speaker makes it understood
that he does not feel bound by these precepts and by no
means accepts them as the basis for literary creation.

In one form or another we constantly come across the
rejection of pedantic criticism of the poetic imagination of
the working people. Ann Yearsley considers that the established set of rules for the composition of verse limits and
stifles the flights of 'Capacious sentiment'. In the poem 'On
Genius Unimproved' she recommends to an 'unlettered
Poet' that he should ignore all these rules and regulations
and give free vent to his inspiration and creative urge, which
she holds to be present in greatest abundance in 'untaught

Minds'.[51] Her own artistic sensibility she described in a similar way, as unbridled by any formal discipline and control.
Many years earlier, Mary Collier had reacted with indignation to the insinuation that a member of the lower classes,
and a woman at that, could not possibly be the author of 'A
Woman's Labour'.[52] And James Woodhouse distanced himself from the established poets of the day in a challenging
comparison, by designating himself the 'Unpension'd Poet-
Laureat, of the Poor'.[53]

The two topics outlined here are neither the only ones,
nor those most frequently taken up by the plebeian poets.
Many deal with biblical and religious subjects, and others
look at classical antiquity. But, from the point of view of a
criticism concerned with the gradual evolution of working-
class literature, they are the themes which point towards the
future, as well as being the subjects which most obviously
reflect the personal sphere and experiences of the writers
themselves.

The relationship between plebeian literature and the bourgeois-aristocratic tradition

As Mary Ashraf says, working-class literature, including its
early, plebeian stages, 'is not an autonomous entity in the
total national culture', although, on the other hand—as our
review suggests—'neither is it a mere appendage' of the
former, 'nor does it follow a completely parallel course'.[54]
The question is how plebeian poetry fits into the literary
scene of the eighteenth century, and how it relates to the
development of the dominant bourgeois and aristocratic
literature.

This complex relationship can only be touched upon here,
but three points in particular are worth bringing to the fore:
1. the problematic circumstances of literary success; 2. the
choice of literary genre; and 3. the increasing interest of the
upper class in the common people.

1. Although in itself an understandable and necessary aim
of the plebeian poets, the struggle for appreciation from a

readership whose interests had nothing in common with their own was full of difficulties, as Southey remarked in his *Lives and Works of the Uneducated Poets* as early as 1831:

A process, indeed, is observable, both in the verses of Woodhouse and Stephen Duck, which might be looked for, as almost inevitable: they began by expressing their own thoughts and feelings, in their own language; all which, owing to their stations in life, had a certain charm of freshness as well as truth; but that attraction passes away when they begin to form their style upon some approved model, and they then produce just such verses as any person, with a metrical ear, may be taught to make by a receipt.[55]

This only applies to Woodhouse to a limited extent. Southey does not appear to have been acquainted with the author's voluminous later work. In the case of Duck, however, conformity to the classicist ideal of poetry had indisputably disastrous consequences. Those who discovered and sponsored Duck and others were never merely content to smooth out irregular grammar and punctuation, but wished to bring about an orientation on current models and the adoption of established forms and conventions. Although individual writers tried to resist this and sought to find their own forms, the pressure towards aesthetic integration (particularly during the Augustan Age) was too strong for the poetic and intellectual capacity of the plebeian poets to be able to escape its effects.

2. Their choice of literary genre makes this particularly obvious. The plebeian writers chose to write verse and thus uncritically accepted the established precedence of this genre over other literary forms. (As mentioned above, it was only towards the end of the century that individual writers tried their hand at other genres.) But also within the sphere of poetry itself, they initially respected the given preeminence of the epic and dramatic forms as opposed to lyrical writing. The result was twofold: on the one hand, there was a preponderance of long, reflective and narrative poems (especially evident in the many imitations and adaptations of subjects taken from the Bible and the Ancients); and on the other hand, a neglect of forms like the sonnet, song or ballad. (The latter form was, of course, in disrepute during

the first half of the century precisely through its association with the vulgar.) It was only in the second phase that in a few cases (Yearsley, Bloomfield) the poetry became more lyrical, subjective and 'enthusiastic', a trend presumably going hand in hand with the lessening rigidity on the established literary scene. So, once again, the plebeian poets were merely following tendencies which had been initiated by the forerunners of the Romantics. The impression therefore remains that even though they were opposed to certain elements of established poetic theory, they were still rooted in it. And that is why their works do not represent a completely autonomous current within the development of the national literature. This does not mean, however, that the authors ignored the possibility of incorporating differing poetic devices, forms and techniques into their works (we know, for example, that it was Duck's intention to write *The Shunammite* in blank verse, but on comparing his first attempts with Milton, he decided that his language was not sublime enough and reverted to the use of couplets),[56] nor does it imply a blurring of the differences between the poetry of the plebeian writers and that of the dominant tradition. The point is that these differences were primarily of content and message; they cannot be shown to exist, and ought not to be sought, on the level of formal composition and technique.

3. The sensational success, both in Britain and beyond her borders, of Bishop Percy's *Reliques of Ancient English Poetry* is just one indication of the growing interest from above in the common people. This work not only brought about the rehabilitation of the folk ballad, but also finally opened the way for the composition of artistic ballads. Yet the attitude of the representatives of the dominant tradition remained throughout ambivalent: on the one hand, they were prepared to look for talent and even genius among the common people—and this gave the plebeian poets a chance; on the other hand, they cultivated a certain image of the 'primitive genius', which had precious little to do with the reality of the common man in the eighteenth century. It is, therefore, only a superficial contradiction when Hannah More, the patron of Ann Yearsley, tried untiringly to find subscribers in order to launch her discovery, but at the same

time did everything in her power to prevent Yearsley from making a career out of her writing. These are two complementary sides of a paternalism—here, and in the relationship between Elizabeth Montagu and James Woodhouse, exercised by women—which can tolerate no opposition, no independence and no subjectivity. The ideal was the naive cobbler sitting at his last or the modest milkwoman, occasionally inspired by the muse. Removed from their inherited station in life, these curiosities were no longer objects worthy of interest. Such a patronising and condescending attitude was, of course, sooner or later bound to wound the dignity and self-esteem of those involved. Thanks to Woodhouse and Yearsley, who had the chance and the courage to articulate their feelings in print, we get an idea of what patronage meant on the receiving end.[57]

2 EARLY SOCIALIST UTOPIAS IN ENGLAND 1792–1848

In the historiography of English utopias, or at least in that part of it which takes its orientation from literary history, the first half of the nineteenth century is not held in high regard.[1] It is seen as a sterile period which produced no works of distinction, nor any significant developments in the utopian form. The sober writings of Robert Owen or the systematised model institutions and organisational forms propagated by English and French utopians of the period, are cited as evidence that the gradual evolution of the utopian genre had come to a standstill at this point, and that, instead of developing from the discursive form of rational argument towards a full-blown fictional form, utopian literature had become subject to the massive intrusion of propagandistic elements.[2] A relatively narrow understanding of utopian fantasy, which centres upon its literary manifestations in novels and short stories, thus leads to the suppression and neglect of almost all utopian projects conceived in the age of the Industrial Revolution.

Another commonly held view is similarly ill-equipped to promote closer scrutiny of the utopian phenomena of this era. One main strand within Marxism, summed up by the (German) title of Friedrich Engels's *Die Entwicklung des Sozialismus von der Utopie zur Wissenschaft* (The Development of Socialism from Utopia to Science),[3] tends to denounce the utopian imagination of the period 1792–1848 as effusive and immature; with the rise of scientific socialism, it is seen to have forfeited any just claim to exist.[4]

Against the background of this widespread unfamiliarity with our object of study,[5] it is necessary, in any reconstruction of utopian ideas in this period, first to present their individual representatives and works, before undertaking a summary in which the material can be ordered and evaluated.

Thomas Spence (1750–1814)

Thomas Spence has enjoyed something of a renaissance in recent years;[6] he is counted by historians amongst the pioneers of agrarian socialism. Certainly his plan for the confiscation of landed property and its use for the common good had an important influence on sections of the English labour movement, from the National Union of the Working Classes of the 1830s through Chartism to Hyndman's Social Democratic Federation at the end of the nineteenth century. This plan, which he advocated, with occasional refinements, for some forty years, can legitimately be seen as the core of his political thought. At the same time, it is possible to discern three further categories of his work which were no less politically motivated than the first. To some extent, the contents of these categories overlap: writings in linguistics, in which he sets forth the advantages of a phonetic alphabet; political songs and poems; and finally, his utopian sketches.

In all these texts, most of which are very short, Spence uses simple, but powerful language; he has the ability to write incisively and with humour, and shows particular skill in his choice of pithy titles. *One Penny Worth of Pig's Meat*, the title which advertised his best-known publication, was an allusion to Edmund Burke's infamous phrase, the 'swinish multitude'—a multitude to which, as one of nineteen children of a poor Newcastle family, Spence himself belonged. He spent his entire life in penury; it was only with difficulty that he was able to scrape together an existence by working as a clerk and teacher in Newcastle. Even after his move to London at the beginning of the 1790s, his situation failed to improve. On the contrary, it worsened; for he placed himself repeatedly in the direct line of fire of state authorities, either by distributing republican writings, which were officially classified as subversive, or through his membership of radical organisations. In the course of the next decade, Spence was arrested and interrogated no less than seven times. Admittedly, he was usually released again a short time later, although he once remained interned (in 1794) for seven months without trial, and was imprisoned for a year in 1801. Far from breaking his rebellious spirit—as had been the case

with other English Jacobins (Thomas Hardy, John Thelwall
and others)—these measures on the part of the State
apparatus clearly had the opposite effect on Spence. His
position seems merely to have been consolidated by the
experiences of these years.[7]

The author's political aspirations, as well as his understanding of himself as a member of the common people, are evidenced by the audience he addressed in his writings. *Pig's
Meat*, for example, explicitly states on the title page that it is
'intended to promote among the Labouring Part of Mankind
proper Ideas of their Situation, of their Importance, and of
their Rights'.[8]

Pig's Meat was also the magazine in which Spensonia,
later defined as 'a country in Fairy-land, situated between
Utopia and Oceana', was introduced for the first time. In
1794, two utopian texts appeared in *Pig's Meat, The Marine
Republic* and *A Further Account of Spensonia*.[9] Spence had
published a work which could be characterised as utopian
as early as 1782—*A Supplement to the History of Robinson
Crusoe, Being the History of Crusonia*, one version of which
was based on his new phonetic orthography. Nevertheless,
there is some justification for considering the various plans
of Spensonia, which were written in the wake both of the
French Revolution and of the formation of a radical mass
movement in Britain, as the more fully developed utopian
works, especially since the phase 1792–1803 represents the
most prolific period in the author's life.

The Marine Republic opens with an allegory. A father,
now advanced in years, call his sons together and reveals to
them his intention to bequeath a ship which he owns, not to
one individual son, but to all of them equally. They are also
to consider ships which they acquire in the future as common
property, dividing such proceeds as may accrue from trade
fairly amongst themselves.

The sons pledge to adhere to these principles, and incorporate them into a written constitution which is also to have
validity for future generations. Yet, committed as they subsequently become to their model shipping enterprise, they
nonetheless have prolonged difficulties in enduring the clearly
unfavourable political conditions of their home country.

Having thus resolved to emigrate lock, stock and barrel to America, they run aground after a storm at sea on an uninhabited but, as it transpires, fertile island where the climate is mild. They settle on the island and begin to administer its affairs according to the same principles as those which governed the free-floating 'island' they had hitherto inhabited; they even go so far as to name the island after the ship, Spensonia.

From now on, their main source of subsistence is farming. Land is consequently declared the common property of all; officials are elected to divide up the land amongst interested parties, in exchange for the payment of rent, and to assume responsibility for the investment of this money in public works. The latter include the construction and maintenance of houses, workshops and roads, as well as—according to the more detailed second work—reclaiming marshland, dredging rivers, mining natural resources, and other public offices not spelled out here. (To later drafts of Spence's utopian plan are added libraries, schools and public assembly-rooms, hospitals and protected bathing areas, grain and fuel silos for periods of emergency, as well as provision for the maintenance of the old and needy.)[10]

Here again we encounter 'Spence's Plan' *in outline*: first the notion, based on natural law, of the just claim of the inhabitants of any country to landed property; and second, the basic features of what one might be tempted to call a welfare state model, had Spence's distrust of centralised power not led him to delegate authority in the most decisive areas of control to local 'parishes'. By sharing the remainder of the rent as a dividend equally amongst all Spensonians—men, women and children alike—the author clearly pushes his ideas much further than Harrington, with whom he nonetheless shares the fundamental belief that political power is founded in economic relations.

The difference between this work and *Oceana* becomes even more apparent in its discussions of political organisation, although these are only elaborated in detail in Spence's next publication, *A Further Account of Spensonia*. In formal terms, *A Further Account* draws on eighteenth-century conventions of travelogue and dialogue. As far as the further development of the community is concerned, it is by now firmly established, prosperous and blooming. As a result, it has become so attractive to the neighbouring indigenous population that they are now settling in increasingly large numbers in this social unit, whose democratic character is the feature which most impresses the fictional author of the travelogue. His interlocutor then describes the two 'pillars' of Spensonian society: the secret ballot and the people's militia. The former, a right extended to all adult female and male citizens,[11] prevents bribery and rotten ballots; the latter insures against tyrannical usurpation of the people's power. The guest is himself invited to attend an exercise of the people's militia, and is visibly impressed, not only by the Spensonians' skill with weapons, but also by the cheerful ease of their approach to the sports competitions and recreational activities which follow. The sight of clean and orderly homes, well-tended woods and fields, orchards and vegetable gardens, moves him at length to admit, 'if ever there be a millenium or heaven upon earth, it can only exist under the benign system of Spensonia.'[12]

In his later writings about Spensonia, the author tends to abandon the fictional form in favour of actual draft constitutions, organised into sections and articles. His source of inspiration was the Jacobin constitution of 1793, the most far-reaching constitution of the French Revolution, which had in fact never been implemented. It is pertinent at this point to mention three further aspects of the Spensonia envisioned here: aspects which, though quite distinct from each other, all bear in their own way the hallmark of their author.

1. In a work entitled *The Rights of Infants* (1797), Spence includes children in the distribution of property, and grants equal rights to children born inside and out of wedlock. (This work also contains some feminist elements.)

2. As repressive measures in Britain became increasingly harsh, the author indulged less and less in the illusion that land was to be made communal property by peaceful means. In his pamphlet *The End of Oppression* (1795), he develops the idea of an inevitably violent expropriation of land from large landowners.

3. The Spensonian week has only five days. Four of these are workdays; according to the final article of the national constitution, the fifth is the Sabbath, 'to promote cleanliness and refresh the spirit of men and labouring animals'.[13]

Robert Owen (1771–1858)

Robert Owen is probably the best known of the utopians presented here; yet the inclusion of an author whose works cannot strictly be considered imaginative literature may seem initially surprising. This is not the place to enter into a discussion of definitions of literature. It would seem somewhat short-sighted, however, to exclude one of the most influential utopian thinkers of the nineteenth century, on the basis of formalist arguments as to the non-literary nature of his work. It is not only in the novel, or indeed any other fictional disguise, that the utopian imagination takes concrete form. On the contrary, it would seem useful to adopt a definition of the utopian genre which spans the whole range of visions of possible alternatives to existing society.

Like Spence, Owen also makes use of the term 'plan'. The concept of the 'Plan' (with a capital 'P') seems to have surfaced for the first time in the 1817 *Report to the Committee of the Association for the Relief of the Manufacturing and Labouring Poor*. At this time, the self-made man Owen was forty years old, and could already look back on a successful career as a silk-spinning and cotton manufacturer. For almost two decades, he had been running what had by now become an internationally acclaimed social experiment in New Lanark, an efficient model enterprise whose paternalistic social welfare provisions were far in advance of their time: a ten-and-a-half-hour working day instead of the normal fourteen hours, uninterrupted wage payments instead of lay-offs in times of market crisis, 'silent monitoring' to replace surveillance and punishment by fine for workers on the shop floor, schooling facilities as a remedy for child neglect.

This experience lent authority to the design drawn up by Owen in the work cited for a community housing around

1,200 members of both sexes including children; for an area of cultivated land large enough to supply the needs of such a community; and for work opportunities, both in terms of spheres of employment, as well as actual work premises. To mention but two characteristic details: adopting the role of educational reformer, in accordance with his oft-repeated motto, 'the character is formed *for* and not *by* the individual',[14] Owen proposed the provision of nursery education for children from the age of three, who would spend the night in dormitories rather than with their parents. He further suggested that children should gradually be introduced to artisanal and agricultural skills. Owen the calculating manager meanwhile joined with Owen the critic of egoism to recommend the installation of central kitchens and the introduction of communal eating facilities.

At this stage the plan represents little more than a response to economic misery in Britain in the wake of the Napoleonic Wars. Yet in the very same year the plan reveals its true nature as a more grandiose project for the future; this is the year in which the idea of 'villages of unity and mutual cooperation'[15] is born, an idea which achieves prominence as a 'model for all others in this country and over the world'.

Full details of the planned community are subsequently developed in the 1820 *Report to the County of Lanark*. Owen insists here on the community being limited to manageable proportions; 800–1,200 inhabitants seems to him an ideal number. Considering his career as an industrialist this excludes, oddly enough, the possibility of dependence on large manufacturing industry. The economic base of collective production is agriculture; although small units of industrial production are accorded a place, they are banished to the periphery of the village site. The expected surplus in production finds its way into central depots, where part of it can be stored in case of emergency. The rest, the exchange value of which is assessed on the basis of the labour invested in it, can be exchanged for goods from other communities in a wider federation. (This plan was later realised in the National Equitable Labour Exchange set up in London, though its existence was admittedly short-lived.) Owen, however, devotes the greater part of his attention to living quarters, meeting-halls and teaching premises in the centre of the community, or to the question of the most convenient 'arrangement for feeding, lodging and clothing the population, and for training and educating the children'.[16]

From this, as well as from the name of Owen's utopia, 'The New Moral World', it becomes clear that he was only superficially concerned with the rational regulation of economic relations amongst a federation of producers. What was at stake for him—as in all positive utopias—was nothing less than human happiness itself, 'a system of society which will ensure the happiness of the human race throughout all future ages'.[17] If and when it became necessary to outline the shape of this humanitarian future, Owen's sober and rational spirit could at times be moved to Biblical heights. 'Even now the time is near at hand . . . when swords shall be turned into ploughshares, and spears into pruning hooks—when every man shall sit under his own vine and his own fig-tree, and none shall make him afraid'.[18]

John Minter Morgan (1782–1854)

In many respects, John Minter Morgan was a model pupil of Owen.[19] As early as 1819, one and a half years after hearing Owen lecture in London, he published a volume of laudatory *Remarks on the Practicability of Mr. Owen's Plan to improve the Condition of the Lower Classes*, under the pseudonym 'Philanthropos'. Similarly in *The Revolt of the Bees*, a utopian work published anonymously in 1826, reference is made to Owen, who appears in the text thinly disguised as a so-called 'experimentalist'. His aim is to bring order and harmony to the bee state, following the unmitigated failure of the entire company of drones—the legislators (House of Commons), the api-economists (political economists) and the social philosophers (Malthus)—to find a solution to the social question. Yet even the experimentalist is at first denied success. 'His arguments were fruitless; for all the powerful bees declared the scheme to be visionary; while they admitted the benevolence and practical experience of the projector. He therefore flew away, and established a colony upon his own principles in a distant region.'[20] The reference here is to the New Harmony community, which had been established in the United States with the support of the Quakers.

Trapped in this apparently hopeless situation, the bees are visited by the spirit of the Scottish poet Allan Ramsay, who invites them to a voyage into the future.[21] They fly to the summit of Ben Lomond, from whence they look out across the landscape of lakes and hills, which is now dotted with a whole series of compact model communities. The scene is set, and the spectator now zooms in, as it were, on images of human life a hundred years hence. The viewer is first struck by the differences in the disposition of the buildings.

Perhaps there is not a more striking contrast between the old and new systems of society, than that which is exhibited in the disposition of their dwellings. Under the former, mankind were congregated in towns or large cities, some of which contained many hundred thousand persons; the houses were so crowded together, that the inhabitants could scarcely move without annoyance, inhaling an unwholesome atmosphere, and deprived of a single green leaf. . . .

Under the new system, mankind have in the first instance selected the most favourable and agreeable situations, and the buildings are so arranged as to afford the advantages both of large cities and country residences, without the inconveniences of either; combining the pleasures of the various and intelligent society of the former, with the pure air and healthful exercises of the latter.[22]

Parkland and bathing areas, colonnades and botanical gardens form further elements in this topography. Homes are so spaciously designed that each individual has two rooms at her or his disposal. It is not obligatory to live as part of a family group. As Owen had envisaged—and he is cited at length at this point—meals are taken communally, although exceptions to this rule are possible.

Since the foundations on which this new society is built cannot be examined in sufficient detail from a bird's (or rather bee's) eye view, Morgan has recourse to another traditional utopian device: he introduces a visitor, and thereby initiates a philosophical dialogue. The guest is a Persian scholar who, though receptive to new ideas, continues to think along individualistic and competitive lines, in accordance with the habits and customs of his native land. His thirst for knowledge gives the inhabitants of the communities ample opportunity to present to him the advantage of the co-operative system.

In this way, the reader learns, for example, of the existence of a series of smaller artisanal and industrial collectives, and even of a cotton factory which is collectively run by four communities, though located at some distance from them. The visitor is struck during his tour of the factory by the cleanliness on the shop floor, and by the high manufacturing quality of its finished products. In terms of the way in which work is organised, it transpires that the community counters the potentially harmful effects of the socially necessary division of labour by implementing the principle of rotation: 'there is no occupation from which any individual is exempt in rotation.'[23] It is hoped firstly that this method will allow all occupations to achieve equal respect in society, even if some community members will be less versed in certain professions than others; and secondly, that rotation will maintain the interest of the community at large in the gradual reduction of hard manual labour. A further consequence of these efforts to bridge the gap between manual and mental labour is touched upon at another point in the text: 'you have beheld none today who are not more or less in possession of these constituents of genuine poetry: it is true that some are gifted with such powers in a higher degree than others, but they are all imbued with the poetry of thought.'[24]

Nominally at least, here too women have accomplished the transition to equal status, although they appear in practice to be employed largely as gardeners and child-rearers —perhaps a sign that the origin of the author's thought lies less in an emancipatory socialist tradition than in Christian philanthropy.

This tableau of future society comprises only one side of the work; the other is a topical critique of existing condi-

tions. We have already encountered the main targets of
Morgan's polemic—parliament, political economy, the
theory of population growth. At this point, the advocates of
emigration for impoverished workers are named as a further
group of apologists of the dominant order. The author's
response to their proposed solution to the social question is
at once ironic and fantastical. The just and sagacious presi-
dent of parliament, to whom the apostles of emigration present their suggestions for reform, is so outraged at their
demand for the producers of the nation's wealth to be
required to leave the country, that he turns the tables on
them by decreeing that these same gentlemen committee
members be themselves deported; their study of all the
relevant documents has, after all, left them so theoretically
well-prepared for emigration that they should have no difficulty in overcoming its adversities. The skilful use of irony in
the speech in which he announces the banishment both of
the supporters of emigration and of their aides and ac-
complices, the political economists, makes it deserving of
lengthy quotation:

Should the fears of a redundant population still annoy
you;—should this hobgoblin pursue you across the Atlantic, and
drive you breathless in the Shawnee Country, there you will dis-
cover no grounds for alarm: for in that thinly peopled continent,
population (to use one of your favourite sentences) may 'go on
doubling' for many centuries to come; and besides, so intermin-
able are the forests of lofty trees and thick underwood, that ages
must elapse ere 'the supply of labour can exceed the demand'.
Each of you therefore may take unto himself a squaw, and culti-
vate connubial bliss, fearless of the consequences either to himself,
to his immediate descendants, or even to a remote posterity.

  If you should be induced to travel towards the south, you must
proceed with the utmost caution, for at every step you will be in
danger of treading upon a rattle-snake. I am however happy to
inform you, that there is a remedy recently discovered for this
calamity, and which proves after a protracted but painful illness an
infallible cure for the severest bite. Among the extensive marshes,
the draining of which will yield you constant employment, swarms
of musquitos will assail you; but, as philosophers have observed,
there is seldom an evil without its attendant good,—the more you
are tormented by these pestiferous insects, the more protection

you will require; and thus increased activity will be given to the gauze manufactories of the mother country.

In these remote and desolate regions, when far removed from the seductive allurements of society, your minds will be abstracted, and you will view all things with the single eye of truth.[25]

This description is relayed through the medium of a fictional letter from a young worker, which is found stored in the communal library.

Finally, at the end of the book, we return to the framing narrative. Impressed by this demonstration of the possibility of harmonious coexistence, even the stubbornest advocates of the bees' old system are brought to their senses, and they formally declare their intention to put an end to it. This boundless trust in the eventual triumph of reason once again betrays the strong influence not only of Owen, but also of Godwin and other eighteenth-century Enlightenment figures.[26] The title, *The Revolt of the Bees*, refers then not so much to the overthrow of a competitive society, as to an older revolution in which the bees had turned their backs on the harmonious laws of nature. According to this scheme of things, the appropriation of social wealth by a handful of individuals appears contrary to nature, as do the process of industrial revolution and its unhappy consequences.

Despite all its naivetés and contradictions, Minter Morgan's utopia remained a popular work until the middle of the century, at least amongst literate workers and craftsmen. By 1839 it had already reached its third edition, and booksellers sympathetic to the labour movement were advertising it under the heading of 'Cheap Books Suitable for Socialists'.[27]

John Francis Bray (1809–1897)

In contrast to this, John Francis Bray's *A Voyage from Utopia*, although written in 1840–1, was not published until the present century (1957).[28] The author probably expected the offensive nature of its contents to give rise to problems—a well-founded fear, in view of the severity of his

attacks on the churches, as well as on British imperialism
and the institution of marriage.

Bray, the son of an actor who had emigrated to America,
was born, like Spence, into modest circumstances.[29] Having
completed his apprenticeship as a typesetter in Yorkshire,
he suffered repeated periods of unemployment and its
attendant poverty. The vagabond years of the journeyman in
search of work constituted for him a simultaneous apprenticeship of a different kind. They opened his eyes to the
economic foundations of class society, and led him to join
the ranks of the labour movement. His journalistic activities
of this period culminated in the early socialist classic,
Labour's Wrongs and Labour's Remedy (1838), which was
later to be liberally cited by Marx.[30]

The publication of this synthesis of Owenism and anti-
Ricardian economy had cost Bray the considerable sum of
£70. His fear of accumulating further debts by publishing the
Voyage may well have been a further reason for withholding
the manuscript. The two works are related to the extent that,
despite predominantly positive reviews, particularly from
Owenite circles, Bray's work also met with the accusation
that the 'cure' he promoted was a utopian one.

*A Voyage from Utopia to Several Unknown Regions of the
World* was conceived of as a response to this reproach. As
the author himself noted thirty years after writing it, 'as the
critics thought I was "Utopian", I wrote this to show what
existed *outside* of Utopia.'[31]

The book thus takes the form of a *voyage imaginaire* in the
opposite direction, away from rather than towards Utopia;
and the conditions in Utopia itself, with which we are
primarily concerned in this study, can only be reconstructed
through the reactions of the traveller, interspersed with the
occasional comparisons he makes with his homeland. In
order to emphasise the objectivity and authenticity of the
report which is addressed to the 'Dear Brethren' at home,
and perhaps also in an attempt to introduce a cautious note
of distance, Bray uses the conventional device of an outside
observer unknown to the narrator. The narrator himself
poses in the preface as a mere mediator and translator, who
claims to have uncovered the manuscript in America. Of
course, the name of the traveller, Yarbfj, is a rather poor

disguise for his real identity, based as it is on a simple rever-
sal of the initials and letters of Bray's name.

The first unknown region into which the traveller
advances is Brydone, whose inhabitants are known as the
Anglos. As in the work of Morgan, with which Bray was
doubtless familiar, the gaze of the traveller alights first on
buildings and homes—here, those of the capital, Londo. In
this context, the reader indirectly learns that the communities of Utopia appear as veritable garden cities in comparison to the bleak urban habitations of the 'commos'. The
two subsequent references to the situation in the traveller's
country of origin reveal similar correspondences with Morgan's work. In Bray's Utopia, there are neither 'soldos' (soldiers) nor 'polos' (police). In *The Revolt of the Bees,* this
absence had been nicely highlighted in the depiction of a
march, which was revealed on closer examination to be not
an army parade, but a column of workers returning home
after helping their allies in the Batavian Republic to recon-
struct a broken dyke.[32] In Bray's work, on the other hand,
we have to content ourselves with a resounding condemnation of militarism, followed by a passing reference to the
absence of a 'soldateska' in Utopia.

A further difference between Bray and Morgan appears in
the former's biting critique of the clergy ('pestos'), and
indeed of any kind of publicly practised religion ('superstition'). His Utopians may not be atheists, for they do
embrace a form of deism: 'In Utopia we are all conscious of
the existence of a power which is superior to and independent of man—which calls into existence and various forms
of animal and vegetable life around us, and wields the ponderous planet in its sphere.'[33] Yet there is no public worship,
nor are there any priests or temples. 'Happy Utopia, where
there are neither soldos nor pestos!'[34]

In a land without wars, without capital punishment or
material deprivation, longevity is enjoyed by the entire
population. This is true above all of women; hence the
horror of the observer, equalled only by his dismay at the
machinations of the pestos, as he notes women's education
into inferiority, their degradation and its most extreme form,
mass prostitution.

Infinitely disappointed by his visit to Brydone, the travel-

ler continues on his way to two further countries, Amrico
and Franco. Where Amrico is concerned, his expectations
are particularly high; for 'These people talked of liberty and
the equal brotherhood of man as though they understood
the terms much better than the Anglos.' He has thus reached
the conclusion that 'their country must be a second
Utopia'.[35] Yet his observations and conversations reveal to
him that nothing could be further from the truth.

The sketches of Amrico and Franco are by no means as
informative as his description of the situation in Brydone. At
the time of writing the author was not yet familiar with
either of these two countries; apart from his childhood
memories of the United States, he had to rely on second-
hand information, as opposed to his own observations.[36]

Nonetheless, a number of his concluding remarks are
interesting, since they offer a few more fragments to add to
our splintered picture of Utopia. Yarbfj, for example,
appears somewhat astonished at the low standard of transport technology. 'None of the nations which I had visited
had any knowledge of the art of navigating the air . . . when I
stated what took place in Utopia, and proposed to show the
people how to construct a flying machine and to generate
motion by gravity alone, they listened with incredulity.'[37]
The flying machines of Utopia, on the other hand, can carry
up to fifty passengers.

Drawing on his own experience of *rapprochment* between
peoples as a result of new modes of transport, the visitor
next recognises the problem of what he calls 'intercommuni-
cation'. 'Without a universal mode of communication there
can be no universal fellowship among mankind.'[38] To avoid
petty national jealousies, he suggests that only one route
lies open: the creation of a new world language. We shall
encounter both these points—the scientific and technical
aspects of air travel, and the question of language—for a
second time in the work of Goodwyn Barmby.

In general it must be said that utopian society is no more
than touched upon in the occasional passing reference. This
in itself corresponds to the author's intention. From his fic-
titious position as editor and translator, he brings a fine
touch of irony to the preface with his remark that he has

excluded statements on this subject from Yarbfj's work, since 'the civilization and institutions of the Utopians appeared to the translator highly absurd and singular in many points embodying some of the aspirations of discontented and irrational enthusiasts in our country.' He further justifies these omissions by noting the traveller's insufferable tendency to glorify the virtues of his native society at every available opportunity. The editor knows himself to be voicing the opinion of the public at large when he writes, 'We *know* that among us there is nothing that needs improvement; whereas other natives merely *suppose* that they cannot be improved; and therefore we alone are in a position to interfere and to direct them, in a manner that must necessarily be to their advantage.'[39] Could one find a more perfect description of the colonial mentality?

The influence of Swift is evident in the layout of *A Voyage from Utopia*, as well as in its satirical use of names. At the same time, the author lacks the capacity (or desire?) to breathe life into his ponderous, if clear and detailed writings. Individual examples of clever neologisms—'pestos', or 'blazo' (for Hell)—together with the one or two humourous passages in the book, cannot alone carry a work with hardly any trace of a plot, and not even a single dialogue—especially since the stereotyped suffix 'o' actually detracts from the satirical effect of descriptions of individual occupations and particular social strata. Bray's strength lies in his clear and precise analysis of society, in his denunciation of social injustice, and in his illumination of relations between individual phenomena which have hitherto been hidden from view.

John Goodwyn Barmby (1820–1881)

One characteristic of all the utopian writers presented here is their missionary zeal and prophetic ardour. Indeed the whole period is characterised by the emergence of chiliastic movements. The social ferment which produced the likes of Richard Brothers and Joanna Southcott (to name but two of many millenarians), and which brought them widespread

support, doubtless also furthered the development of utopian social projects. It is by no means uncommon to encounter similarities between the vocabulary of the chili-
asts and that of the utopians.[40]

Yet this messianic tendency is nowhere so clearly marked
as in the work of the man who can justly claim to have
introduced the concepts 'Communist' and 'Communism' to
the English language: Goodwyn Barmby, a comprehensively
educated autodidact, a Chartist agitator, writer of poems
and pamphlets, socialist and feminist, as well as a preacher in
the partly religiously, partly politically inspired Communist
Church, of which he was the leader.[41] Barmby was barely
twenty-one years old when, having returned from a stay in
Paris, he founded the Central Communist Propaganda Society in 1841 and published his first journal in 1842. Its
title, *The Promethean*, was inspired by Shelley.[42] Barmby's
unfinished utopian work, 'The Book of Platonoplos: or,
The Perfect Commonwealth. A Romance of the Future',
appeared in 1846 in the perodical *The Communist Chronicle*. Right up to the present day, both the journal itself and
Barmby's utopia remain largely unknown, even amongst historians of the period.[43]

Spence, as we have seen, had no qualms about using the
name 'Spensonia' for his ideal state. Yet this appears the
height of modesty in comparison with Barmby's efforts to
orchestrate his own part in the coming of the millennium. In
response to the question, put by the visitor to Platonopolis,
'How came this change?',[44] his guide and interlocutor tells
the tale of a 'divine man' who one day arose and spoke the
following words: 'Brothers and sisters! The good spirit has
sent me to ye. Blessed be its name! Why compete ye with
one another, when there is enough plentifully for all?" The
same man subsequently founded a church and began to
preach the doctrine of 'communion', resisting persecution
and repression until such time as 'the village was deserted
for the communitorium, and the city for the communistery,
and the province became a commune, and the nation a
communarchy, and the whole planet one great commonwealth.'[45] The significance of this passage lies in its extension
of the concept of utopia beyond the boundaries of any iso-

lated island, to encompass the world at large. The name 'communistery' has its origins in the non-individualistic arrangement and function of living units, which bear the names either of famous utopian models or of the founding fathers of the utopian tradition. Moreville is represented, as is Soliscivitas, Atlantis as well as Harringtonia, even Jesuville. The early socialists too, Babeuf and Owen, Weitling and Saint-Simon, are deemed worthy of dedication by name. Another point which should further be noted here is Barmby's intention to publish a library of utopian classics—one of many bold projects which he was never able to realise in practice.[46]

In good utopian tradition, the architectural style of the 'communisteries' favours geometrical forms. Only in relation to the height of his centrally situated temple does Barmby deviate from the traditional scheme of things; as a committed supporter of the decimal system—he designed, for example, his own calendar with a ten-day week[47]—he equips his place of workship with a total of ten floors.

Harmony is the prevailing principle of life in Barmby's 'Perfect Commonwealth'. Animals as well as human beings live in the spirit of this principle; indeed, even the relationship between them is one of harmony. The visitor encounters lions in harness drawing large carts, and the author's ingenuity does not stop there. The transport sytem of his visionary future includes submarines and aircraft of various kinds. Once before, in a different context, the same author had formulated demands for safe air travel and for the free provision of air-balloon transport.

Regrettably, the three chapters of the utopia which were published before *The Communist Chronicle* went out of circulation contain no details of the social and political organisation of the community. It would have been instructive to know the extent to which Barmby might have modified the views of social needs which he had earlier propagated, following his own later experience of social experiment through his work as the architect of a real, if short-lived community in 1843.[48] In his platform of forty-four 'societarian wants', formulated in 1842, he had, for instance, made what now seems a topical reference to the principle of rotation in the exercise of government powers by elected representatives of the people.[49] A community should aspire not merely to communist forms of distribution and consumption, but also to the formation of communal units of production. Another point of interest is his exposition of the relationship of human beings to nature; in spirit if not in name, what may be called an ecological mode of thought is discernible here. Medically irreproachable food—in other words, organically grown—is explicitly deemed essential. In addition, Barmby demands the immediate summoning of an international conference to secure world peace (this too has highly topical echoes today). Amongst other things, he further proposes the formulation of a new world language, which in the long term would act as an instrument in the overcoming of national differences. Working out this new language will be the task of a discipline delightfully entitled 'philanthropic philology', whose first representative is none other than Barmby himself.[50] But there is a note of comfort for the Anglo-Saxon world; after careful consideration of the pros and cons, Barmby proposes English as a transitional language on the road to the goal of communism.

Although it is neither explicitly mentioned here nor in his utopia, any exposition of Barmby's social philosophy is incomplete without some reference to his demands for the complete equality of women. In what was for both him and his wife Catherine a question of principle, he did not even hesitate to cross swords with the Chartists, whose six-point programme included only male enfranchisement. (It should further be noted that it is to Catherine Barmby that we owe one of the most far-sighted and eloquent pieces of feminist polemic of this period.)[51]

Conclusion

Having sifted through these individual works, we are now better placed to determine the similarities between them, and thus to assess the historical position of this phase of the utopian imagination. In this summary we shall be dealing above all with questions of content, structural and formal characteristics being mentioned only in passing.

1. The final work discussed above is the only one to bear the title of 'romance', thereby anticipating the further development of the genre in the second half of the century. All the others tend to represent utopias in the real world. There is an insistent workability about them; their characteristic feature is their practicability. In reality too, almost all the authors were involved in concrete projects: Spence elaborated his draft constitutions. Owen founded a model colony in the USA, Minter Morgan developed plans for 'self-supporting villages' under the aegis of the Church of England,[52] Barmby experimented with communal living in the Moreville Communitorium which he himself had set up. Their works bear the traces of experiences they had gathered in these real communities.

2. The ideal community was to be compact and manageable. Spence's 'parish', Owen's 'villages of industry' (or later, 'townships'), Morgan's 'community' (or 'self-supporting village'), Barmby's 'communistery'—not one of these community forms housed more than 2,000—2,500 inhabitants. On the one hand this was a reaction both against the anarchism of the new northern industrial towns and against the sprawling colossus of London; a reaction which revived old yearnings for the restoration of the small-scale artisan and peasant communities of the past. Yet this conception of community does contain something more, namely a positive attempt to overcome the fatal opposition of town and country. Minter Morgan's claim, cited above, that the new system united the advantages of both forms of social life, while at the same time eliminating their disadvantages, expresses a conviction shared by all these authors.

3. The utopian designs discussed here give primacy not only to the principle of compactness in the social unit, but also to its transparency. In terms of political organisation, 'grass-roots' democracy is given precedence; a centralised state is rejected and government power reduced to a minimum; the inhabitants of the community regulate their affairs for themselves. Large-scale projects or communal undertakings which place too great a burden on individual communes are taken care of by the confederation, to which individual

communities belong as autonomous units bound together by
an understanding of their mutual solidarity.

4. From Spence through Owenism to the feminism of
Barmby, there emerges an understanding of democracy
which explicitly embraces the rights and equality of
women—a fact which marks this as a turning-point in history. The famous declaration of their contemporary,
Fourier, to the effect that the progress of human history was
to be measured by the extent of women's emancipation,
accords entirely with the ideas of early socialists in England.

5. It is, however, not only social aims which are associated
with these utopian projects, not merely the elimination of
economic misery, or of social differences between classes
and genders; their goals are also moral ones. Whether in
terms of the abolition (or reduction) of crime and vice, and
the concomitant abolition (or humanisation) of a barbaric
criminal law, or in relation to the curse of egoism (private
property, the profit motive), or in the struggle against ignorance and superstition—in every way the early socialists
reveal themselves as the heirs and executors of the Euro-
pean Enlightenment. With their firm belief in the perfectibil-
ity of humankind, they envisage a 'new moral world', whose
cardinal social virtues are order and harmony. In some individual cases (Morgan's adaptation of the community to the
contours of the surrounding landscape, or Barmby's taming
of wild beasts) these principles of a society in which all dis-
cord is resolved are extended to include the relationship
between nature and humankind—a relationship characterised in reality by the despoliation and subjection of the
former by the latter. From a modern perspective, one can
thus begin to talk here of the emergence of ecological
thought.

6. The formal principle of 'isolation', which one critic has
attempted to establish as an essential characteristic of all
utopias, cannot be maintained as such in relation to the
period dealt with here.[53] No longer is a remote island of
utopian happiness projected into a sea of selfishness, suffer-

ing, wars and diverse misfortunes. All these works are inspired by a notion of social progress which embraces the whole humankind. As early a writer as Spence expects the radiant energy of his system to convince the Indian peoples of its virtue, once they have learned to distinguish between the brotherly spirit of the Spensonians, and the colonialists and missionaries who aim to subjugate and indoctrinate them. Owen directs his writings to 'all classes and all nations'. Morgan's Persian guest intends to give his all to spread the idea of the model community in his own country after his return. And finally, Barmby sees the earth as a whole being spanned by a network of 'communisteries.'

7. In the period with which we are concerned here, utopian literature undergoes a transformation from travels in space to travels in time, a change which is both clearly determined by the notion of social progress outlined above, and which comes at a time when the realisation of the utopian ideal seemed to have moved within reach. While Spence still used the conventional motif of shipwreck on an island, Barmby's Platonopolis is displaced into the year 2000. Between these two lies Minter Morgan's *The Revolt of the Bees*, the first book in English utopian literature to tread this particular path.[54] (In the lineage of French utopias which dominated the eighteenth century, the same development had already taken place at least fifty years earlier with Louis Sébastien Mercier's *L'an 2440*.)

8. One weak point shared by all these texts is similarly bound up with their faith in social progress. The question of *how* utopian society has been established is hardly ever posed, let alone answered. We know of Owen's appeals to the good judgement of the regents and governments of Europe and America. Minter Morgan's deliberations on the matter are never pursued beyond the banishment of the political economists. For Barmby, though he at least poses the question, Creation seems to have taken pity on the wretched of the earth; for London and Paris, those two sinks of corruption, have been swallowed up by the sea. As has been shown above, only Spence at one point weighs up the

possibility of violently expropriating land from large land-owners, and develops a rudimentary strategy for the seizure of power by the people.[55] Bray's watchful observer Yarbfj certainly registers any social tendencies which might bring about a transition to a utopian state of affairs; yet apart from his emphatic insistence that, 'a change, then, is inevitable—a revolution certain',[56] he too has nothing further to offer. If and when he mentions the past history of Utopia, he makes only extremely vague references to struggles and defeats on the way to eventual peace in society. It was not until fifty years later that this question was posed amongst the ranks of socialist utopians, when Morris, armed with the historical experience of the '48 revolution and the Paris Commune, addressed himself to it in a key chapter in *News from Nowhere*, 'How the Change Came'.

9. It is striking that all these authors are not only relatively well versed in an older utopian tradition, but also that they make reference to each others' work, so that the utopian features which appear for the first time in Spence have already been consecrated as part of an early utopian socialist tradition by the time of Barmby's work. Spence himself could not have attended Owen's first public appearance in London; but Owen, generally so reserved when it came to admitting to influences on his own thought, confesses in his autobiography that he was familiar with Spence's plan.[57] The direct influence of Owen himself on Morgan has already been discussed. The fact that Morgan was familiar with Spence is clear from his other semi-fictional work, *Hampden in the Nineteenth Century*.[58] Bray deals amongst other things with Spencean and Owenite ideas. And finally, Barmby was influenced from the outset by Owen, a lettter of recommendation from the latter having accompanied him on his trip to Paris in 1840. I have found no direct reference to Spence in his work; yet the motto cited on the title page of *The Communist Chronicle* might perhaps be an indication that the agrarian socialist ideas of the Spenceans were not unknown to him. It read, 'God is the only true Landlord.' Barmby also sought to establish contact with Morgan, yet the hurt tone of Barmby's reaction indicates that he was politely but firmly rejected by the latter.[59]

10. There remains finally the question of the reasons for the breakdown of this particular tradition. Clearly it is the year 1848 which was to become 'the great twilight year of the utopians'.[60] Three developments can be seen to have played a role here: the defeat of Chartism and other revolutionary movements in Europe, which simultaneously put an end to particular forms and notions of activism in the early labour movement; the extended phase of prosperity which had been dawning in British capitalism since 1849–50, and which also improved the material situation of the working population; and the claims of an emergent Marxism that the humane society of the future should be built on the basis of scientific planning, far removed from visionary utopian inspirations. Nonetheless, 1848 did not bring a total rupture with the past. The dream and romance elements characteristic of Barmby's utopian fragment have already been identified as part of a form which was later to achieve dominance in the utopian tradition. A further link between the utopias of the first half of the century and the later path of development of this genre is Bulwer Lytton, who was familiar with the ideas of Godwin and Owen, and is likely also to have known Morgan's widely-read works. One passage in *The Coming Race* (1871) makes clear reference to early English and French utopian socialists, even though they are not referred to by name.

Now, in this social state of the Vril-ya, it was singular to mark how it contrived to unite and harmonise into one system nearly all the objects which the various philosophers of the upper world have placed before human hopes as the ideals of a Utopian future. [61]

The fact that Bulwer himself opposes the 'levelling' tendencies aspired to here, or that he reveals deep-seated fears of a technologically controlled future, is the beginning of a different story.

Translated by Erica Carter

3   THE HISTORICAL BENT OF THE CHARTIST NOVEL

The treatment of Chartism is symptomatic of the insularity that has overtaken so many academic disciplines: whereas the historians' fascination with the period manifests itself in dozens of publications every year, students of English have so far deemed it worthy of little more than the occasional footnote. It is not a question of parity, for Chartism's socio-historical significance clearly exceeds its standing in literary history. But if we agree with one definition of Chartism as 'a response of a *literate* and sophisticated working class, different in tone and temper from earlier protest movements',[1] then questions arise as to the scope, nature and artistic value of its literary output—questions, surely, to which students of English should be addressing themselves.

It would be presumptuous to attempt a comprehensive discussion of Chartist literature within the confines of a brief chapter, given its diversity and unwieldly profusion. Martha Vicinus lists 'speeches, essays, prison letters, dialogues, short stories, novels, songs, lyrical poems, epics, and, later in the century, autobiographies.'[2] To complete the tally, we should perhaps add politically committed literary criticism and the emergence of industrial reportage ('trades grievances').

In view of the multiplicity of genres, there is much to be said for concentrating at this stage on one particular area, that of the novel. But even here we immediately come up against a difficulty which is peculiar to Chartist literature as a whole, namely the virtual inaccessibility of the texts. Most Chartist fiction—indeed, most Chartist literature—was published in newspapers and journals, and it was only the odd exceptional work which reached its readers in book form.[3] The serialisation of narrative and other works was of course not uncommon in the mid-nineteenth century, and many of the best-known novelists of the period availed themselves of the device (Dickens, Thackeray, Gaskell and others). However, when we examine the immediate context of such serial fiction, it is clear that most serial publications are at odds with the particular political and cultural ambience which radiates from the pages of the Chartist press. For a proper understanding of the Chartist conception of literature, it is vital at the outset to establish the nature of that journalistic context.

I

If there is one area which bears out Disraeli's apprehensive observation on the development of two separate 'nations' within one state, it is that of the press. The rise of a pauper press can be traced historically to the inability and unwillingness of the established periodicals to articulate any interests other than those of the ruling class. It was a state of affairs which continued fundamentally unchanged right up to the rise of Chartism as a mass movement at the end of the 1830s. Indeed, the war of 'the great unstamped' that had raged during the preceding two decades served merely to exacerbate the polarisation. When the struggle was over, effectively by 1836, it was clear that neither censorship nor the stamp tax could keep the poor men's newspapers down permanently. Individual papers may well have been killed off, but the journalism of the workers, artisans and radicals as a whole survived unscathed. And so it continued in the Chartist period: most Chartist periodicals had an extremely short life-span, but their impermanence was frequently overshadowed by the enthusiastic launching of yet another new publication.

The slogan, 'Knowledge is Power', which heralded the appearance of the *Poor Man's Guardian* (1831–5), was still redolent of enlightenment didacticism and hence not necessarily at odds with certain radical middle-class positions. In the Chartist press, however, an additional and decisive impulse is at work which is alien to bourgeois journalism, that is the emphasis on mobilisation and organisation. Ernest Jones, with whose work as a novelist we shall shortly

concern ourselves, characterised this impulse, and thus the
ideal conception of a Chartist organ, in the following terms:

The very first, the most essential requisite of a movement is to
have an organ to record its proceedings, to communicate through,
with its several branches—to appeal through, to exhort through, to
defend through, and to teach through. It is the fundamental bond
of union, the ensign of progress, and the means of organisation.[4]

The function described here was fulfilled for many years by
The Northern Star (1837–52). But besides this most durable
of all the Chartist publications, the Chartist movement threw
up a huge number of other papers and journals during its
barely twenty-year history. All told there were nearly a
hundred, but it is perhaps less their number than the fact
that they were produced in centres throughout the regions
which is most immediately striking. Wherever there was
mass support for the six points of the Charter, efforts were
made, using handbills, leaflets, tracts, newspapers or journals as the media of instruction to rally and mobilise the
artisans and workers. The written and printed word carried
many of the movement's great hopes for the progress and
spread of reason. A proletarian public was thereby constituted which—for the first time in history—assumed national
dimensions and expressed national aspirations, yet at the
same time resisted unifying and centralising tendencies. The
innumerable regional Chartist newspapers and magazines
are therefore in no sense offshoots of a metropolitan-
oriented paper—as tends to be the case of the ruling class's
political press in the great provincial cities—but represent
rather the outcome of self-discovery, solidarity and feelings
of identity on a local level.

A further difference concerns disposition and status of
literary texts in the newspapers of the period. It would be
wrong to generalise and thereby gloss over the fine distinc-
tions between one paper and another, but here again the two
camps reveal clearly divergent tendencies. What is noticeable in the Chartist newspapers is that the literary columns,
far from being consigned to a separate 'feuilleton' or arts
section, enjoy equal prominence alongside the political, historical, temperance or whatever sections. Moreover, as often

as not they have a close thematic or ideological affinity with the other columns. The literary texts published in the bourgeois press, on the other hand, are frequently found to bear little or no relation to the rest of the paper. Even when they are not actually hidden away among the political news, among the advertisements and—as industrialisation proceeds apace—the increasingly substantial economic section, they nonetheless constitute to an ever larger extent a foreign body in a whole that is directed by the principles of utilitarianism.

By contrast the Chartist press makes a constant programmatic point of emphasising the intimate relationship between literature and politics. Take, for instance, this statement from *The Labourer*:

We, however, had one great goal before our eyes—the redemption of the Working classes from their thraldom—and to this object we have made the purpose of each article subservient . . . we have placed poetry and romance side by side with politics and history.

Arguing in a similar vein, the editor of *The Chartist Circular* adds that in selecting material strict criteria were applied:

No silly romance—no coarse or immoral anecdote was to be admitted. In this generally fascinating walk of literature, all the biographical and historical sketches, all the narratives, stories, and occurrences written or selected for our periodical were to be such as would not only induce our youths to read, but have a tendency to impart to their minds a high moral tone—to inspire them with a noble love of liberty, and an honest detestation of every species of delusion and oppression.[5]

Ultimately, of course, the intermingling of literature and politics in Chartism is expressed most clearly in personal terms, in the fusion of poet/novelist and activist. The movement can no more bring forth the 'impartial' author or the author who writes about reality from a respectable distance than it can spawn 'specialists' or 'freelance Chartist writers'. In this it foreshadows a feature of the subsequent development of the working-class movement: just as all the most eminent Marxist theoreticians up to the beginning of the twentieth century put their principles into practice in the front ranks of the movement itself, so Chartism's most significant artistic contributions are made by authors who were active on its behalf as speakers, organisers and journalists. To take only a few examples from the field of fiction: Thomas Doubleday was editor of *The Northern Liberator* and one of the principal speakers at the 1839 mass rally in Newcastle; Thomas Cooper and Ernest Jones served two-year prison sentences for making inflammatory speeches; and Thomas Martin Wheeler was secretary of the National Land Company.

II

We have already detailed the many different genres which comprise the ensemble of Chartist literature. In so far as it is possible to draw any conclusions from an examination of a dozen of the more important periodicals,[6] the novel is very much a minority form, and particularly so during the first Chartist decade (1837–47). It is all the more instructive, then, to note the tendencies manifested in these early works. Serialisations such as *William Tell, or Switzerland Delivered; Calefi, an Authentic Tale of a Ferrarese Carbonaro*; *The Incendiary, a Tale of the German Peasant Wars*; or *Albert, or the Spirit of Freedom*, have a number of features in common. First they are set in foreign countries; second, they revolve around struggles for freedom; third, they are rooted in the past (even if their message points to the present); fourth, they are all translations. Just how rudimentary the Chartists' own production of fiction was at that stage is confirmed by Wheeler's prefatory remark in his novel *Sunshine and Shadow*. Looking back at the literary record of the movement he notes:

The fiction department of our literature has hitherto been neglected by the scribes of our body, and the opponents of our principles have been allowed to wield the power of imagination over the youth of our party, without any effort on our part to occupy this wide and fruitful plain.[7]

Wheeler perhaps overstates his case, but if what he has in mind is literary prose that focuses on the worker and renounces fanciful flights into the realms of the aristocracy, he is right. Jones's 1847 romances, for instance, continue to exhibit blatant concessions to the popular literary taste of melodrama, even if he is clearly concerned to portray the corruption and wickedness of those who seduce his working-class heroines as symptomatic of social conditions generally. But—and this is decisive—it is still the nobility and the military élite who are held to blame for such vices. The other principal enemy of the Chartists, the industrial bourgeoisie, does not figure at all in these romances. There was precious little innovation, either, in that early Chartist fiction which derived its themes from the freedom struggles of other peoples and other historical epochs. When *William Tell* was published in *The English Chartist Circular* in 1842, there were already at least four other versions of the story in circulation.[8] Works of this kind represented essentially an attempt to adapt the received form of the historical novel to more radical interpretations of the past.

Only two longer tales, both published anonymously and buried in obscurity for 140 years, stand out from the general run of early Chartist efforts: *Political Pilgrim's Progress* (1839) and *The Pioneers* (1842). *Political Pilgrim's Progress*, which has recently been attributed to Thomas Doubleday, first appeared in *The Northern Liberator*.[9] As its title indicates, it borrows a great deal from Bunyan, an astute move on the author's part, given the popularity which the original enjoyed among the literate artisans and workers. The visionary dream, the motif of the journey, the allegorical form, the use of personified abstractions—all these features reappear. Philosophically, however, *Political Pilgrim's Progress* marks a radical turn toward secular and contemporary political concerns. The obstacles and opponents that stand in Radical's way, as he moves from the City of Plunder to the City of Reform, are the oppressive powers and institutions of contemporary England as well as the intellectual and political adversaries to Chartism. Each and every confrontation which the protagonist has to win through, whether by argument or by struggle, is designed to raise the political awareness of the readers and, where necessary, to arm them in readiness for real struggles.

Similarly, *The Pioneers, or a Tale of the Radical Rising at Strathaven in 1820*, to give its full title, attempts to update and put to effective use a traditional form. It may well have been intended to become a large-scale project, but the Scottish *Chartist Circular*, in which it was serialised, ceased publication after the fourth instalment, and so it remains a fragment. *The Pioneers* distinguishes itself from the derivative historical novels mentioned earlier in two important respects.

For the first time, the struggle for freedom is no longer transposed to another country or an earlier epoch, but is located in the still-continuing historical present. The character of the novel therefore ceases to be metaphorical; it reflects the contemporary situation without resorting to complicated mediating devices. 'If we succeed', says one of the insurgents, 'it will not be a rebellion, it will be a revolution, and instead of punishment, we will receive the gratitude and thanks of a free and happy nation.'[10] As in *Political Pilgrim's Progress*, where Radical's companion, Moral Force, falls by the wayside, the reader can hardly fail to notice the warning that it may be necessary to prepare for armed struggle.

Secondly, the author is not afraid to deviate occasionally from Standard English when it comes to the dialogues, the use of Scottish dialect underscoring his solidarity with the people. In one scene where the fighters are requisitioning weapons, we find the following sentence: 'jist gae wa' and gie us thae guns, as we hae na' muckle time to palaver wi' ye'.'[11] Such unselfconscious use of the Scottish vernacular had of course been given considerable impetus by the breakthrough achieved earlier in Sir Walter Scott's novels, and it is noteworthy that there are no comparable passages in the prose of the English Chartists. In England even Elizabeth Gaskell, with regard to the use of working-class speech the most audacious of the social-problem novelists, felt obliged to defer to her readers' sensibilities by adding footnotes to, or translating into Standard English, the colloquial utterances of her working-class characters.[12]

It is true that *The Pioneers* (together with *Political Pilgrim's Progress*, though the character and thrust of the latter work is quite different) is something of an oasis in what is otherwise a fictional desert. Nonetheless, it does anticipate, and prepare the way, for developments later in the 1840s, when the Chartist novelists strove to consolidate its tentative advances. What were those developments and tendencies? First and foremost, continuing recourse to the historical novel as a generally appropriate genre; secondly, thematic concentration on events from the national past—or, more precisely, on the turbulent political history of the preceding fifty years; and thirdly, the taking up of local struggles and conflicts.

III

There are two particular novels which embody these tendencies at their most highly developed. They are generally regarded as the greatest achievements in the history of the Chartist novel—and, indeed, in contemporary socialist prose generally. Thomas Martin Wheeler's *Sunshine and Shadow, a Tale of the Nineteenth Century*, was published in 1849–50, and Ernest Jones's *De Brassier, A Democratic Romance, The History of a Democratic Movement, compiled from the journal of a demagogue, the confessions of a democrat, and the minutes of a spy*, appeared in 1851–2. The subtitles announce the choice of genre, and in fact the authors make no bones about it. In his foreword Jones declares, 'Fiction does no more than frame the historical picture', and Wheeler concludes his novel with the remark, 'Our object was to combine a History of Chartism, with the details of our story.'[13]

It is, then, all the more puzzling that the critics have made so little of the sense of history which both novels display. Martha Vicinus stresses the formal borrowings from the conventional melodramatic romances as one of their essential characteristics, whereas Jack Mitchell sees both works as examples of the political journalist gaining the upper hand over the novelist.[14] The presence of such elements, which

militate against a realist narrative style, is undeniable, but
they can only partially explain the strengths and weaknesses
of the two novels.

The most immediately noticeable innovation in both
novels is that they take Chartism itself as their subject matter. *De Brassier*, it is true, is written as a parable about the
dangers that threaten 'every democratic movement' (the
term Chartism is not used), but Wheeler, in accordance with
his stated objective, actually mentions the movement by
name. At this point a short summary of the two novels may
help to make it clear that in neither case is Chartism treated
peripherally.

De Brassier follows the progress of an impoverished
nobleman to the leadership of a popular movement. After
denouncing all his rivals and thereby eliminating them, he
exploits the movement for his own private purposes and
finally allows it to collapse in ruins. Some readers and critics
have read the novel as a condemnatory attack on the Chartist leader, Feargus O'Connor, but the character study of a
demagogue is only one aspect of the whole, and not a central
one at that.[15] Jones is more concerned to represent the
movement and its enemies in all their political, ideological
and sociological complexity. He does this by means of extra-
ordinarily complicated plots, constant changes of setting and
a motley array of characters that need not detain us here.
The novel is anyway most memorable for its individual vig-
nettes: the description of an impressive torchlight procession embracing thousands of workers and artisans, for
instance, or the caricature of a Cabinet meeting (which was
probably not too wide of the mark). And beyond that we are
left with an overall impression that the author, for all that he
criticises the desperado elements in the movement and,
more generally, the corruptibility of the popular masses,
never falters in his confidence in the ability of those selfsame
masses to learn.

By comparison with the expansive, frequently melodramatic and bombastic scenic representations of Jones's
novel, Wheeler's *Sunshine and Shadow* is a remarkably con-
cise, sober and at times even lifeless work. The plot revolves
entirely around the proletarian protagonist (and, in the early

stages at least, his bourgeois counterpart), and follows his life with all its vicissitudes—one of the several levels of meaning of the 'sunshine and shadow' metaphor. But after a certain point Arthur Morton's life story is overtaken by developments in Chartist political history, and from then on the fate of both are seen to be inextricably interwoven. After making a rousing speech at the Birmingham Bull Ring, which leads to a riot (1839), the hero is forced to disappear into exile. It is not until 1842, when the next great wave of agitation is sweeping across the country, that he reappears in England. Given this interlocking construction, it is clear why Arthur—and not Edward, the colourless mechanic and ineffectual opponent of De Brassier—should have become the first 'broad prototype of the proletarian hero'.[16]

Both works end with the failure of the movement. Jones puts his finger on the smouldering internal disputes, the subjective factor, as the main cause; Wheeler, however, goes further and refers to 'the power of adverse circumstances'[17]—in other words, objective difficulties. There is yet another point of difference: Jones's (unfinished) novel breaks off at an earlier stage, whereas Wheeler brings his story almost up to the time of writing. Which leads us back once more to that aspect of the novels which has already been mentioned, the diminution of the gap between the time that is being narrated and the narrative time itself. In this case the process is pushed to the point where history appears to have actually caught up with the authors. Or to put it another way: the fact that the novel can now encompass Chartism—and in this context we should also mention *Alton Locke, Tailor and Poet* (1850) written by the Christian socialist, Charles Kingsley—is the surest indication that the movement is in decline.[18] For in order for it to be able to do so, certain conditions must obtain, particularly as far as the protagonists are concerned. The movement needs to be in all essentials 'reviewable', relatively complete and historically as close as possible. Only thus can it become the objective of aesthetic reflection—and it is important to stress 'aesthetic', because considerable differences can open up between the imaginative grasp of historical reality on the one hand and theoretical or political utterances about it on the other.

While Jones—in the very periodical in which his novel was published—was still campaigning for the renewal of the Chartist movement, and while Wheeler was still championing the Land Plan at the time he was writing *Sunshine and Shadow* in O'Connorville, their novels convey the aesthetic recognition that the movement is finished, even if they do so without a trace of defeatism.[19]

What reasons prompted the Chartists to turn to the historical genre, what were their anticipations, what did they hope to achieve by their choice? The first thing to mention is that Chartism went hand in hand with a marked increase in historical consciousness. Ample evidence is provided by the movement's press, for there is hardly a journal that does not carry regular 'historical sketches'. But this concern with history, the interest in historical writings, and of course the predilection for the historical novel are not by any means peculiar to Chartism but common throughout the literate classes of the age. By the same token, there was nothing original in the fact that the Chartist novelists turned their attention to the nation's past and attempted to politicise the genre. The redoubtable Bulwer Lytton, highly esteemed by Wheeler as a practitioner of this particular form, had already trodden a similar path. He, too, viewed the terrain of history as a sounding board for the articulation of political propaganda, albeit in the interests of Disraeli's Tory democracy.

What sets the Chartists' understanding of history apart from most other contemporary conceptions is its operative principle. Characteristically, Jones's column in *Notes to the People* is entitled 'Lessons from History'. The writings of Bronterre O'Brien, the 'schoolmaster of Chartism', stress the role of the masses as the agents of history and introduce the concept of class as a historical category.[20] Historical consciousness thus comes to be regarded as a necessary precursor of class consciousness. In their novels Wheeler and Jones suggest as much when, faced with the problem of resolving the class conflict they have depicted, they adopt an uncompromising position. This is in stark contrast to the attitude of their middle-class contemporaries, the authors of the social-problem novels, who are more concerned to eliminate class conflict altogether, whether through a change of heart on the part of an individual or through pleas for mutual understanding.

The Chartist conception of history performs another function, too. It serves to keep in check the potentially overwhelming elements of melodrama and romance, as well as distancing the novel in terms of subject-matter from the elevated realms of the aristocracy. Wheeler at least was fully aware of this: 'We might have made our tale more interesting, by drawing more largely from the regions of romance, but our task was to combine a History of Chartism, with the details of our story.'[21] Similarly, Jones's novel represents a marked advance in terms of realism on his earlier romances, *The Confessions of a King* and *The Romance of a People*, although the latter work, a 'historical tale, of the nineteenth century' to some extent presaged the new tendency.

The Chartists were right to contend that 'the voice of Romance must die before the words of History',[22] but the new direction they were taking imposed its own special burden on the novel. The novelist now ran the risk of descending to the level of a mere historiographer. And in fact there are long passages in Wheeler's work which are best described as narrative reporting rather than graphic representation. The author is constantly obliged to take himself in hand, as he does, for example, after a digression on the city of Birmingham: 'But we are not writing a political essay, and therefore must discontinue this theme.'[23] Moreover, his characters generally lack life because he insists on 'characterising' them directly, seldom allowing them to develop in the course of the action and almost never through dialogue.

Having escaped one dilemma, then, the socialist novel seemed to be moving towards yet another impasse. But even if one set of difficulties had replaced another, this is not to suggest that the novel was simply marking time. A number of advances had in fact been made without beat of drum. At the level of subject matter, for example, the goal of representing a worker in a positive light and making him the central figure in the story had been realised. When it is borne in mind that 'As recently as the 1830's it had often been doubted whether the middle classes were sufficiently interesting to have novels written about them',[24] then the fact that here was an even lower social class which had yet enforced its claim to be represented in literature is undoubtedly of major significance. Additionally, and of particular relevance to the aesthetics of literary production and reception, the leading Chartists recognised that the terrain of the novel could no longer be simply left in the hands of the upper classes; it was now the task of the working class 'to occupy this wide and fertile plain'.[25] And thirdly, the bourgeois entrepreneurs, in the shape of Walter North in *Sunshine and Shadow* and Dorville in *De Brassier*, were now clearly identified as the principal social adversaries of the working class, whereas in the romances the reader's outrage had always been directed against the nobility.

IV

It seems to me more fruitful to view the emergence and development of the nineteenth-century socialist novel as a history of such small steps forward (with of course the occasional reverse), rather than to get involved in the discussion as to why the Chartist novel did not advance beyond the rudimentary stage. If the assumption were to be proven that the nineteenth-century socialist novel cannot stand comparison with the socialist poetry of the same period, then we should indeed be confronted with a problem of general aesthetic relevance—and one, moreover, which could not be dismissed simply by pointing to the lack of creative talent among the working-class and socialist novelists. But the history of the genre is still too incomplete to warrant any such claim, and in any case the arguments which have so far been advanced, although correct in some respects, leave many questions unanswered. The most common contentions are:[26]

a. whereas the poem (hymn or song), a short form that is easy and quick to compose, can be made politically operative at any time and in any situation, the novel is by comparison an unwieldy medium;

b. poetry is rooted by tradition in popular culture, but the novel demands of author and reader alike a high level of education;

c. the Chartist poets (and their successors) were able to call
   for inspiration on the revolutionary example of the English Romantics (Shelley, Byron), whereas there was no
   such point of reference for the novelists;
d. the nineteenth-century socialist novelists too often
   regarded the novel as merely a vehicle for ideas.

Even the most recent and ambitious attempt to transcend
such partial explanations and throw new light on the problem fails to lead us much further forward. Jack Mitchell, who
regards everything that comes before Tressell's *The Ragged
Trousered Philanthropists* as under-developed, argues that a
proletariat that is still caught up in the process of developing
and shaping itself will of necessity lack a coherent proletarian conception of man. Hence, he concludes, a highly
developed socialist novel was a historical impossibility during the Chartist era. Referring to Wheeler and Jones, he
writes:

> the proletariat was not yet really aware of its new type of
> revolutionary human validity. . . . although, in Chartism, the pre-
> 1850 proletariat had a working-class Idea to set against the
> bourgeois Idea, it was a partly utopian Idea which misunderstood
> and underestimated the present and future role of the working
> class in history.[27]

The trouble with this explanatory model is that it proceeds in
almost hypostatising fashion from a proletarian conception
of man that has been fixed once and for all, whereas of
course that conception, like the structure and social position
of the working class itself, is subject to historical change.
Apart from that the argument fails to tell us how it was that a
quite different literary form of the period, the working-class
autobiography, did in fact contain clearly delineated features
of a proletarian conception of man. But the main weakness
of Mitchell's case is that it is based on an over-estimation of
Tressell, who seems to emerge like a giant out of nowhere.

My concern is not to gloss over the shortcomings of the
Chartist novel, nor to belittle Tressell's achievement and
talent. But given the present state of research, I believe that
general aesthetic discussions should cede priority to the task

of reconstructing the tradition itself. Without that knowledge, all attempts to clarify theoretical questions are bound
to remain speculative. This is just one of several reasons for
my asserting that the study of the Chartist novel, with all the
artistic shortcomings referred to above, can be a meaningful
and rewarding undertaking.

The Chartist novel merits critical attention because it
occupies an early stage in that long if sporadic and uneven
tradition which has seen working-class and socialist writers
attempting to appropriate productively a literary form
which, given its close ties with the rise and history of the
middle class, turned out to be a major stumbling block. It is
thus important not to approach the Chartist novels with false
hopes. Generally speaking, 'working-class literature does
not come on the scene with a triumphant succession of great
artists.'[28] Hence the proposal to proceed from the small
advances and successes and to take account of the reverses.

To concern oneself with the Chartist novel is to take stock
of demands made of literature that are seldom encountered
in modern literary theory, namely that it should be both
operative and agitational. To put it crudely, the Chartists did
not conceive of their works as art for art's sake, nor did they
write in order to make money. Their best works are informed
by the aim of contributing to the consolidation of the movement and driving a wedge into the hegemony of aristocratic
and bourgeois culture. This they achieve by validating in
aesthetic form the collective experiences of the working
masses.

The period in which the Chartists were grappling with the
problems of the novel form, the 1840s, is of special interest
because it was then that the oppositional elements of proletarian culture began to acquire a literary dimension on an
unprecedented, and even in later times rarely equalled,
scale. With this development the ensemble of literary areas,
practices and interests, was first properly constituted, which
is still with us today, albeit in modified form. By this I mean
the essentially different, if overlapping and contested areas
of 'high-brow art', literature for mass-consumption—and,
now, working-class and socialist literature.

Finally, a hint on method. The Chartist novel need not be

studied in isolation; not only its aesthetic shortcomings, but also its promise and potential can best be worked out by undertaking an analysis that contrasts it with a novel written from a middle-class perspective that has a similar thematic orientation. The reverse also holds good: the works of Disraeli, Gaskell, Kingsley, Dickens and others should no longer be represented as the only examples of the early Victorian social-problem novel, but ought to be confronted with their Chartist opposite numbers.[29]

4 FORMS OF MINERS' LITERATURE IN THE NINETEENTH CENTURY

The following sketch of the beginnings and first stages of miners' literature in Britain ought to be read as a bibliographical essay rather than a thoroughgoing investigation. It is intended as a first mapping of the field. A more detailed critical and historical consideration of the genres and works introduced here would of necessity have to re-create much more of the context in which these were written and first used or enjoyed. Nevertheless it is hoped that despite its brevity the present survey—the first of its kind for the literature of any industry or occupational group[1]—is not without interest and will stimulate further research and extended critical enquiry.

By miners' literature I understand first of all the literary expressions of the coalminers themselves. But works produced by outsiders, who were not born into a mining community yet take a sufficient *and* serious interest in a mining subject, also qualify for inclusion. Broad as such an approach may be, it remains a working hypothesis which needs to be tested in the course of the study.

Edward Chicken's *The Collier's Wedding* (1720), the earliest known work in which coalminers figure prominently, provides a first opportunity to do so. It deals with the encounter of a collier lass and lad, their courtship and wedding. To devote oneself poetically to such a 'low' theme, warranted some kind of 'apology' in the early eighteenth century. This the author duly delivers, but without wasting his time. Soon a colourful ethnographical tableau unfolds before the reader, in which unbridled vitality and ancient rituals combine to unleash a fascinating spectacle of plebeian festivities. Here is just one of many amusing passages that would be worth quoting. When the villagers and other guests find the church-door locked and the parson absent, they

> Knock, swear, and rattle at the Gate,
> And vow to break the Beadle's pate;
> And call his Wife a Bitch and Whore,
> They will be in, or break the Door;
> .   .   .   .
> The Gates fly open, all rush in,
> The Church is full with Folks and Din;
> And all the Crew, both great and small,
> Behave as in a common Hall:
> .   .   .   .
> They scamper, climb, and break the Pews,
> To see the Couple make their Vows.[2]

During the ensuing banquet the couple and their guests finally throw off whatever fetters might have restrained them so far:

> Impatient for the Want of Meat,
> They feak, and cannot keep their Seat;
> Play with the Plates, drum on the Table,
> And fast as long as they are able;
> .   .   .   .
> Some eat the Bread, some lick the Salt
> Some drink, and other some find Fault.
> .   .   .   .
> Swift to the smoking Beef they fly;
> Some cut their Passage through a Pye:
> Out Streams the Gravy on the Cloth;
> Some burn their Tongue with scalding broth:
> .   .   .   .
> Now Geese, Cocks, Hens, their Fury fell
> Extended Jaws devour the Veal
> .   .   .   .
> Dead drunk some tumble on the Floor,
> And swim in what they drank before:[3]

Faced with such scenes, more puritan-minded contemporary observers were complaining of a return to barbarism and heathendom. Chicken lets no such sanctimonious and paternalistic considerations enter his picture. He contents himself with a truthful description of the sequence of events as he must have witnessed them many times; though, interestingly enough, he situates his narrative 'In former Days when Trade was good'.[4] The author (1698–1746) was an outsider, but one endowed with a remarkable gift of observation and a sense of coarse humour. And as a weaver's son, whose formal education had stopped at the level of a Newcastle charity school, he was, socially and geographically, not too far removed from the object of his work, even if he had meanwhile become a schoolmaster and parish clerk.[5] In any case, he makes no bones about his keen interest in the 'COLLIERS and their WIVES' and their 'drunken, honest working lives'.[6]

The same thing cannot be said about the poems of industry of the eighteenth century. In John Dalton's *A Descriptive Poem Addressed to Two Ladies at Their Return from Viewing the Mines near Whitehaven* (1755), for example, we come across the following lines:

> Agape the sooty collier stands
> His axe suspended in his hands.
> His Aethiopian teeth the while
> 'Grin horrible a ghastly smile',
> To see two goddesses so fair
> Descend to him from fields of air.[7]

Here, as in other examples of this type of writing,[8] the author's attention rests only momentarily and, one cannot fail to notice, incidentally on the miners. These poems celebrate in elegant diction the technical progress of their day, and its invigorating consequences for the commerce of the nation.

Aesthetically elaborate views from within the mining communities cannot be expected at this stage. Miners do not figure amongst the plebeian poets of the age.[9] What we find, then, in the eighteenth and early nineteenth centuries, are not elevated forms and works but only a rudimentarily formed kind of writing. Yet what evidence of literacy has survived—letters, handbills, speeches and early pamphlets —is at times a fascinating record and as often imaginative as not. The emergence of this kind of writing is an indication not only of the growing literacy amongst miners but also of their likewise developing confidence in themselves as a class of useful workmen.

Letters

One of the earliest letters on record comes from the hands of five Scottish miners who in 1746 sent a petition to Lord Prestongrange asking permission to work elsewhere during the temporary suspension of works in his colliery, lest they should starve to death.[10] Deference is the prevalent note, and yet the very wording of the letter makes it an outcry against a situation in which, until 1775–96, the Scottish coalowners held total control over the life of the miner and his family, not just in immediate practical terms but with the full sanction of the law of the country, which had reduced colliers (and salters) to the state of serfdom.

An open *Letter to Coalmasters in Scotland* from 1787, about whose existence we are informed in a later publication (1799),[11] refers to the barely satisfactory statute of 1775, under which the emancipation of the miners remained a piecemeal and highly bureaucratic affair. Only new entrants to the industry were henceforth automatically free. It is all the more remarkable, therefore, that the author(s) of the open *Letter* insist(s) on the principle of equality among men by pointing both to the more favourable condition of the miners in England and the ongoing discussion about the inhumanity of the cotton-slave trade.

An altogether different epistolary tradition is the anonymous threatening letter, a genre which has been described as 'a characteristic form of social protest in any society which has crossed a certain threshold of literacy, in which forms of collective organised defence are weak, and in which individuals who can be identified as the organisers of protest are liable to immediate victimisation'.[12] The occasion of such notices aimed at intimidating the rich and the mighty, or impressing a particular message on fellow-workmen, was as a rule a specific social grievance such as high bread prices or, in an agrarian context, an impending enclosure. The addressee may be a local food-hoarder or speculator, or a justice of the peace who may have protected the former in his court-rulings. Obviously such letters are not a peculiarity of mining communities; they can be found in many districts, in almost all trades and industries as they develop. Nor do these letters necessarily take up grievances at the workplace. They are directed against all kinds of measures that threaten the livelihood of the labouring poor. Pushing them under doors, dropping them in the street, affixing them to trees or pillory posts, their authors seek the shelter of anonymity because on identification they would face severe punishment. As a Newcastle collier remarks in 1765, not without a tinge of humour: 'I Wauld Tel you My Name but My Simplicity Will Not Let Mee.'[13]

The following specimen differs in two ways from the more traditional type of anonymous threatening letter: first the *fait* is already *accompli*, though further acts are announced; and second, it justifies by sophisticated reasoning the intrusion into the house:

I was at yor hoose las neet, and myed mysel very comfortable. Ye hey nee family, and yor just won man on the colliery, I see ye hev a greet lot of rooms, and big cellars, and plenty wine and beer in them, which I got ma share on. Noo I naw some at wor colliery that has three or fower lads and lasses, and they live in won room not half as gude as yor cellar. I don't pretend to naw very much, but I naw there shudnt be that much difference. The only place we can gan to o the week ends is the yel hoose and hev a pint. I dinna pretend to be a profit, but I naw this, and lots o ma marrows na's te, that wer not tret as we owt to be, and a great filosopher says, to get noledge is to naw wer ignerent. But weve just begun to find that oot, and ye maisters and owners may luk oot, for yor not gan to get se much o yor awn way, wer gan to hev some o wors now. I divent tell ye ma nyem, but I was one o yor unwelcome visitors last neet.[14]

The incident reported here took place in a village in County Durham in 1831, the recipient of the letter being a viewer in the nearby colliery. The letter stands at a turning point in the history of many mining communities. To consume in kind what has been withheld, as a way of making up to a fair wage, while simultaneously taking pains to leave the furniture of the house untainted, reveals a thinking along lines of a moral economy, and this is traditional. The hint to recently acquired knowledge, on the other hand—which could allude either to the activities of the Methodists in the region or to a proletarian motto of this period, 'Knowledge is Power'—foreshadows germinating class-consciousness, and this points to the future. The whole genre of the anonymous threatening letter is rather backward-looking; but, then, this genre has been adapted here to such argumentative purposes as to almost assume the character of a pamphlet, which is a more representative literary document emanating from the working class in this period.

Speeches

'A new type of speech based on fluent colloquialism grew up with the radical labour movement.'[15] Not parliamentary oratory or dinner speeches delivered in a cultivated ornate style are meant here, but the use of the platform in order to address mass audiences in the open air.

A whole and as yet not properly explored tradition of radical working-class oratory opens after the end of the Napoleonic Wars as part of the agitation for parliamentary reform, and leads then on via the repeal of the Combination Laws to the mass meetings of the Chartists, in which very articulate speakers gave rhetorically impressive performances.[16] Given the clandestine and discontinuous existence of the early trade unions, it is no surprise that initially such evidence as we have of speeches by miners' leaders tends to be based either on court proceedings or the reporting of a biased middle-class press. One can only assume that during the strikes of 1810 in the north-eastern coalfield and 1816 in South Wales, or during the intense union activity in Scotland in 1817–18 travelling delegates must have addressed quite a significant number of meetings.[17] But from the 1831–2 Durham strike onward, the evidence for the use of public speeches and proclamations is clearly available; and as the unions gather strength organisationally and ideologically, speeches by miners' leaders are more and more exploited as propagandist weapons. They might be distributed as handbills or pamphlets amongst the non-organised or specially hired blackleg miners. In the first miners' newspapers, *The Miners' Advocate* and *The Miners' Magazine*, both founded in 1843 in the north-east, lectures and speeches by union leaders form a regular feature.[18]

In Durham and Northumberland, the most consistently

militant coalfield of the first half of the nineteenth century, the rhetoric of miners' leaders is often strongly pervaded in tone by chapel preaching. Owing to the triumphant incursion of Methodism since the 1820s, the fusion of preacher and agitator was here a common phenomenon. The entire leadership of the strike of 1831–2, for example, was made up of Methodists.[19]

Speeches in the nineteenth century are also embedded in aesthetically more elaborate works, serving a didactic, propagandistic or revealing end, as the occasion might require. Thomas Cooper's monumental verse epic *The Purgatory of Suicides* (1845) begins with a speech which the Chartist author made before miners in Staffordshire,[20] and for which he received a two-year prison sentence. In Thomas Wright's *Grainger's Thorn* (1872), not strictly speaking a mining novel but still a work in which colliers and pit-bank girls are involved in a strike, the device is also used. In this case, however, we get not only the speech of the strike leader but also that of his enemy, the tyrannical capitalist Grainger, himself a former miner who has made a fortune as a gold-digger.[21] Only in the twentieth century do speeches become increasingly rare in miners' fiction and the socialist novel generally.

Pamphlets

No clear demarcation line can be drawn between this genre and the preceding one. The difference is essentially one of the audience aimed at: whereas in speeches miners addressed other miners, a considerable number of pamphlets, though by no means all of them, were directed at a wider public.

Among those addressed to the miners figure the published statutes of the unions which sprang up in many places after the repeal of the Combination Acts in 1824–5. It would be instructive to compare and contrast the extant rules of the Operative Colliers of Lanark, Dumbarton and Renfrewshire with those of the United Association of Colliers on the Rivers Tyne and Wear.[22] There is no space here to do this in detail, but one interesting difference is that the Scottish colliers did explicitly include a strike clause and generally employ a more self-confident, if not aggressive language.

At the same time, tracts and pamphlets were now being published with the aim of disseminating information among enlightened members of the middle class or workmen and artisans in other trades. The focus here is on injustices and grievances experienced daily almost everywhere: inadequate safety regulations in the pit, a tyrannical disciplinary system often leading to fines, the truck system (frequently continuing despite its official banning in 1831), the habitual cheating out of a fair wage through the weighing of the coal by overseers.

A typical example of this category, dated 1825, is entitled *A Voice from the Coal Mines; or, a Plain Statement of the Various Grievances of the Pitmen of the Tyne and Wear: Addressed to the Coal Owners—Their Head Agents—and a Sympathizing Public.* Its authorship is claimed collectively by the colliers of the already mentioned United Association of Colliers of Durham and Northumberland:

O! that in a moment like this, our masters would consider our situation, and amend our condition. Were they for a short time to change conditions with us, they would then fully understand, what the *oppression, insults, and injuries* are of which we complain. How miserable would they be, with the slender comforts of a collier's cottage: existence would then be intolerable, and happiness would only live in name. O! that the voice of RELIGION, REASON, and HUMANITY, (the sacred things, in the name of which we plead) might be heard and obeyed in our behalf.[23]

The juxtaposition of religion and reason indicates the main sources of inspiration. Religion, however, comes first, not only in enumeration, but also in the Biblical colouring of the language. How strongly this document is impregnated by a religious spirit becomes even plainer, when the passage quoted is set against some excerpts from a Scottish pamphlet published almost a generation earlier and entitled *Observations on the Laws Relating to the Colliers in Scotland; and Remarks on a Bill Proposed to Be Brought into Parliament, for Regulating the Service, Mode of Hiring, and Rate of Wages, of the Colliers & Other Persons, Employed in or about the Coal-Works in Scotland* (1799):

when the sales decline, particularly during summer, it is a common practice for Masters to restrict their Colliers to work only four or five days in the week. Is the Collier to obtain no redress for being thus thrown idle? It may be likewise asked, What provision is made for the Colliers, if, through the unskilfulness or parsimony of the Master, the Machinery should become insufficient, and the pits be filled with water, so as not to admit them to work? What provision is made for them, when days occur so stormy that the men and horses above ground, cannot stand to receive the coals, which the workmen are ready to furnish?

Instead of pleading, the second author demands; in lieu of moderation and patience, he utters a warning:

The inevitable consequence of coercive laws is, a mutinous disposition in those against whom they are enacted; . . . They would excite stubbornness and cunning in some, and outrage in others; and, in all, a want of that hearty exertion which is uniformly the result of free choice.

The writer also reflects in solidary manner on the negative consequences which a suppression of bargaining rights in one industry might produce for other working people:

if such regulations were adopted with regard to the Colliers, they would appear to be the forerunners of similar restraints, for all those employed at other mechanical or laborious employments in the kingdom.[24]

Perhaps the difference in diction and argument between the two pamphlets can be explained by attribution of authorship. The *Voice from the Coal Mines*, with its continuous use of the 'we', has the ring of authentic miners' writing. By contrast, the author of the *Observations*, quite apart from his more sophisticated style of debate, speaks of 'the Colliers' as if he was not one himself. A good guess as to the identity of the writer is that it was the Glaswegian law-agent Wilson, whom the colliers of Lanarkshire entrusted with their case in 1799, asking him to mobilise public opinion against certain planned clauses in the amendment to the

1775 Act.[25] The concerted action of petitioning miners and a stirring public debate, in which even a number of coalmasters voiced objections against the Bill, was a complete success. In 1799 the last remnants of serfdom disappeared from the Scottish coalfields.

However, the Tyne and Wear pamphlet did not remain unanswered. In the year of its publication alone, it provoked at least two replies.[26] A pattern of accusation and defence, initiated from either side of the industrial arena, is discernible here, a pattern which was to reappear for many years to come. Obviously it does not lead very far to generalise about the tone and attitude of these controversial writings. But by and large one gets the impression that the pamphlets produced on the coalowners' side are more frequently filled with an indignation that lets their language swell to ridiculous exaggerations, whereas the publications written or commissioned by the miners display, amidst a general tone of sobriety, the occasional note of humour and sarcasm. In reply to the suggestion of a middle-class pamphleteer to bring all the rebels to the gallows, one pamphlet-writer retorts drily: 'Poor fellow, if he had his own way he would hang all the Pitmen, and then his gains would be all at an end.'[27]

This tendency to mockery and ridicule at the expense of the class enemy or, for that matter, the class traitor, based as it is on a display of confidence and self-reliance, is perhaps more prevalent during the great trial of strength of the 1840s. From the long heroic strike on the north-eastern coalfield of 1844 the following parody of the Ten Commandments has survived:

I. Thou shalt have no other Master but me.

II. Thou shalt work for no other Master, neither shalt thou give thy services to any other man, for I thy Master am a jealous man, and I will visit thee with heavy fines and punishments if thou break any of my commandments.

III. Thou shalt say no manner of evil of me, but shalt say I am a good master although I act as a tyrant towards thee; for I will not hold thee guiltless if thou say any manner of evil of my name.

IV. Remember thou work six days in the week, and be very thankful that I allow thee the seventh day to recruit thy exhausted strength, for I, thy Master, want as much work out of thee as possible, and if it suits me to give thee only two, three, or more days in the week, be very thankful that I give thee any work at all, for I only look at my interest, not thine.

V. Honour me thy Master, honour my Viewers, My Overman, and my Agents, so that thy days may be long in my service.

VI. Thou shalt work thyself to death and commit self-murder.

VII. Thou shalt exhaust thyself with work to hinder thee from committing adultery.

VIII. Thou shalt not steal anything from thy Master altho' I give thee no money for working for me.

IX. Thou shalt not bear witness against me or any of my agents for any misdemeanor we may commit.

X. Thou shalt not covet thy Master's house thou shalt not covet thy Master's wife, nor his servants, nor his lands, nor his carriage, nor his horses nor any thing that is his.[28]

Summing up, one might say that the great variety of pamphleteering shows an endeavour not only to present an argument convincingly but to achieve some imaginative quality which would enhance its impact. Letters, speeches and pamphlets thus anticipate and prepare the way for the artistically more elaborate and demanding genres that were to follow. However, they did not automatically become obsolete when those more elevated forms appeared, but continued for a long time to be used as effective forms for rallying and instructing fellow-workmen, for voicing complaints and articulating urgent needs.

The verse tale

Thomas Wilson's *The Pitman's Pay* (1826) can be regarded as the first aesthetically shaped literary work—even according to conventional definitons of art—from the pen of a (former) miner. Born in Gateshead, the author (1773–1858) had toiled in the mines of Northumberland from the age of eight, and worked his way up from trapper to hewer, until he left the pit for good when he was nineteen. Owing to his tireless efforts at self-education, he had managed to secure himself a position as a teacher, eventually obtaining a clerkship and ending as a respected business partner in some mercantile establishment.[29]

His verse tale treats of the living and working conditions in the north-eastern coalfield as they existed in his boyhood in the 1780s. Wilson consciously established a connection with his predecessor Chicken, but *The Pitman's Pay* differs from the earlier *The Collier's Wedding* in at least three respects.

1. It draws a more comprehensive, if idealised, picture of everyday life in a mining community by not concentrating exclusively on a festive event but taking in several domestic and communal aspects. Although Wilson's locale is an ale-house on pay night, the use of dialogue enables him to illuminate various aspects of the pitmen's condition.
2. The author is not content solely to entertain his readers, but sets out to instruct them. With an eye to a middle-class public, he is at pains to qualify the prevalent image of the miners as a brutal, savage and drunken race—an image which *The Collier's Wedding* had unwittingly done much to confirm. At the same time, Wilson the Methodist and proponent of self-help wants to impress certain values such as honesty and sobriety on his proletarian readers. His ideal is domestic bliss, 'the happy hyem', which no degree of poverty or adverse circumstances can ultimately impair:

   'We labour hard te myek ends meet,
      'Which baffles oft the gentry's schemin';
   'And though wor sleep be short, it's sweet,
      'Whilst they're on bums and bailies dreamin'.

   'There is a charm aw cannot nyem,
      'That's little knawn te quality:
   'Ye'll find it in the happy hyem,
      'Of honest-hearted poverty.[30]

3. In resorting, in dialogue, to his native Northumbrian dialect, Wilson introduces an inimitable touch of class and locality. To give one more example of the rich, concrete and graphic quality of this language: the author

describes, in the following two stanzas, how the coalmasters lull the miners through drinks into near-insensibility so as to make them willing to sign the yearly bond without paying attention to the terms:

> 'Just like wor maisters when we're bun,
>   'If men and lads be varry scant,
> 'They wheedle us wi' yel and fun,
>   'And coax us into what they want.
>
> 'But myek yor mark, then snuffs and sneers,
>   'Suin stop yor gob and lay yor braggin':
> 'When yence yor feet are i' the geers,
>   'Maw soul! they keep yor painches waggin'![31]

Wilson's Scottish fellow-poet David Wingate (1828–1892) similarly turns to the past in his verse tale *Annie Weir* (1866). An old miner tells his nephews the story of his early days in the pit, and of his love for the barely seventeen-year-old Annie who was employed as a coalbearer. The work demonstrates that more than twenty years after the formal prohibition of female labour underground this ignoble chapter of industrial history was neither forgotten nor forgiven. Annie and Reuben one day find themselves trapped in a flooded pit. The girl could have escaped in time but chose to return to the seam in order to warn her workmate and lover of the imminent danger. Now they are both cut off and face certain death as the water rises incessantly:

> We didna tear our hair,
>   But it surely was despair,
> That made us ither's hauns sae wildly tak';
>   For our heavy hearts aye sunk,
>   As wi' hollow, dismal, clunk,
> The water slowly rose and drove us back.
>
> For hope there was nae room,
>   There we saw and kent our doom,
> Nae skill, nor faith, nor prayer could scaur't awa;
>   It would creep up pace by pace
>   And to reach the farthest face
> It could but tak' a day, or maybe twa.[32]

What lifts Wingate's work above the ephemeral, is the absence of any sentimental or bathetic undertone in this desperate situation, at a time when this was one of the chief characteristics of the poetic effusions of not a few of his Victorian contemporaries. Long passages are written in a simple, yet effective down-to-earth manner. The narrative ends with a typical colliery superstition: the two narrowly escape death, but Annie only in order to die within a year, 'ere she was a mither',[33] the suggestion being that the mine has nonetheless claimed its own.

Verse tales like the ones discussed here often recount occurrences from everyday life. And mining disasters were a common feature of nineteenth-century pit-life. The verse tale is thus, in Mary Ashraf's words, a suitable genre for giving 'significance to the experiences and feelings arising out of the normal setting of life and to make didactic use of these examples'.[34]

With Joseph Skipsey (1832–1903) we return to the Northumbrian coalfield. This miner's life story, with its combination of more than average hardship inflicted at an early age and, again, a rather atypical closeness to established literary circles, makes fascinating reading: the father shot dead by a constable during the turbulences of the 1831–2 strike; the boy 'apprenticed' as a trapper at the age of seven; teaching himself to read by the occasional light from candle-ends while attending to the trapdoor; repeatedly attempting to earn a livelihood other than by hewing coal but invariably failing, as if magically drawn back to the pit; patronized (in the dual sense of the word) by the Pre-Raphaelites; at one time given custodian's post at Shakespeare's birthplace in Stratford-upon-Avon showing American tourists around, but not able to stand it; always taking up the pick again.[35]

Skipsey's most striking poems are short lyrical impressions like 'Get up!':

> 'Get up!' the caller calls, 'Get up!'
>   And in the dead of night,
> To win the bairns their bite and sup,
>   I rise a weary wight.

        My flannel dudden donn'd, thrice o'er
        My birds are kiss'd, and then
    I with a whistle shut the door,
        I may not ope again.[36]

But on one or two occasions he does also resort to the verse
tale—as in 'Bereaved', where a woman mourns over the
loss of her husband and children from a variety of causes.

In later life, the author developed a predilection for
natural and spiritual themes. He is the first of a number of
miner writers who now resist the label 'pit-poet', as they
cherish greater ambitions and move increasingly beyond the
range of subjects provided by the mining milieu.[37] Despite
advice to the contrary by his patrons and mentors, Dante
Gabriel Rossetti in particular, Skipsey persisted in these
efforts, exploring in a number of allegorical poems the state
of society and of the human soul. Isolated, misunderstood
and impoverished, he nonetheless drew creative energy out
of his unwavering conviction that here at last, in the alle-
gorial mode, he had discovered a congenial style.[38]

Documentarism

Had Annie and Reuben, the protagonists of Wingate's verse
tale, been real-life figures, they might have numbered
amongst the thousands working in or around the mines who
in 1841 gave evidence to the Children's Employment Commission just as the author of *The Pitman's Pay* was interviewed.[39] As is well known, when the Commission finally
submitted its findings to parliament, their publication created a stir and prompted the abolition of child and female
labour underground. Beyond that, what has made these
bulky volumes such an invaluable source of social history, is
the sheer amount of primary material accumulated from all
the British coalfields; mostly short interviews with the men,
women and children themselves, but also with overseers,
doctors, clergymen and teachers.

From the perspective of a cultural and literary historiography, which takes an interest in the reconstruction of lived

social relations and past consciousness, the value of this source material is, of course, somewhat diminished by two circumstances: first, the informants were only allowed to reply to a set catalogue of questions; second, in most cases their answers were reproduced in Standard English. Did eleven-year-old James Cargill from Barnsley speak like this?

I am turned 11. I work as trapper in Messrs Day and Turbell's pit. I went to pit about four years ago and then I hurried. I go to all pits where my brother does. I go at seven in the morning, and I come out at half past five. They use me very well: they don't lace me, because I have got a brother in the pit. I go to a Sunday-school sometimes. I don't know my letters . . . I am quite sure that I never heard anything about Jesus Christ coming on earth to save sinners. I don't know how many weeks there are in the year; there are 12 months. Ireland is a town, but I do not know what Scotland is.[40]

On the other hand, depending on the individual approach and commitment of the respective sub-commissioner, one may come across more authentic-sounding testimonies like this statement from six-year-old Margaret Leveston from Mid-Lothian:

The work is na guid; it is so very sair. I work with sister Jesse and mother; dinna ken the time we gang; it is gai dark. Get plenty of broth and porridge, and run home and get bannoch, as we live just by the pit. Never been to school; it is so far away.[41]

J. R. Leifchild, who had been appointed to investigate the conditions in Durham and Northumberland, went about his work in a methodologically more reflective way than most other sub-commissioners. Not only did he, for example, take into account the natural distrustfulness of the miners vis-à-vis any outsider, but also made himself familiar with the 'northern provincialisms, peculiar intonations and accents, and rapid and indistinct utterance',[42] in short, learnt the pit-talk of at least some mines and added—like Thomas Wilson before him—a glossary to his report. However, despite his avowed intention to reproduce the answers of his 668 informants—the highest number interviewed anywhere—in an unadulterated manner, there can be no question of his having made any concessions to dialect. In fact, he even had the predicate in his informants' sentences changed to the third person singular.

Leifchild represents the kind of philanthropic bourgeois of this period in whom sympathy for the miners' intolerable conditions and downright hostility to their trade-union activity meet. The author spent many more years in the northeast relentlessly collecting geological and technological data about coalmining as well as recording the everyday life of the pitmen, and eventually brought the fruits of his research to the attention of the public. His anonymously published book *Our Coal and Our Coal-Pits; The People in Them, and the Scenes around Them. By A Traveller Underground* (1853)[43] was the best informed and most substantial account of coalmining to date, however unreliable in certain details such as the *mentalités* of the miners it might have been.

What is important, however, is the fact that contemporary middle-class opinion accepted the truthfulness of his descriptions. There was obviously a demand for authentic, semi-scientific and popular accounts of the industry and its workforce, which until only recently had been regarded with horror and contempt, and whose often isolated, closely-knit communities had for a long time precluded the leaking out of inside information. Soon Leifchild's work went through a second impression, and other publications in this vein followed in the 1860s. Some of these have not the least merit, such as, for example, *Life amongst the Colliers* (1862), despite its anthropologically promising title. Other writers developed a more historical approach like the work of an Ignotus, whose *The Last Thirty Years in a Mining District; or Scotching and the Candle vs. Lamp and Trade-Unions* (1867) surveys the advent of 'civilisation' in the Welsh coalfields. By 1873, Fynes could thus note, 'The miners have now come to be regarded as objects of universal interest.'[44]

This attention accorded to the miners is also part of a wider documentary impulse, active around the middle of the century. Henry Mayhew is another prominent early social investigator, whose preoccupation with the causes of poverty led him, empirically as well as linguistically, to much more fruitful results. *The Morning Chronicle*, for which he worked, was renowned for its regular column 'Labour and the Poor'.[45] This is then the period of the first great ethnographical explorations by enlightened and disturbed middle-class travellers of what would eventually be called the proletarian 'abyss'. A now shuddering, now sympathetic, public is offered factual inside views of hitherto undocumented scenes from the everyday life of the British Isles. The more empathetic and culturally oriented of these documentary accounts ought to be distinguished from the purely fact-finding, statistically oriented reports current in the 1830s and 1840s.

Songs and Ballads

The reason for dealing with miners' songs so late in this survey, when in keeping with the chronology they should have come first,[46] is simply a generic one. Musicologists have rightly insisted on the need to treat songs and ballads as a cultural form in its own right, not to be lumped with literature *tout court*.

The particular quality of the songs and ballads may also account for the fact that of all the forms and works sketched here none is more popular or more easily accessible. This situation owes a lot to the pioneering anthology *Come All Ye Bold Miners* (1952, 1978),[47] and the many new recordings of songs that followed in its wake.[48] A further indication of the actual interest in the song culture of the miners is the lively debate that has gone on for some time about the origins, nature and function of the genre. A. L. Lloyd, who initiated the serious study of the industrial folk-song in Britain, has on one occasion proposed the following definition: 'songs made originally within, and for circulation among, the in-group of workmates and their families, more or less agreeing in style with traditional folk song in creation, shape and destiny'.[49] The emphasis laid here on the original situation of the composition and reception of the songs stems in part from Lloyd's aim to distinguish industrial folklore from other types of workers' song, such as revolutionary anthems or the workers' chorus. But this has not prevented it from being attacked for what was seen as an idealised picture of the real conditions of industrial folk-song production. David Harker, for example, has argued that, at least in the case of the miners, only a minority of songs were actually written *by* them, whereas the great majority of songs in circulation came from outside the mining communities, that is, were written *for* them. A whole number of supposedly authentic and doubtless popular miners' songs can thus be shown to be doctored versions or written with a definite commercial aim.[50] The problem with this kind of approach is, however, that it tends to over-estimate the importance of the class background of the song-writer. Relevant as questions of authorship and transmission are, they ought, as we have pointed out at the beginning of this chapter, not to be taken as the only criteria. There is much to be said for concentration on the actual contents and function of the songs. Indeed, the cultural use of the form seems beyond dispute: 'the songs of the pit community can be seen . . . as much a part of the pitman's daily experience as the wage he hewed, the ale he drank.'[51]

The immediate value of such songs becomes obvious when their subjects are set alongside those of famous socialist hymns like *The Red Flag* or *The International*. The latter type, written in an elevated style or agitational manner, takes up more general political issues (oppression, injustices, martyrdom for the cause, visions of the future). By contrast, the miners' songs and ballads remain firmly located within the boundaries of the pit community. Leisure and love, work and industrial conflict, pit disasters and general coalfield conditions are the recurrent themes. The great variety of moods and attitudes with which subjects from this repertoire are treated cannot be specified here.

It is, however, possible to note a few general tendencies, characteristic of the evolution of the genre in the nineteenth century:

1. the growing importance of the individual song-creator accompanied, on the level of mediation, by a shift from oral transmission to channels like the leaflet, the newspaper or the songbook;
2. the impact of the Music Hall, in the latter half of the

century, on song-writing;
3. the invariable attempt to turn songs into an operative genre in moments of struggle (e.g. during the 1831–2 and 1844 strikes in the north-east, or the two lock-outs of 1892–3) and for particular charity uses such as fund-raising after pit-disasters;
4. the outstanding contribution of the north-eastern coal-field, and the evolution of a regionally coloured style whose main features are the use of dialect, a local patriot-ism (Geordie-ism) and the caricaturing of the milieu.

After the turn of the century, the miners' song tradition ran dry, to be revived again in the 1950s, at a time when the industry itself was in steady decline. It was fitting that in those years a new kind of song would see the light, the farewell tribute to collieries closed by the National Coal Board. In output and distribution, no less than in longevity and popularity, miners' songs have thus outstripped all the other forms introduced here.

Autobiographies

Why is it that, compared to some other industries or trades, autobiographies by coalminers are a rarity in the nineteenth century and so late in coming?

The first known printed work, *Autobiography of a Colliery Weighman* (1874) by George Hanby, is a slight affair, written in verse and not exceeding three pages. Like *The Early Recollections of Moses Horler* (1900), it does not even come from the pen of a pitman proper.[52] Hanby had never worked underground, and Horler was employed as a mason by the colliery of his native village of Radstock (Somerset). Owd Mo's *From Coal-Pit to Joyful News Mission* (c. 1890) might have been a different story, had the author not actu-ally begun his account with his conversion to Methodism.[53] As it is, all we get to justify the first part of the title are a few meagre hints to his early gambling, drinking and fighting days, after which 'The Devil's Servant' becomes 'The Ser-vant of Jesus Christ'.

So we have to wait until the publication of Edward Allan

Rymer's *The Martyrdom of the Mine, or, a 60 Years Struggle for Life* (1898), before we get a comprehensive life-story of a miner who had not only worked in all conceivable capacities in the pit but had, uniquely, in part as a result of frequent victimisation, in part as a service to his union, set his foot in all the principal coalfields of England.

From the outset, Rymer's recollections reveal a feature which is distinctive of an entire group of working-class autobiographies. Though he spares his readers no details of his many misfortunes and struggles, these are never told for their own sake but with the aim of illuminating general 'wrongs, evils, grievances, and abominations of mining life', and of driving home the message 'that not a single miner out of the half a million working underground should be found outside the miner's unions'.[54] Blind in one eye, almost crippled at one stage, twice imprisoned, many times victimised and blacklisted, Rymer had from early childhood borne more than the average brunt of hardship and deprivation. But as an indefatigable fighter for the Cause, his individual destiny is always related to the wider issue of the emancipation of the miners, and it is to the union that his first and last thoughts belong. The wish not to over-personalise the narrative is already apparent in the title, when compared to those previously quoted. But it is also there in a typical silence in the text which the author shares with the great majority of proletarian autobiographers: a reticence to speak about his private life,[55] an experience not deemed fit or relevant enough to be of value to the fellow-workmen to whom this kind of autobiography was primarily addressed.

Some of the tendencies spelled out in connection with Rymer's memoir—notably the individual narrator as spokesman for his occupational group or community—can also be found in a group of life-stories that begin to appear before the First World War: John Wilson, *Memories of a Labour Leader* (1910); and George Parkinson, *True Stories of Durham Pit Life* (1912). Thomas Burt's posthumously published *Autobiography* (1924) also belongs here. Contrary to Rymer, however, these three authors, without exception public figures from the north-eastern coalfield, relate their experiences from a position of social recognition and financial security. Burt (1837–1922) belonged to the first generation of working-class people who had been elected to the Commons after the Second Reform Act of 1867. Wilson (1837–1915), another MP, had for many years acted as General Secretary of the Durham Miners' Association, whose history he wrote. Parkinson (1828–191?) had achieved celebrity as a Methodist preacher. Not surprisingly, therefore, their memoirs offer much beyond the description of mining life at the time of their boyhood and early manhood. Wilson gives prominence to his political reform activities; in Parkinson's case the largest space is taken up by an account of his missionary work; and Burt's story, which is only brought to the year 1874, has been updated by his biographer Aaron Watson so as also to cover his parliamentary career.

Yet the charm and interest of these works clearly lies in those early parts which evoke the atmosphere in the mining communities around the middle of the century. Burt, the most vivid and humorous story-teller of the three, recounts some tragi-comical incidents from the heroic struggle of 1844. Parkinson's narrative is most persuasive in its treatment of two occurrences that were to figure time and again in future autobiographies and novels: the 'first days in the pit' and a fatal accident. Wilson is very good in his recollections of the stamina needed for the courageous insistence on one's rights in the days of non-existent unions, and the suffering it usually entailed either through vicious treatment by the overseer or through threat of dismissal. In Wilson's work, once again, the impersonal quality of working-class autobiographies, noted above, is very prevalent, leading the author to assume the third person singular for his narrative.

To return to the initially posed question, then: even allowing for the existence of hitherto unearthed material,[56] the fact remains that it is only the second generation of miners' leaders, active on their men's behalf from the 1860s onwards, who put their pen to paper with the purpose of making their reminiscences useful public knowledge, while the pioneers of the 1830s and 1840s left no such record behind. Many of the Chartist radicals were eager autobiographers in later life; but, as it happens, no miner rose to any significant rank in the movement. On the contrary, it was the Chartists and militants from other trades who provided advice and agitational 'know-how' to the early miners' unions so that it can be said of the organisation of the 1840s that 'Most of the top leaders of the Miners' Association (with the exception of Swallow and Jude) appear to have never worked in the coal industry'[57]—a circumstance that provided ammunition for anti-union propaganda. Even the first two miners' magazines published from the north-east were edited by outsiders, though in Scotland, with its better provision of education, the situation was different. The shortlived *Colliers' and Miners' Journal* actually appears to have been run by a working miner.[58]

And this is the most plausible explanation for the long absence of autobiographies; the social and cultural isolation of most mining communities, a general lack of educational facilities, and hence for a long time a low degree of literacy—to say nothing of the harsh and disabling working conditions.

Novels

The first fictional treatment of miners that I have come across dates from the 1840s and early 1850s, the heyday of the 'industrial novel'. In 1844 *The New Monthly Magazine* serialised a tale entitled 'The Miners: A Story of the Old Combination Laws'.[59] The author, 'The Medical Student' alias Robert Douglas, was a young Scottish surgeon in the Royal Navy who died prematurely in the year of the story's publication.

The title is somewhat misleading, for the miners as a class lead only a shadowy existence in the background of the story, whose plot revolves entirely around the relationship and worldly progress of two brothers. They are miner's sons sure enough, but have used all their energy and talent to rise above their class; Edmund, the younger, by obtaining eventually, through intrigue and marriage, the ownership of a colliery; Mark, the older, by organising and leading a powerful clandestine combination of miners. Nominally Mark is still on the side of labour, but his methods are so ruthless, his self-interest and corruptibility so revolting, that this is pure masquerade. For example, it transpires that he has not only misappropriated union funds but is actually a double-dealer with contacts with the Home Office.

It is clear that Douglas's tale is not based on first-hand knowledge of mining life and that, ultimately, the author's interest is with the intricate and deadly enmity of two kinsmen and not the rather coincidental setting. But when it is remembered that 'The Miners' was first published at the height of the 1844 strike, it is difficult not to read it as a condemnation of all trade-union activity, even if there is, as is usual in the social-problem fiction of the period, the inevitable sympathy for the 'poor creatures', the sullen mass of the working people. The very least that can be assumed is that the reception of the work by the readers of *The New Monthly Magazine* would have been along these lines.

Though G. Wharton Simpson's basic attitudes in his tale 'Colliers and Coal Mining', serialised in *The Working Man's Friend and Family Instructor* (1851), are not altogether dissimilar, one difference is that the blame is now laid at the door of union officials who have arrived at the troubled spot from outside and have led the decent mining folk on a disastrous path. This is a familiar kind of argument. But in many ways this story is written with greater insight into the industry. In fact, the author misses no opportunity to intersperse facts, figures and footnotes, and concludes his work with a statistical appendix.[60]

Simpson agrees that the present appalling conditions of the miner cannot be tolerated, and is even prepared to admit that it is a disgrace to the whole nation. But his solution is no less patronising: the necessary improvement has to be initiated from above, not through the exertions of the miners themselves. In the year of the Great Exhibition, which figures prominently in the columns of *The Working Man's Friend* and is also mentioned in the tale, it was appropriate to end on a note of cautious optimism. The author bases his hopes on the progress of the Total Abstinence Society and the spread of Mechanics Institutes.

Like the last-mentioned periodical, the anonymous author

of the novel *Jane Rutherford; or, The Miners' Strike* (1854) poses as 'A Friend of the People'. The person behind this pseudonym is Fanny Mayne, in whose journal *The True Briton* the novel was first serialised. Artistically flimsy, ideologically an unequivocal reflex of the 'industrial novel', her work is vaguely reminiscent of *Mary Barton*. There is the figure of the embittered labour leader Jonathan Rutherford, whose ambition, selfishness and guilt are such that they can only be redeemed in a death in delirium (in its excessively drawn negative traits this portrait ends in real caricature); his sensitive, discreet and religious daughter Jane; and finally the motif of emigration. Mayne's Tory ideals are embodied in the noble—in both senses of the word—mine-owner Lord Westerland. In order to lend authenticity to her picture, the author employs several methods: she quotes extensively from Leifchild's just published documentary account; she reproduces verbatim speeches of the two main antagonists, Rutherford and Westerland (though she cannot refrain from continually intruding with comment); she claims to have visited a coalmine herself; and she adds to the book edition a congratulatory letter from a miner, who wholeheartedly agrees that the pitmen have too often been duped by demagogues. None of this is particularly convincing, but the real blunder comes when she attempts, by use of phonetics, to reproduce the miners' dialect.

Enough has been said of this kind of prose to substantiate the point that it has no claim to be considered as miners' literature. Indeed, as in the case of the autobiography, it was to be another forty years before a novel of mining life, written from a diametrically opposite perspective, would appear. The honours go to W. E. Tirebuck (1854–1900) for his work *Miss Grace of All Souls'* (1895). Born in Liverpool and endowed with only a minimal formal education, this novelist had worked in a variety of manual and clerical jobs before becoming a journalist and, in his last years, a free-lance writer.[61] *Miss Grace* focuses on the lock-out of 1893, which originated in a decision by the mine-owners to push through a twenty-five per cent wage reduction, a measure against which the colliers of Yorkshire, Lancashire and the Midlands, who then formed the Miners' Federation of Great Britain, put up a stubborn and desperate resistance.

The novel demonstrates the full force of the struggle, the deployment of troops at the request of the coalmasters and its inevitable consequence, the senseless killing and injuring of people; but also the daily hardship and suffering endured by the miners and their families during fifteen weeks without pay. It further exemplifies the many virtues of a typical mining village in the North of England in times of struggle: the determination and solidarity of a united community, the singular dedication and tenacity of the young miners, their indifference to the propaganda of compromise and class reconciliation, their humanity and moral superiority.

With some justification *Miss Grace* has been characterised as 'the most important industrial novel to be published in England since *Hard Times*'.[62] Like the mid-century novelists, Tirebuck presents the social conflict as a clash between 'two nations'. But there the parallels end. For the author displays a far greater understanding of the motives of the strikers. He wonderfully re-creates the cultural texture of a mining family and its neighbourhood. And he is unambiguous in his attack on the profit-mongering mine-owners and the coverage of the events by the press; and in his indignation at the role of the Church. False religion is embodied by a vicar who publicly preaches moderation to the miners, while inwardly fearing for his coal shares. The true Christian values of brotherhood and sincerity, Tirebuck proclaims, have to be sought elsewhere; in the miners' backyards and in the courageous behaviour of the vicar's daughter, Grace Waide, who changes sides in the course of the struggle.

Miss Grace is a novel which would demand a far more detailed treatment. Its differentiated characterisation both of the women and of the leading working-class figures, the fine atmospheric and linguistic rendering of the working-class environment, and the stance it takes on the miners' side, will secure it an honoured place in the history of English socialist fiction—which is another way of saying that, above all, it deserves to be reprinted.

This, then, is the opening of the militant miners' novel

tradition. But the decisive breakthrough, the taking-up of the genre by working miners, had still to come. This is the achievement of the generation of miners born around the great lock-out: James C. Welsh, Harold Heslop, Fred C. Boden, John Swan, Lewis Jones, and others.[63] Their novels, however, only begin to appear after the First World War and thus lie outside the confines of the survey of this chapter.

5 HAROLD HESLOP: MINER NOVELIST

Harold Heslop occupies a unique place in the history of English socialist fiction of the first half of the twentieth century. Born of mining stock and a miner himself for fifteen years, he had his first novel published in a mass edition in the Soviet Union before any of his writings found their way to the press in his own native country. He represented the still unorganised British worker-writers at the Kharkov Conference of Revolutionary and Proletarian Writers in 1930 which brought together more than a hundred delegates from twenty-two countries. And last but not least he had one of his novels compared and contrasted not too unfavourably with Joyce's *Ulysses* in a key text of Marxist literary theory of the 1930s, Alick West's *Crisis and Criticism*.[1]

To explain how Heslop reached his singular position is the purpose of this chapter, the interest of which is largely biographical, though cross-references are made in a number of places to worker-writers in similar positions. In drawing attention to an author who has so far escaped the current interest in the thirties I hope, of course, to be able to rescue him from obscurity.[2] Indeed, the once internationally recognised author is so little known today that most people will be surprised to learn that he died as recently as 10 November 1983.

The portrait that follows is based on a cursory reading of a number of twenties and early thirties periodicals of the left (*The Sunday Worker, The Worker, Plebs, Labour Monthly, The Communist Review, International Literature*, etc.) and on information provided by Heslop himself.[3]

To say that the emphasis is biographical and historical rather than literary is to counter in advance the reproach that occasionally shortcuts are made between the 'real world' and the world of the novels which, from a strictly critical viewpoint, may be contestable or at least warrant circumspect mediations.

I

Harold Heslop was born on 1 October 1898 at Hunwick, a village near Bishop Auckland, into a family which had worked in the mines of the north-east for four generations. In what is the author's least known but arguably finest novel, *The Earth Beneath* (1946), Heslop has erected a monument to his ancestors, portraying their life from the time they first took to coalmining in the 1840s to the definite breakthrough of union organisation two generations later. His father, however, had moved two steps upwards socially by attaining the position of a colliery manager. This family background may help to explain why the manager in his novels is never quite such a sinister and lecherous figure as, for instance, in the works of James C. Welsh, that other formidable miner novelist of the twenties. From *Goaf* to *Last Cage Down* the author appears anxious to represent the manager as no less exposed to the law of the labour market than the miners themselves. At any rate, the father's position allowed him to offer his son an education at Bishop Auckland Grammar School which he might otherwise not have received. This, however, came to an abrupt end after only one term owing to a family move resulting from the father assuming his first managership in an iron-ore mine in Boulby (Cleveland). Since there was no grammar school within reasonable distance, the boy, at the age of fourteen, had to go 'the way of all mining flesh—into the mines',[4] as the author remarks of one of his characters. From 1912 to 1924 Heslop worked thus in iron-ore and coalmines, interrupted only by a spell in the cavalry towards the end of the First World War during which, however, he saw no fighting. Most of those years were spent in the South Shields colliery district where he had found work after having practically been driven from home by his stepmother. It is in this area that his major works (*Goaf, The Gate of a Strange Field, Last Cage Down, The Earth Beneath*) are situated. And the actual place-names in these novels are so thinly disguised that one wonders why he chose to do so at all.[5] The peculiarities of the Durham coalfield come out not so much through the use of a particular kind of dialogue as through the description of characteristic local traditions, such as the cavilling system by which lots are cast every three months among the miners for the particular sections of the coalface to be worked, so as to avoid a permanent unjust distribution of hard and soft areas. Other local customs and sports, vividly described particularly in *The Earth Beneath*, include the celebration of New Year's holiday, 'knurr and spell', which is a kind of golf, and 'pitch and toss', one of the few games played on a Sunday.

Heslop knew his Durham so well that on the publication of J. C. Grant's pseudo miner novel *The Back-to-Backs* (1930), which purports to give a realistic picture of the north-eastern colliery districts but actually treats the miners as revolting brutes living a monstrous life in a hellish environment, he could easily pin down as a scurrility without any documentary value whatsoever the sensationalist exploit of someone with only a superficial knowledge of pit life. This sound judgement stands out well against the contemporary chorus of voices, including parliamentary labour leaders, which praised Grant's work for its supposedly stark realism.[6]

It appears that Heslop had already completed his first novel when the event occurred which took him out of his community and in the long run changed his entire life. In 1924 he won, after a series of examinations, one of four scholarships for the Central Labour College in London which the Durham Miners' Association awarded annually to its members. Another successful candidate that year was John E. McCutcheon, in later life also a well-known miner writer of the north-east.[7] The two-year scholarship included not only free board and tuition but also a weekly maintenance grant from his Lodge. Yet his stay at the College—where he crossed paths with Lewis Jones, a future NUWM organiser and fellow miner novelist—was not apparently all sunshine. Heslop was perhaps unlucky to arrive at a time when one scandal followed the other and 'the Labour College was in a state of almost constant political turmoil',[8] with the students voicing complaints ranging from the spartan discipline of the establishment to the incompetent lecturing of the three members of staff.

The internecine conflicts raging in the labour college movement were another problem with which Heslop must have been confronted. The controversy was over the question of how best to advance along the path of independent working-class education, whether by means of a resident central college which could train only a limited number of particularly gifted students but who would then serve as teachers back in the country, or through a chain of non-resident colleges which would reach out for the wider ranks of the organised working class, the latter idea being promoted by the Plebs League and the National Council of Labour Colleges (NCLC). There was then a situation of objective competition between the Central Labour College and the NCLC for trade-union support, but there were also personal animosities at work. That Heslop was eventually drawn into these, is evident from an extremely polemical article written later and entitled 'Raymond Postgate. A Memoir'. This he had the audacity to submit to *Plebs* where, inevitably, it was turned down, before being published, after some revisions, by *The Communist*.[9] Yet, however much Heslop may have been influenced in this by the hostile feeling fostered in Central Labour College circles against the intellectuals of the Plebs League, he displays here a tendency which is also glaringly present in some of his early novels and seems to betray a personal weakness. The harsh and indiscriminate nature of his attacks on trade-union officials, notably in *The Gate*, by far exceeds the kind of bitter jibes at fellow-workers to be found, for example, in a work like *The Ragged-Trousered Philanthropists* and constitutes a major difficulty for an assessment of the political and ideological stance taken in these early works. In this particular case the contempt was reciprocal. When *The Gate* came out, *Plebs* hit back by deploring the publication of such 'half-baked, silly mush'; and N. (ess) E. (dwards), the author of the review, used the opportunity to question the methods of a political education, when a worker, after a two-year training at the College, could produce such 'mud'.[10] Though the reviewer was not very eloquent on this matter, the fierceness of the attack may also have been provoked by the fact that Heslop in one passage of the novel had deplored the 'monstrous schism'[11] in working-class education between the university-oriented WEA and the more Marxist-inclined NCLC rather than speaking out in favour of the latter.

As a resident of the Labour College from 1924 to 1926 Heslop witnessed the Nine Days of the General Strike in London. It is an experience re-enacted in *The Gate*, though what is pertinent here is less the militancy of the strikers than the combative mood of the middle and upper classes:

In the part of London where they lived there was no revolutionary outlook. There was nothing but glittered hatred. All available forces were being mobilised to quell the tumult, a mobilisation which spelled danger. . . . He saw the undergraduate and the member of the Universities swoop down on Piccadilly.[12]

As in Ellen Wilkinson's novel *Clash* (1928), when it comes to the other side in the struggle, the focus is on the higher reaches of the trade-union hierarchy instead of on the activities of the rank and file. This allows the author to criticise the timorous handling of the strike by the London leaders: the somewhat enigmatic title of the book is actually a quotation from H. G. Wells's General Strike novel *Meanwhile* (1927) in which the General Council of the TUC had been spoken of as behaving like 'sheep at the gate of a strange field'.[13] But this self-same concentration on the national leadership is clearly a handicap which prevents Heslop from conveying the motivations and actions of countless men and women behind the strike. The result is, as Alick West pointed out, a lack of felt energy in the presentation of social struggles: 'Heslop can show social organisation in productive activity as a living reality. When it is a question of the change of that organisation through class-war, he becomes abstract and aloof; what he describes, is an empty unreal show.'[14] Taken on its own, the author's absence from the coalfield during the crucial period of the Nine Days and its immediate aftermath cannot account for this weakness. Others factors of a more general artistic and philosophical nature are also undoubtedly involved. After all, Heslop had been actively engaged in earlier industrial struggles (1919, 1921), in 1923–4 he had been council delegate of his union, and after his return to the coalfield in the summer of 1926 he had been quite active in the Minority Movement. Perhaps the fact that the author takes his central character to London at all, where he has no hand in the preparations for the strike and is almost taken by surprise at its outbreak, is ultimately due to the larger autobiographical construction of the plot. *The Gate* is built around a central figure, Joe Tarrant, whose initiation into mining, love and trade-union activities is clearly based on lived experience, even if there is an attempt, in the earlier parts of the book, to endow this individual story with a representative dimension.

The most important aspect of Heslop's first London sojourn, his literary debut, still remains to be described. While in the metropolis and at the centre of the publishing business, he quite naturally tried to market the novel, which, as one reviewer claims, was written in part on bits of greaseproof paper during rests down the pit. It is perhaps difficult to visualise the odds with which an aspiring working-class writer in the middle twenties had to contend.

It is true that Herbert Jenkins Ltd and, from 1924, the Labour Publishing Co. brought out a number of working-class novels, but they tended to promote authors who had already made a reputation for themselves such as Patrick MacGill, Ethel Carnie Holdsworth or James Welsh. The Communist press issued no creative literature at all; the meaning of the word literature was narrowed down to party literature, i.e., pamphlets, textbooks, etc. Martin Lawrence published the first novels in 1929—translations by Soviet authors (Gladkov's *Cement*, Fadeev's *Nineteen*, etc.). The literary intellectuals who were to play a prominent role in the launching of working-class literature in the thirties did not as yet take any interest in the working class at all, either as a social force or as a subject for literature.

Not surprisingly, then, Heslop had his manuscript rejected by Herbert Jenkins. Yet the move to submit it to this publisher turned out to be a lucky choice. For the reader, a Rochelle S. Townsend, while having to turn down the novel in the name of her firm, actually recognised its virtues and was prepared to make use of her contacts. As in the case of Robert Tressell then we owe the discovery of a working-class author to a sympathetic woman reader. Rochelle Townsend became Heslop's Jessie Pope. Once she had taken matters into her hands, everything went remarkably smoothly. It was she who arranged for Heslop to meet a secretary at the Soviet Embassy, Ivan Maisky, who became ambassador in 1932 and remained at his post throughout the difficult years of the Fascist expansion in Europe and the tenacious, if futile, moves for an Anti-Hitler Coalition between the Western powers and Soviet Russia. A translator was found in Zina Vengerova-Minsky, wife of the Russian emigré poet Nikolaj Minsky, an expatriate since the days of the Czar, and in 1926 the book was duly published by Priboj in Leningrad with a preface by Maisky. Shortly afterwards, a cheap edition followed which sold more than half a million copies. When in 1934 the book eventually reached the British public under the title of *Goaf*, it still carried the dedication to R. S. T. and V.-Z. M. While this novel was widely reviewed by Soviet papers, Heslop remained virtually unknown in his own country. The first time his name crops up in the English press is when A. B. Elsbury of *The Sunday Worker* sent in this report from Russia:

I was entirely unprepared for a Russian version of an English novel which has not yet appeared in its native language. This was 'The Price of Coal' by an English writer, 'G. Gislop' (which, I imagine, must be H. Heslop). On inquiry I was informed that the novel is one written by a Durham miner and rejected by the London publishers. In an extremely attractive cover the book was selling well.[15]

A minor mystery surrounds the title of the book. What Elsbury denotes as 'The Price of Coal' is called 'The Wilderness of Toil' in a review by *Isvestya* and identified as 'Under the Sway of Coal' by E. Elistratova in an early piece of Heslop criticism in *International Literature*.[16] To add to the confusion, the book came out in Britain in 1934 under the title of *Goaf*, essentially unaltered, it appears, except for an addition of the year 1926 in a summary of dates relevant to the miners' postwar struggles.

The term 'goaf' needs perhaps a word of explanation. It is an abandoned working in the pit from which all the coal has been extracted. At one point Heslop gives an awesome account of it:

There is no more sinister death-trap in the earth than the goaf of a mine. . . . The goaf is the home of a tremendous darkness—a darkness which is soundless as the uttermost depths of the sea. It is the most terrifying spectacle in a mine, and no miner, except when in the last extremities, will venture into the goaf for the distance of one yard. There is a superb dignity of danger about the goaf. Nothing is more awe-inspiring, more fearful. It seems to stand at the edge of the coal with the gaping jaws of some immense hell, awaiting the intruder.[17]

Its relevance for the story lies in the fact that after a roof-fall two miners, political and personal adversaries, are trapped, with the goaf as the only, if seemingly hopeless escape route open to them. Given the dread of the goaf one of them prefers to wait entombed for the rescue operation to arrive, whereas the other chooses to pierce through the goaf thereby losing his way and almost his sanity before being discovered. This underground incident is in various ways entwined with the rivalries in the union lodge above ground and the personal evolution of the Marxist leader Tom Drury, one of the trapped miners, from militancy to moderation. It is in the narration of such accidents that Heslop's writing is at its best and, indeed, excels that of most other miner novelists (James C. Welsh, Lewis Jones, Len Doherty).

II

At the time Heslop was not even aware of his mention in *The Sunday Worker*. He had returned to South Shields after the expiry of his scholarship in the summer of 1926 to find the coalfield still in an undeclared state of war and the lockout in full swing. When work was eventually resumed, on starvation terms and with tacit victimisation, as in the rest of the country, he went back to his old job as a putter at Harton Colliery. This, he insists, was an unusual step to take for anyone who had been at the Central Labour College, since most leavers secured themselves a position in the union, as insurance agents or tutors. Heslop also did his share of lecturing at the local (non-resident) labour college, but on top of his mining job, as a gesture of his debt to his union. He also immersed himself once again in local politics contesting, although unsuccessfully, the Shields Ward of the South Shields Town Council. He stood as a Labour candidate but had been nominated and sponsored by the Miners Lodge. In November 1927 he found himself among 900 men turned away from the colliery as redundant. Heslop saw this with mixed feelings. Nobody in his right mind could have welcomed the near-hunger of unemployment. But during the last six months of work underground he had become aware of a growing aversion to pitwork, and it is significant that he did not even attempt to ask his father or brother, who held important positions in other collieries, whether they could find him a job. Like so many other miners over the next few years—the name of fellow writer Idris Davies springs to mind—Heslop thus left the coalfield for good, returning with his London-born wife to the metropolis at Easter 1928. There is a certain irony in the fact that, while the family now went through varying periods of unemployment and short-term occupations, handsome royalties were accumulating in Russia, of which only a modest portion could be converted into foreign currency. But Heslop made the best of this time by producing two novels within the next two years, *The Gate of a Strange Field* (1929) and *Journey Beyond* (1930). *The Gate* came out in March 1929 under the imprint of Brentano and was almost immediately followed by an American and a Russian edition. German and Japanese translations were also planned but do not seem to have materialised. The book was widely reviewed in Britain though commercially not a great success. Of the Labour press only *The Communist Review* was downright hostile, its critic finding the novel 'full of clichés' and 'unending literary jargon' and stating rather haughtily that 'we had a right to expect far more from comrade Heslop'.[18] Yet the general tone of the reviews was one of warm welcome, and several times comparisons were struck with MacGill's *Children of the Dead End* (1914).

'Comrade Heslop' meanwhile was furious that a quarter of the original manuscript had been cut so that it conformed to the standard novel length of 300 printed pages. One and a half years later, in Kharkov, he was still bitterly complaining about these cuts, maintaining that they had been of a political nature and amounted to censorship. This claim, however, is not accepted by Elistratova who, after having had access to the complete version, declared the political insights of the excised sections to be of the same 'rather poor calibre'.[19]

Notwithstanding the reservations expressed in some left-wing quarters, the success of this novel gained Heslop access to the publications of British socialism. He now became a regular reviewer for *The Worker*, the organ of the Minority Movement, until its demise in 1932. It ought to be borne in mind that reviewing in those days, at any rate in the socialist press, was not quite so compartmentalised a job as it is today. Heslop would write on a variety of subjects, one week on the economic causes of the Reformation, another on Mayakovsky's death.[20]

Of his new contacts on *The Worker* the relationship with Robert Ellis, another former Labour College student, now a journalist and trade unionist with international associations, proved particular enduring. Early on, it survived the fairly critical judgment which Ellis, under the pseudonym of KERN, passed on *Journey Beyond* (1930), a work that anticipates the unemployment novels of the thirties (Lionel Britton's *Hunger and Love*, Walter Greenwood's *Love on the Dole*, Walter Brierley's *Means Test Man*), but fails, as they do in large part, to give adequate treatment to the political dimensions of this theme; to the representativeness as opposed to the purely personal aspect of the tragedies of its characters.[21] KERN wrote under the heading of 'Which would you shoot—The Prostitute or the Scab?':

Here we are in a world aflame. Comrade Heslop poses the problem: should a man live on the immoral earnings of a woman? . . . There are bigger questions cogitating the workers to-day. Ninety per cent of women are prostitutes if by this is meant the sale of sex.[22]

By the time this article appeared in print, reviewer and reviewed had arrived by ship in Leningrad, their real destination being the Second International Conference of Revolutionary and Proletarian Writers which was to open at Kharkov on 6 November 1930.

III

In order to understand the dealings of this forum, it may be useful to sketch some of the stages in the formation of the International Union of Revolutionary Writers (the name was only adopted at Kharkov). Its origins lie in the International Provisional Bureau for Proletkult set up during the proceedings of the Second Comintern Congress in 1920. Two basic tenets of the Marxist tradition can be seen going into this foundation: the great importance accorded to cultural and artistic matters and the internationalist outlook of the labour movement. Both are to be found in the proclamation with which the Bureau called on 'The Proletariat of All Countries' to convene national conferences dedicated to the study of proletarian culture, to give regular space to this subject in the labour press, with the ultimate aim of building up organisations that were to stimulate the growth of a truly proletarian culture, art and literature. As, however, the proletkult school came subsequently under attack by the CPSU and was finally disbanded, an ideological reorientation became apparent which denied the leading role of proletarian writers claimed by the followers of proletkult, conceded equal space to the literature of peasants and fellow-travellers and revalued the (bourgeois) literary heritage. This more cautious approach to the realm of literature, mediating as it did between the rivalling factions, culminated in an important resolution of the Central Committee of the CPSU of 18 June 1925 which interestingly rejected the demand to solve literary controversies by administrative measures and assigned the role of guardian of the literary sphere to a Marxist literary criticism raised to new standards.[23] In the same year a new office was set up in Moscow which was to hand on these guidelines to fraternal organisations abroad and to co-ordinate the up to then rather sporadic and often individually based exchanges between progressive writers all over the world. This was the International Bureau for Revolutionary Literature (IBRL) which met in regular plenary sessions. Henri Barbusse from France, Bertolt Brecht from Germany, Nazim Hikmet from Turkey are just some of the writers who associated themselves with this platform over the following years. No British writer of comparable status can be cited. Indeed, apart from some interest in the work of Proletkult which subsided as the twenties went on, all these developments largely bypassed both the left and the intelligentsia in Britain. Thus the only British 'writer' present at the First International Conference of Proletarian and Revolutionary Writers (1927), which marked the next stage in the organisational history of the internationalisation of proletarian literature, was the journalist Robert Ellis. This conference took place on the occasion of the tenth anniversary of the October Revolution, and some of its preoccupations were political enough. The defence of the Soviet Union and the support of the struggle of the colonial peoples figure prominently in its resolutions. But it did also issue some more strictly literary calls, such as the need for the creation of worker-correspondents' movements and the launching of a multilingual journal. It would appear that here the idea of *International Literature* was born. Significantly, the organs of the British left, while giving ample coverage to the celebrations of the Revolution, contained no hint of all these literary debates.

Although Ellis at least, as a regular visitor to the Soviet Union, must have been aware of them, Heslop was clearly put to shame when confronted at Kharkov with reports of the activities in Germany, the United States, Hungary, the Far East and elsewhere. As there was in Britain, apart from the Workers' Theatre Movement, no organisational nucleus to speak of, he confined himself in his speech to a survey of more recent English fiction with an interest in the working class:

A new school of writers has branched off from the old. I speak of such writers as Richard Aldington, Rhys Davies, Henry Green, James Hanley, and, of course, Liam O'Flaherty. These people are products of the new phase of modern capitalism in Britain. They are creatures of its vast and implacable contradictions. They are influenced by such writers as James Joyce and the late D. H. Lawrence. Some of these writers, especially James Hanley and Henry Green, are of proletarian stock. They express a revolt against capitalism that is in itself quite interesting. However it is quite discernible in their novels that their revolt is against the *decay* of capitalism rather than against capitalism itself.[24]

With the benefit of hindsight it is easy to ridicule this list of names. One can see why they are considered as potential allies of the working class: Davies because he comes from, and writes about, the mining village of Clydach Vale in his powerful first novel *The Withered Root* (1927); Green, who of course was of thoroughly upper-middle-class stock, on the strength of his factory novel *Living* (1929); Hanley—the only one of them later actually to join the Writers' International—for his compelling early short stories and, particularly, his first novel *Drift* (1930); O'Flaherty, another visitor to Soviet Russia in 1930, for his tales and novels about the Civil War in Ireland.[25] But instead of criticising the list for its lack of critical judgement and insight, it is more interesting to note Heslop's dismissive treatment of some older working-class writers:

It is now five years since [John S.] Clarke sold out to the capitalist class. James Welsh is a similar case. His *The Morlocks* visualised revolution, but the content was clearly counter-revolutionary. It might easily be called the first novel of the social-fascist in England. The great disappointment is Joe Corrie. Here again we are faced with a writer, who is lacking any degree of Marxist training. His revolt seemed to express itself in a negative criticism of the priest-class, a strange fact when one considers the great amount of non-religious proletarians in Great Britain. His recently published book, with a preface by Ramsay MacDonald, is the final condemnation of this writer.[26]

Finally one ought to be aware of the omissions from this survey. A number of writers such as Ralph Fox, Ellen Wilkinson, Frederick Le Gros Clark, and Charles Ashleigh, all of whom had published promising novels with a socialist perspective during the preceding few years, and who would be prominent figures on the left in the thirties, simply do not figure in it.

It is not quite clear what moves Heslop and Ellis undertook on their return to Britain, to carry out the pledge signed at Kharkov 'to establish a British Section of the Union at the earliest possible opportunity'.[27] In 1931 a loosely organised group called the Robert Tressell Club was apparently founded.[28] The choice of name is telling, as it reveals the proletarian as opposed to the later dominant popular front tendency of the group. But too little is known about the Club, which foundered within a year, to be quite certain that it originated from their endeavours. Clearly, however, they were not involved with *Storm* (1933), the revolutionary fiction magazine, whose albeit short-lived existence marks another step towards the eventual foundation of the Writers' International in February 1934. This is evident from some fairly critical remarks in the correspondence between Douglas Jefferies, the driving force behind *Storm*, and his Soviet counterparts.[29]

IV

Heslop meanwhile had taken up work at the Intourist Office in London, a job which permitted him to see a good many (fellow-) travellers board the regular steamer to Leningrad. His writing career took a new turn with the publication in 1934 of *The Crime of Peter Ropner* which is an attempt at a crime novel from a left-wing perspective. Instead of providing a mystery as in the standard detective story of the day, Heslop here investigates the conditions and motives that drive a man to murder. The hero, who returns from a business trip to Russia, finds a letter from his dead wife disclosing the fact that during her loneliness she had been unfaithful to him, and, unable to face her husband, had determined to end it all in suicide. Ropner's only concern now is revenge on the lover whom in due time he tracks down and throws into the river. For this act he is sentenced to death, a sentence commuted afterwards to a prison term. When it later leaks out that the lover is still alive, Ropner on his release declares his intention of doing the job properly next time.

As in Christopher Caudwell's comparable novel *This My Hand* (1936), the influence of Dostoevsky can be strongly felt here.[30] Neither novel is particularly successful, but they can be seen as provocative literary interventions, on the part of two socialist writers, to break up a genre dominated by an ossified set of rules and a highly conservative ideology. Dorothy L. Sayers, who disliked the style and 'unnecessary tendentiousness' of Heslop's novel conceded that it had 'a crude and sordid power that leaves its mark' and she thought it wholesome 'that we murder-fans should occasionally be reminded that in real life a murder is not a pretty piece of pattern-making, but an ugly mess of lust, greed, violence, and spiritual degradation'.[31]

With *Last Cage Down* (1935) Heslop returns to familiar territory. It is his one work which echoes the Communist line most unequivocally. It is not that the author has chosen a Communist as his protagonist and mouthpiece. Rather he gradually reveals the limitations in a man who is otherwise a splendid example of courage and generosity. Jim Cameron, a passionate and loyal miner, is drawn with understanding and affection. Yet Heslop makes it clear—partly by contrast with a highly informed Communist—that despite Cameron's undoubted qualities as a natural leader of the men, despite his efficiency as lodge secretary and his human warmth—his class-consciousness is more rooted in instinct than in thought and study. Thus he sees an industrial conflict in terms of a personal fight against his class enemy. This conflict, interestingly, arises out of an ambitious scheme of rationalisation which the new company agent, Tate, a product of the universities, wants to push through regardless of the risks involved: electrical coal-getting is to replace traditional hewing, mechanised transport is to be substituted for the pony and the main and tail system of haulage. The 'advanced' thinking of Tate also emerges when in an act of perversity he quotes from the actors' scene in *Hamlet* to instruct the mine-manager how to go about buying off the lodge secretaryship after Cameron has been imprisoned for threatening behaviour. The novel culminates once again in a mine disaster, which directly results from the irresponsible introduction of the new machinery in an unsafe shaft as Cameron had feared and predicted all along. It testifies to the humaneness, that is to say, the class-transcending solidarity, of Cameron and his like that he does not hesitate for a moment to place himself at the head of the rescue brigade after he has been informed that Tate, his class enemy, is actually one of the victims.

With this book, Heslop's career as a novelist had almost come to a close. In fact there was to be a late sequel in 1946,

The Earth Beneath, which once again takes the reader to the Durham coalfield but which in tone and temper no less than in historical setting differs considerably from the previous more narrowly political works.

Why is it that his work achieves at times a power unmatched by any of its predecessors? Clearly, in basing his narrative on the history of his own family the author was partly relieved of the difficulty of devising a plot, which was never one of his strengths. In concentrating on the communal customs and folk heroes, instead of on the rivalries and bickerings in the union lodge, Heslop could exploit his keen interest in, and intimate knowledge of local history to the full. There is a magnificent portrait of the legendary hewer Bill Tempest, and the scenes of local games or the visit of the forthright miner John Akers to the Bishop of Durham are no less memorably fleshed out in graphic detail. For the first time, too, the local dialect is employed here, adding a further note of colour and vividness to the story. Though focusing on the destiny of one family, the Akers, Heslop neither idealises nor isolates his characters. In the diametrically opposed paths chosen by the two brothers, Simpson and John Akers, the author shows that there were always two alternatives open to the gifted workingman: the road to individual improvement imbued with opportunism and ultimately leading to the bosses' side, and loyalty to and remaining within the working class. And in connecting the destiny of these men and women with wider social issues such as the role of the Primitive Methodists,[32] the terrible mining disaster at Hartley Colliery in 1862 and the arrival of the ideas of co-operation and trade unionism, Heslop successfully re-creates some major stages in the history of the Durham coalfield without succumbing to either historiography or to biography.

Finally a somewhat unusual work, still from the thirties, deserves a mention. This is *The Abdication of Edward VII* (1937), a book jointly written with his old friend Robert Ellis and published under the pseudonym of J. Lincoln White. It is a day-to-day factual account of the events leading to the abdication of the King, from the first press reports reaching Britain through American newspapers to Baldwin's handling of the crisis and the famous BBC broadcast by

Edward. A vividly written piece of journalism supplied with a generous amount of documentary material, it conveys effectively the anxiety and tension of the closing months of 1936. Yet, for two socialist authors, it is also a curiously detached piece of writing, taking a neutral stance and abstaining even from arranging the material in such a way as to reveal a definite standpoint. Edward's sympathies for the unemployed are duly recorded, but, if anyone, it is Baldwin, 'a modern Cromwell',[33] who emerges triumphantly from these pages. Read today the book is still a useful and reliable source of information but it betrays no ambition beyond the immediate reproduction of facts. Set beside the zealous undertakings of Mass-Observation, then underway and further precipitated by the abdication crisis,[34] it emerges as a fairly pedestrian effort.

We may conclude with a brief glance at the author's political affiliations. At one stage, before 1924, Heslop had joined the ILP. Yet, if the presentation of Joe Tarrant in *The Gate of a Strange Field*, who makes a similar choice, is any guide, that decision was never taken wholeheartedly. By 1926, Maisky, in his preface to the Russian edition of *Goaf,* could already describe Heslop as 'standing somewhere between the ILP and the CP'. Subsequently his contacts and, more importantly, his public statements prove him to be sympathetic to a Communist position, though he never became a card-carrying member. This near-Communist stance, most evident in *Last Cage Down*, lasted throughout the thirties. In the 1940s, however, after a move to Somerset because of the war, Heslop joined the Labour Party of which he remained a member until his death. In 1948 he won a seat in the municipal elections for Taunton Town Council, and some years later he stood for Parliament in the North Devon constituency, one of his opponents then being the young Jeremy Thorpe. (Neither of them got in on that occasion.)

Heslop's novels have never been reprinted. But that fact alone cannot account for their extreme rarity today. Perhaps they are to be found treasured in the homes of miners in County Durham and in miners' libraries elsewhere in the country.

6   SOCIALIST NOVELS OF 1936

Since I first wrote about the socialist fiction of the 1930s (1975), the situation in which both scholars and general readers find themselves has continually improved. The process of recovery of forgotten texts, though not yet complete, has given way to the stage of investigation and assessment of individual works and authors, and this in turn has facilitated the move to recirculate the texts. The next threshold, of appropriation and appraisal beyond radical academia, has yet to be crossed. But there is now at least a tiny band of active, devoted and exchanging researchers in the field, and it is of particular importance that they have lately been joined by native enthusiasts. For the strange situation in the middle of the 1970s was that what interest there existed in English working-class and socialist literature came almost exclusively from students outside Britain.[1]

This lack of academic interest in Britain in one strand of its own literary heritage has had serious consequences. For example, while so many of the erstwhile practitioners of the genre were still alive, no sustained attempt was ever made to interview these writers and get first-hand accounts of how they had been discovered, sponsored, made much of and dropped again. Not that recovery through memory could dispense with the need for a critical reconstruction and assessment of the period, but what a great missed opportunity in the age of oral history nevertheless! From two cases, where the evidence is readily available (Walter Brierly and Harold Heslop), we know quite positively that the fact that nothing was published after 1940 and 1946 respectively does not mean that these authors had stopped writing novels. It was rather that the channels which had temporarily opened had closed once again, that the sudden interest of intellectuals and publishers had gone, and that the public was no longer sympathetic to this kind of writing.

Or was it? The latter statement, with its ring of familiarity, warrants a number of questions: which public? the novel-buying readership as it existed in the minds of publishers and their staff? The users of public libraries and of working-class institutions up and down the country? A letter to the *Daily Herald* of 15 March 1939, by the chief librarian for Dagenham, tells a different story. It speaks of 'the unceasing demands' of working-class readers for 'novels with an economic and social background'.[2] Was this a purely local phenomenon, a mere individual estimate based perhaps on an obsessive preoccupation with a narrow area of writing? Could our valiant librarian not read the signs of the times? Or did he read them only too well, sensing the end of a remarkable period in the history of working-class and social-ist fiction?

I

Working-class and/or socialist? This is a first difficulty, giv-ing rise to confusion and argument, for the potential rela-tions between these two terms, as they are applied to actual novels, range from interchangeability to mutual exclusive-ness. Between a book like Robert Tressell's *The Ragged-Trousered Philanthropists*, which is by common judgement both a working-class and a socialist novel, and a work of the order of J. C. Grant's *The Back-to-Backs* (1930), which seems to endorse the subordinated position of the working class in society, there stretches a vast middle ground of intermediate possibilities. The following analytical distinc-tion between 'working-class' and 'socialist' novels cannot then dispel all the difficulties. To submit that 'working-class' is a *descriptive* term denoting the fiction produced by worker-writers (that is, authors still in the production pro-cess or subjected to unemployment) and by writers with a working-class background depicting their milieu of origin, is thus an ideal-type definition, but one which at least yields two criteria, authorship and subject matter. There are periods for which these sociological and thematic orienta-tions are particularly useful, for example, when one thinks of the incessant outpouring of novels about working-class life in the 1950s and early 1960s.

Yet when one takes a long-term historical perspective and examines such decades as the 1880s or the 1930s, the usefulness of the overall category 'working-class' is more open to doubt. Not only are there individual works to which such a descriptive term is hardly applicable, but there will also be whole groups of novels which simply defy such a label. Thus at some stage the need for another concept becomes urgent, one which grasps the *ideological* quality of works. It is this requirement which the term 'socialist' seeks to fulfil. Indeed, it could be argued that the term 'working-class' will become less useful and specific in proportion as more working-class prose and verse from the past is recovered, and more new works are published or performed in the new media.

To insist on an ideological grounding—those to whom the term is suspect might replace it by philosophical or *weltanschaulich*—is not an original proposition. Indeed, a detailed enquiry into the history of the usage of such terms as 'working-class' and 'socialist', and of the older 'democratic' (in Chartism) and the not-so-old 'proletarian', in relation to literature, would, I think, show a clear preference in most times for terms which capture the function and value of literary works for the Cause, and its potential role in the lives of their readers.

This link with the labour movement, and the condition of the whole working class, can then only be severed at the risk of emptying the concept of any meaningfulness whatever. And it is for this reason that I start from a definition of the socialist novel as one which, by being written in the historical interests of the working class, reveals a standpoint consistent with that of the class-conscious sections of this class.[3] Under this rubric there is also room for the work of socialist intellectuals, irrespective of subject matter.

II

It is important to realise that the cultural significance of the 1930s lies not only in the fact that representatives from the *under*privileged sections of British society are drawn into the artistic ambit, but also in the political awakening of an *over-*

privileged group and their consequent literary intervention in the interests of the objectives posed by the radical wing of the working-class movement.[4] During the decade a surprising number of at least temporarily socialist-oriented intellectuals accepted and promoted in their imaginative work the emancipatory role of the working class in the liberation of society. Others chose not necessarily to treat working-class themes and problems, but to lay bare the mechanisms and contradictions of society, and to throw light on the driving forces of history, by setting their work in a particular historical 'moment' where social conflict comes to the surface. Hence we get a major contribution to the historical novel. In 1936 alone, no less than four socialist intellectuals used this evidently popular form: Phyllis Eleanor Bentley, *Freedom Farewell!*; Robert Briffault, *Europa*; Jack Lindsay, *Adam of a New World*; Sylvia Townsend Warner, *Summer Will Show*.[5]

Another aspect of this cultural intervention is the truly remarkable range of socialist novels produced by women writers. Not only Bentley and Townsend Warner, but also Carmel Haden Guest, Winifred Holtby, Storm Jameson, Ethel Mannin, Irene Rathbone and Gabrielle Vallings came forward with interesting works in the same year. Their novels merit critical attention—as a body of work they have never been studied—but this is a task beyond the limitations of this chapter.

III

Any closer look at one moment, genre or group of novelists in the thirties thus forces one to make a choice.[6] For the corpus of fictional writing eligible under the rough definition given above is far greater and more varied than even my own first bibliographical excursion into the field allowed.[7]

And it is the following group of socialist novels produced in one year that I propose to discuss: Ralph Bates, *The Olive Field;* Mulk Raj Anand, *The Coolie*; John Sommerfield, *May Day*; James Barke, *Major Operation*; all published in 1936. Four male writers in their thirties (excepting the somewhat younger Sommerfield), of mostly working- or lower-middle-class origin, who take their material from contemporary struggles and who are, as will be seen, also united in the particular brand of socialism which they embrace. In 1936 these four had reached approximately the same stage in their novelistic careers. None of them was an entire newcomer to the genre, like for instance Cecil Day Lewis with his *The Friendly Tree*, nor were they such experienced and established practitioners as the above-mentioned women novelists.

With at least one novel each to his credit, these writers now embarked on more ambitious projects which were to show advances, in narrative as well as ideological and political terms, over their first endeavours. In *Lean Men* (1934), Bates had offered some exciting scenes of revolutionary action and insights into the cultural context of Catalan dockworkers, but his work suffered at the same time from a lack of controlled story-telling and an unconvincing treatment of its central figure, an English Comintern agent in Spain. Anand's *The Untouchable* (1935), a book rejected by no less than nineteen publishers before Wishart under Edgell Rickword brought it out, with a preface by E. M. H. Forster, relates a day in the life of a young Indian latrine cleaner and street sweeper whose awareness both of his own hopeless position and the forces of change gradually unfolds before the reader. It is easily the best novel of the four: the plot and psychology of the hero are very skilfully built up, but the choice of a protagonist from the lowest level of humanity precludes any wider vista of Indian society. Sommerfield's *They Die Young* (1930), published when he was twenty-two, reveals that the author's interest in experimental novel-writing antedates *May Day*, yet the vagaries of the adventures of his young bohemian-turned-sailor clearly mirror the uncertainty of direction at this point in the author's own life. Much the same can be said of James Barke, in whose first novel *The World His Pillow* (1933) a dispossessed crofter drifts through Glasgow, devoid of any clear philosophical or political outlook.

IV

Of the four, Ralph Bates (born 1899) enjoyed the greatest success at the time. His books went through several impressions on both sides of the Atlantic, including an early Penguin of *Lean Men*. As Spain was the setting of his work in the thirties from the short-story collection *Sierra* (1933) onward, the author came to be regarded as an authority on the social revolutionary struggles on the Iberian peninsula which sharpened as the decade progressed. Bates had acquired inside knowledge of the Spanish scene through extended stays in Catalonia since 1923. Despite his long absences from Britain he managed to write regular reviews for *Time and Tide* from 1934. Among his political friends and contacts he counted André Malraux and Ralph Fox[8] who were, like himself, present at the famous International Writers' Conference for the Defence of Culture, held in Paris in 1935, and who were equally to play major roles in the International Brigades.[9]

The Olive Field, a work which uses a wide canvas and a large cast, falls into two parts of unequal length, of which the first, dealing with life in a pueblo in Southern Spain, is the more detailed, varied and colourful, and thus holds greater interest. In Los Olivares the livelihood of most of the inhabitants depends on olives so that when a great part of the crop is destroyed in a hailstorm, the whole community is affected. Given the reigning semi-feudal system under which the olive-gatherers are hired for the harvest only and paid by the basket, it will inevitably increase the competition among them and lower the price a basket of fruit will fetch. It is this combination of 'natural' and economic factors which leads to the Anarchist-inspired rising of the olive-gatherers, and with it the author has skilfully interwoven the destinies of a group of revolutionaries. Though Bates by no means concentrates exclusively on this group, but takes in the entire social structure of the pueblo and draws some very memorable portraits of a reactionary priest and of a book-collecting, music-loving aristocrat, he focuses nevertheless on the community of the revolutionaries or, more precisely, on the dialectics between the internal relationships of the group and the revolutionary action. One example of this is the immediate cause of the riot which is constructed in such a way as to bring the most personal of relationships to have a bearing on the rising. In a situation of unbearable tension any trivial incident will trigger off a riot, but the incident which actually sets everything off is the major-domo's sneering at one member of the group, the pregnant Lucía.

I have used the word 'revolutionary' to denote the political outlook of the group. Indeed, it is the only fitting description, the common denominator for its members, who in party political terms are divided into a strong Anarchist and a much smaller Communist wing. This division of opinion is a constant source of conflict and reaches a particularly critical stage when Caro, a figure who has all the sympathies of the author, breaks with Anarchism and moves gradually to a Communist position. But the real test for the coherence of the group comes when Mudarra, the leading Anarchist, sleeps with Lucía, the girl on whom Caro, his friend and up to then fellow-Anarchist, has set his eyes. It is the resulting pregnancy which provokes the major-domo's reaction, which in its turn releases the passions of the Anarchists.

As might be expected, the peasant rising ends in defeat. But what is significant is the author's decision not to end the book with its suppression. He has undertaken to disclose the quasi-religious nature of Anarchism, its worship of action, its unquestioning obedience, its mystical love for its leaders. But since he cannot but admire other features of this movement, such as the courage and selflessness of its adherents, their craving for equality and closeness to the people, and since he wants to show the Spanish peasants and workers on the move, ready to learn their lessons, he adds a shorter, less fictionalised and less panoramic account of a much more promising rising, namely the story of the Asturias insurrection of miners and dockers of October 1934, which can properly be regarded as the prelude to the Spanish Civil War. The link between these two politically quite different events is established by the imprisonment, expulsion or emigration of the Los Olivares leaders to the north of Spain. In this later rising, the virtues of the Anarchists can be fully deployed, because they are coupled with, and controlled by, the discipline and organisation provided by the Socialists and Communists with whom they have formed an alliance, the *Alianza Obrera.*

Two things stand out in Bates's treatment of the Worker Alliance. First, he makes Caro enter the Alliance before the Communist Party has actually given its seal of approval, so that his allegiance appears to be with the *Causa* rather than with the organisation. Secondly, the forming of the Alliance is not a defensive measure, but clearly intended to prepare for the takeover of the country by the labouring classes. I emphasise these points, because in this solution the novel differs sharply from the popular front strategy propagated at the same time by the Communist Parties in Western Europe, or from the line taken by the Spanish Communists during the Civil War, a line, incidentally, which Bates later came to accept for a considerable time, before he broke with Communism altogether.

The political concept of working-class unity has also a bearing on the internal relationships of the revolutionary group. Torn apart by ideological differences, Lucía's pregnancy and Mudarra's imprisonment following the events in Los Olivares, the group is once more drawn together in the moment of revolution. But this newly found unity now has stronger foundations, for it is forged together in the struggle for a better society and, in the end, in the fight for survival under the onslaught of the Moorish troops. The strength that the survivors Caro and Lucía draw out of this reunion will help them in their future struggles. And Bates leaves no doubts in his readers that the fight will be carried on. In this *The Olive Field* resembles the earlier *Lean Men* in which a dockers' rising in Barcelona was likewise defeated, but the spirits of the survivors remained similarly unbroken.

If *The Olive Field*, despite its final tragedy, does not end on a defeatist note, it closes nevertheless with a certain ambivalence, that is Caro's and Lucía's decision to return to Los Olivares. Even if one interprets this step as only a necessary rejuvenation of power, it is, judged from the overall structure of the novel, implicitly acquiescent and contradicts Caro's final statement that he will continue to work for the revolution. It also betrays his own evolution into a Communist who would have to know that a revolution is not made in an Andalusian village.[10]

V

In this respect Mulk Raj Anand's novel *The Coolie* is less ambiguous. For Munoo, the coolie, there is no return to the mountain village once he has left it behind. In fact, for very obvious reasons there could not plausibly be any such return. Munoo is an orphan who, after reaching the age of fourteen, is literally sold by his uncle as a servant to the family of a small bank employee. Since he suffers maltreatment at the hands of his mistress, he runs away to find work in a primitive pickle factory. Once more on the road after the bankruptcy of this firm, he ends up in a huge jute mill in Bombay where he eventually witnesses the preparations for a strike which is, however, averted by police agents. He dies, still a boy, of tuberculosis which he acquires by pulling the rickshaw for an Anglo-Indian lady. Had this story ended with the protagonist's return to his native village, it might have led one to assume that the feudal rural order could serve as a viable alternative to capitalism. For the sequence of these episodes, far from being accidental (as e.g. in the picaresque tradition which the author has critically appropriated), follows a distinct historical pattern: Munoo stands for millions of Indian peasants who are dragged into the city by forces beyond their control or understanding. His bitter experiences in the 'jungle of the cities' therefore exemplify the long and painful process of adaptation of the Indian people to the capitalist mode of production.

In such a presentation there obviously looms the danger of naturalism, of reducing the human being to a mere victim of the social process. Anand avoids falling into this trap by enlarging his vista in the Bombay chapter. Though Munoo is shown to be more or less accepting of his lot, the Indian working class clearly is not, certainly not in its entirety. In the figure of the former wrestler Ratan we have a vigorous and intelligent mill-worker, a man who does not crouch in the presence of the foreman, who is, on the contrary,

actively engaged in the preparations for the strike. It is true
that the strike never comes off, but despite its failure there
remains a glimmer of hope throughout the rest of the book,
because the human resources of defiance and resilience have
been seen at work and are kept alive in the final anticlimactic
chapter in the conversations Munoo has with a Communist.

And on one occasion, just before the meeting of coolies
and factory workers is dispersed, when the crowd is still
shouting the demands put forward by the union leaders on
the rostrum, there is a remarkably metaphorical passage
which briefly reveals the slumbering potentialities of the
Indian working class:

> The words of the charter rose across the horizon. At first they were
> simple, crude words, rising with difficulty like the jagged, broken,
> sing-song of children in a class room. Then the hoarse throats of
> the throng strained to reverberate the rhythm of Sauda's gong
> notes, till the uncouth accents mingled in passionate cries assas-
> sinating the sun on the margin of the sky.[11]

I take this passage to anticipate the growing strength of the
Indian working class. The rather simple straightforward sentences of the charter are enriched and reveal their deeper
meaning, as more and more workers join in their rhythmical
shouting, that is as one after the other symbolically enters
the ranks of the labour movement. Though the movement
may at present still be in its infancy, once united it will be in
a position to go beyond all existing barriers, may indeed be
capable of storming heaven.

The latent power of the labour movement is further
underlined by the string of virile sexual associations that runs
through the passage: the swelling rising chorus of voices,
the reverberating rhythm, the passionate cries redolent
perhaps of an orgasm which symbolises revolution, itself
both an act of violence ('assassinating the sun') and an act of
liberation.[12]

The novels of Bates and Anand deal with the theme of
exploitation and human resistance in places far removed
from Britain, but their relevance for, and connection with,
the struggles on the 'home front' must have been fairly obvious to readers in the thirties. Anand was, of course, born in

India (1905). But, like Bates, he received some of his major formative influences in 'exile'. By the time *The Coolie* came out, he had already spent some ten years in Britain, and it is inconceivable that this book, and even more so its predecessor, would have offered the same Marxist perspective for the Indian road to the future or, for that matter, that he would have had an opportunity to publish this work, had he not been in close touch with the politicised literary intelligentsia in Britain (indeed the whole genre of the Indian English novel is very much a form used by Indians living or having lived in the western world).

In Anand's case, however, this long residence abroad (1926–45) does not affect the setting of his novels which are always firmly located in India, a contemporary India that is subjected to the workings of imperialism and hence in touch with his host country. Anand, on the other hand, again resembles Bates in that his political commitment is older than that of most of the thirties writers. It stems, in fact, from his being beaten up during the General Strike for refusing to blackleg, and his reading of Marx's series of articles on India at about the same time.[13]

VI

When we turn to the two remaining novels, the difference from those already discussed is apparent not only in their concern with domestic issues but also in their openness to formal experimentation. Where Bates had written in a grand manner, vaguely reminiscent of Tolstoy, and Anand, apart from occasional recourse to a simple version of the stream-of-consciousness technique (notably in *The Untouchable*), had drawn on similarly conventional fictional modes of structure and narration, John Sommerfield consciously sought a new method with which to record London (working-class) life on the eve of May Day. The result is the kind of pieced-together, fragmentary novel of fact which, in a different cultural context, provoked in 1936 the polemic of Georg Lukács. What the Hungarian critic wrote about Dos Passos, could also have been directed against *May Day*:

'In *Manhattan Transfer* people do not run into each other on the
road but meet in the most natural fashion'. [Lukács is quoting
Sinclair Lewis here.] 'The most natural fashion' implies that the
characters either fall into no relationships at all or at best into
transient and superficial relationships, that they appear suddenly
and just as suddenly disappear, and that their personal
lives—since we scarcely know them—do not interest us in the
least, and that they take no active part in a plot but merely prom-
enade with varying attitudes through the externalised objective
world described in the novel.[14]

Lukács, as is well known, bases his judgements on the concept of the totalising, 'organically moulded', critical realist
novel of the nineteenth century. But if one does not accept
this tradition as a model for the contemporary writer, many
(though not all) of his criticisms become irrelevant.

In the first place, Sommerfield simply starts from different
premises. *May Day* is a deliberately de-centred and open
work, with only the barest of characterisations, no central
hero and hardly a plot to speak of. The author is clearly not
concerned with the presentation of round characters and the
dramatisation of personal lives. Instead he focuses on events
and situations as they act upon men and women, and are
themselves in part the result of human agency. In part,
because the motto of the book is precisely Marx's 'Men
make history but not as they please'.

At least two significant influences, one immediate and of a
non-literary nature, the other very literary indeed, can be
discerned in *May Day*. The first of these is the documentary
movement which, at the time of the novel's composition, was
just beginning to take a more socially committed stance in
films like *Housing Problems* and *Enough to Eat?*, or in Bill
Brandt's photographic collection *The English at Home,*
though it would take another two or three years before the
documentary impulse would manifest itself as a major cultural practice.[15]

Yet in *May Day* the camera-eye can already be seen at
work, almost like a searchlight over the city, stopping here
for an instant, penetrating the curtains of a terraced house,
catching a glimpse of happiness or misery, making a halt
there, over an office, recording the hammering of the type-

writers and the conversation of clerks, then moving on
to a wealthier residential area, illuminating the idleness and
preoccupations of those at the top. For both societies, the
class which owns the property and means of production as
well as the class which has to sell its labour, are present in
the book. Also present, unfortunately, are the limitations of
the documentary method, its tendency to spell things out by
name, in a general way, but not to concretise and individual-
ise them. Take this passage:

Blondes and brunettes, beauties and uglies, good girls and bad girls,
virgins and tarts, so much flesh, so many thoughts and feelings, so
many drab, cheerless destinies, so many who might have been at
some other time, in some other place to live the lives of human
beings. At least once the moment will come in each of these lives
when they will stop and think, 'What have we been born for, why
do we live as we do, toiling only to eat, eating only to toil.'[16]

Quite often the variety, colours, smells and noises of London
life are simply enumerated in this manner. Because it is not
fleshed out in concrete experience, the final moving reflection is, in this case, robbed of its power. In Lukács's terminology, the author here describes, but does not narrate.
    The other perceptible influence, and one that is better
absorbed, derives from *Mrs Dalloway,* the most famous
London novel of the previous decade. One of the key
aspects of modern city life with which Virginia Woolf was
concerned is the experience of alienation and the search for
ways by which people can overcome the damaging atomisa-
tion of their existence. In *Mrs Dalloway* certain relationships, albeit vague ones, are established by the chimes of Big
Ben or the aeroplane which different people in different
places hear or see simultaneously, some of whom will meet
at the party in the evening. The equivalent of these devices
in *May Day* is the newspaper headline about an air race
around the world and, more significantly, the political
slogans painted on the wall ('Forward to a Soviet Britain' for
example). The use of the latter is particularly interesting
because it is more than an artistic tool. The people who see
these slogans or read the leaflets demanding 'All out on

May Day' have more in common than the mere fact of living in the same city at the same time. The many millions of individual destinies, coexisting in London, 'the different currents of its lives . . . strive to run all ways, confusedly, each trying to follow its own separate course'. But, the quotation continues, they are in fact just 'lines that make patterns of confusion, the invisible spiderwebs that lead, through a million routes, to the factory chimneys'.[17] What shapes the lives of these people, is their common position as wage (or salary) earners, and the production process as the determining and regulating instance in these lives is shown to extend right into their recreational time. But, the novel insists, the factory is also the focusing point of resistance, the cradle of the idea of solidarity, and, thence, of new forms of social organisation. Though it is as yet only a small section of the working class which has entered the political arena, the relationship between this vanguard and the apathetic unpolitical majority has, by virtue of their common class position, a more real foundation than the rather mystical bonds uniting the characters in *Mrs Dalloway*. Thus also the march which, at the end of *May Day*, unites so many different people beneath the same banners has a deeper, more active meaning than the party which concludes *Mrs Dalloway* and brings together people who have little in common apart from being members of the upper class.

It would be against the inherent purpose of the socialist novel to leave Sommerfield's work without briefly noting its telling capacity to capture the mood of militancy amongst the organised London working class. Though the author, in a prefatory note, warned against interpreting his work as 'making any kind of historical forecast', the events of the following year vindicated his picture of the industrial scene in such a way as to invest it with a highly prognostic quality. I quote from a passage in which a trade-union leader, a thinly disguised Ernest Bevin, is pondering over the question of how he can thwart the activities of the more militant members of his organisation:

Mr. Albert Raggett, secretary of the United Transport Worker's Union . . . sat in his study composing an anti-communist encyclical to be issued as a last-minute appeal to the busmen.

He was writing 'Paid Agents of Moscow are trying to disrupt our trade union movement, that has been built up by so many years of—' And he looked up from his paper, trying to think of a good juicy expression comprehending 'patient endeavour', 'selfless sacrifice', 'loyalty', 'devoted leadership' and all that, and then he saw the rain.

Rain, he said to himself. Rain, oh good! Maybe it meant the end of this month's fine weather and that the rain would come pouring down all tomorrow, and he thought of a straggling miserable little procession of Communists with drenched banners huddling into Hyde Park. . . . If only the rain would stay.[18]

Mr. Albert Raggett's worries are caused by the activities of the indefatigable London Busmen Rank and File Movement, which, set up in the early years of the decade, had become a formidable industrial force by the mid-thirties and was now the driving force behind the moves for a strike of the busmen. As John Saville has commented:

It was a situation Ernest Bevin found exceedingly irksome since he was pushed into negotiations in support of demands which he often considered too advanced. After negotiations in 1937 had dragged on for at least two months past the time appointed for a new agreement, the Union officially gave a month's notice to strike, and every bus in London came off the streets at midnight on 30 April.[19]

A Londoner himself, John Sommerfield (born 1908) brought the feeling of the locale and the invaluable experience of having worked in many places, situations and capacities, for example as a carpenter, a bookshop assistant and a stage manager, to his novel. Like Bates, he had also felt the urge to go abroad and had responded to it, characteristically, by going to sea. Under the guidance of his former schoolmate Maurice Cornforth he eventually came to adopt a Communist position and was, again like Bates, to see service in the International Brigades.[20] At one time reported killed, he returned to England in 1937, published his *Volunteer in Spain,* threw himself into party work and began work on the next London-based fiction, a novelette about a successful rent strike entitled *Trouble in Porter Street* (1938), which met with greater response, commercially and politically, than anything he was ever to produce again.

VII

With James Barke's novel *Major Operation* we move from London to Glasgow. The book contrasts the lives of George Anderson, a coal merchant, and Jock MacKelvie, like the author himself a shipyard worker, whose paths eventually cross in a hospital ward. Both are victims of the economic crisis, but whereas Anderson's reaction is one of utter despair and helplessness, MacKelvie becomes a leader of the unemployed. It is a much longer story than this very brief summary indicates, and the author tries to liven it up by frequently changing his style. In this he is at his best when he lapses into a staccato version of stream-of-consciousness thereby giving us an insight into the muddled thoughts of the middle-class representative. Here we have Anderson, still in business, though already sensing the impact of the Depression, walking through the streets of Glasgow, his mind wandering and jumping:

Moderates mediocre. Labour Party just as bad though. Need a dictator: Mussolini. Not Hitler. Ignorant, dangerous type Hitler. Shoots pals. Caesar Borgia was it? Hun not dead yet. Prussianism: new disguise, Jews rotten. Still, old Sam a Jew: not bad fellow. Control finance. No Jews in Ireland? And yet . . . what about that story of Jews cornering candles at Dublin Eucharistic Congress? Deserved to get away with it. Clever people. Think about business in their sleep.[21]

Then he encounters an NUWM march:

Unemployed demonstration. Hadn't seen anything about that in the papers. Unemployed becoming a menace. Silly of them demonstrating during business hours. Dislocating traffic. Silly at any time, come to that. Break into a riot, loot shops. Give police lot of bother. Addition to rates. High enough already. Too high. Hadn't they got the dole? Want jam on it. Sapping morale. Terrific burden on country.[22]

Anderson is by far the better executed of the two principal characters. And the reason is that he is allowed to have his doubts, his worries, and his tragedy, qualities that are completely absent in his opponent and eventual 'conqueror'. It is the collapse of his world, initiated on a personal level by the infidelity and eventual desertion of his wife, continued on an economic and social level through the bankruptcy of his business and given its final blow on a physical level by the duodenal ulcer which demands treatment in hospital that make Anderson 'ripe' for the operation on his mind to be performed by MacKelvie. After an extensive series of discussions and arguments in the hospital ward between the two of them (running over a hundred pages), Anderson is won over for the cause of the workers, sealing his decision by settling with the MacKelvies in the slum area of Glasgow after his release from hospital. Whereas Anderson, once his accepted tenets of faith are shattered, is thus driven to a new outlook, painful though this process may be, MacKelvie, by contrast, remains a static and bloodless figure throughout the book, devoid of any inner struggle or contradiction. The one transformation he undergoes, from a worker solely caring for his trade, disappointed about the outcome of the General Strike, but with no serious interest left in politics, in the first part of the novel, to a militant activist, an inexhaustible source of energy, in the second, is not dramatised, but simply stated in terms of its results, in retrospect. Once he has reached that point, he remains unperturbed by whatever happens to him, including long spells of unemployment. Judging from this figure alone, the unemployed do not feel the strain of enforced idleness very much, and one wonders therefore why they should be marching in the streets of Glasgow. Nor does MacKelvie's relationship with his wife seem to suffer in the least. The problem is, however, that all the evidence from the thirties points to the contrary. One needs only to look at Walter Brierley's *Means-Test Man* (1935) or the interviews collected by Beales and Lambert to get an idea of the debilitating effect on the minds and souls of people living on the dole. Now there would be nothing wrong in singling out an atypical case, if it were accompanied and thus relativised by glimpses of other responses. But these we are not offered in the book.

The idealisation of the working class in the figure of Mac-Kelvie corresponds to the downright negative portrayal of

the middle class. Jack Mitchell has trenchantly described the
dangers resulting from such a schematic characterisation.
A number of writers, he says,

> *romanticised* the workers and then embraced their own romantic
> creation. Their attitude had more of moral idealism than of histor-
> ical materialism. The proletariat is seen not so much as a histori-
> cally developing class but rather as an absolute and therefore de-
> historicised *moral category* whose superiority over the bourgeoisie
> lies in its moral excellence and lack of that inner conflict which
> ham-strings the middle class and its intellectuals.[23]

Mitchell ascribes this attitude to the intellectuals. But James
Barke (1905–1953) was, rather like his Scottish fellow-
novelist Lewis Grassic Gibon, 'a son of the soil', born in Gal-
loway and brought up in a village near Kincardine. Driven
from the land 'to tenement life in the crowded, smoky
noisy, bustling city of Glasgow',[24] the author found work in
the Clyde shipyards, first as an engineer, later as a shipping
clerk. Of all the writers considered here, he was the only one
actually to follow a proletarian trade at the time of writing
his novel.

The courageous thing to do for the newly converted
Communist in the mid-thirties was to confront and give
embodiment to the idea of the popular front. For this is what
the outcome of the hospital debate ultimately symbolises.
Whether this conception, as it is artistically executed, can
stand up to intent scrutiny, is another question. One objec-
tion is that if it takes an ordeal such as Anderson goes
through to make sections of the middle class susceptible to
the idea of the popular front, it seems a pretty hopeless
enterprise from the start. And a sociological flaw in the
whole treatment of this policy is the fact that Anderson is,
half-way through the novel, already no longer a representative of the bourgeoisie, but rather of its de-classed elements.

VIII

What common features emerge from, and cut right across,
the wide thematic range of these novels? First of all, their

ideological slant can hardly be described in any other terms than revolutionary socialism as opposed to social democratic or any other gradualist versions of socialism. The point does not need any proof in the case of *The Olive Field*, nor does it have to be explained at great length for May Day. When one recalls the slogan under which the workers assemble and march on May 1st (which, significantly, is not the Labour Party's day to commemorate past struggles or engage in present ones), namely, 'Forward to a Soviet Britain', the emphasis is quite clearly on the building of workers' councils at factory level, the very locale of Sommerfield's novel. With regard to Anand's work the claim appears to be more debatable. The difficulty here arises from the choice of the protagonist, a low-caste boy who is unlikely to become involved in revolutionary activities. Though this is a technical handicap which limits the author's possibilities, it does not prevent him from disseminating revolutionary ideas in passages like the one quoted above. This overall politico-ideological assessment of the four works under review holds, I would argue, even for *Major Operation,* despite its overt attempt to embody in a novel the popular front. The final march in which the middle-class representative turned socialist gives his life for the unemployed leader, who has already been battered down by the police, the moment when Anderson stands above the prostrate MacKelvie protecting him with his body and waving the red flag has revolutionary undertones which vividly recall similar shots in Russian revolutionary films.

Given the fact that in 1936 all four authors were Communists, card-carrying or not, the remarkable thing about this particular accentuation is that it conflicts at first sight with the popular front line taken by their Party, a policy which postponed working for the revolution until after the defeat of fascism and the elimination of the danger of war, a policy moreover in which the cultural apparatus around the CP also had a major role to play in order to attract middle-of-the-road intellectuals and artists for the common task of defending liberal democracy. Paradoxically, in that cultural apparatus the same writers were active who, in their fictional work, expressed aspirations and hopes that went way beyond such immediate objectives. This seeming contradiction can partly be accounted for by the composition dates of the works. In 1935–6 two fundamentally different Communist strategies overlap and intermingle, the class-against-class line adopted in 1928 and in effect until 1934–5, and the popular front policy which replaced it from 1935 onward. By the time Sommerfield's novel came out (May 1936), the slogan 'Forward to a Soviet Britain' referred to above had, as a consequence, already been dropped by the CP (October 1935).

On the other hand, the former revolutionary policy under which quite a few intellectuals and writers or artists had actually found their way to Communism—among them Bates, Sommerfield and Anand, but also James Boswell, Alec Brown, John Cornford, Montagu Slater, Randall Swingler and Edward Upward—had not yet receded to a distant past and was quite likely to have still been cherished by a not insignificant number of party members. Just how many writers still embraced it, might be established by a close analysis of their works produced in the second half of the thirties.

Another instance of common ground between the four novels is of more general aesthetic interest. It concerns the vanishing hero, a question also of relevance for the socialist novel. In fact, in only one of the works discussed here do we find anything like a central individual hero, namely in *The Coolie*. In the others, it has been replaced by a new element, the revolutionary group or the working class. And even Anand is not so much concerned with the uniqueness of his hero's destiny as with its representativeness and typicality, a fact underlined by the dropping of the definite article in the title in subsequent editions.

According to Goldmann, who presupposes a structural homology between the novel form and the system of exchange in the capitalist social formation, the hero begins to disintegrate and finally to disappear, as the shift from one stage of capitalism, a competitive *laissez-faire* type economy, to another stage, an economy of monopolies and cartels, takes place.[25] In its general emphasis, this view is suggestive as far as it goes. But Goldmann's whole argument is too firmly located within the problematic of the bourgeois novel to help us with our own enquiry. In the heyday of the bourgeois novel, the critical-realist phase, its socialist counterpart was often absent or, when it was there, not yet fully developed. However, when the socialist novel matures in works like W. E. Tirebuck's *Miss Grace of All Souls'* (1895) or Robert Tressell's *The Ragged-Trousered Philanthropists* (*c*. 1906–10), it does so, almost from the outset, by downgrading the role of the central individual hero. Instead of presenting unique individuals in extraordinary circumstances, the socialist novel tends to emphasise the representativeness of its characters and the commonness of their position. Indeed, as early a writer as the Chartist Thomas Martin Wheeler says of his hero: 'Arthur Morton is a type, a representative of his class.'[26]

The whole question has also a more historico-philosophical side to it, which becomes of greater importance as socialist writers consciously tackle the novel form with the requirements of a Marxist analysis of the social and historical processes in mind. It is striking that not only Sommerfield but also Barke prefixes a Marxist motto to his book, this time from Engels who compares and contrasts the forces operating in nature with those of society. Another phrase of Engels's, 'Freedom is the recognition of necessity',[27] was in all probability the most widely quoted Marxist aphorism of the time. Generally speaking the thirties was a decade in which writers were perhaps more consciously experiencing their time as history in the making than in any other period this century. Evidence for this preoccupation can be found in works as diverse as Auden's 'Spain' and Grassic Gibbon's trilogy *A Scots Quair*. Now, though one would obviously have to examine the notion of history in every single case, and though it seems doubtful that the subordinate clause of the 'Men make history' sentence, namely 'under circumstances not chosen by themselves, under circumstances directly encountered, given and transmitted from the past', was given its due emphasis at the time—so doubtful indeed that the Marxism of the thirties has been characterised as voluntaristic—,[28] this immersion of the literary works in a historical fluid may have contributed to further shifting the balance from the individual (hero) to a wider human agency, the revolutionary group, the working-class community etc. And in the end it may have promoted an understanding of the role of the class struggle, its effect on human lives as well as their impact on its course.

The problem confronting the socialist novelist was thus never simply one of substituting a positive socialist hero for the worn-out 'problematic' hero, as some writers assumed in the thirties, but was rather how to relate the central fact of the class struggle to the lives of individuals. And this implies, in Brecht's words, that

the whole social causal complex can no longer be used as a mere prompter of inner experiences. To say this is not to deny the value of representing psychic processes or, more generally, representing individuals. . . . The old technique [of empathy] entered a state of crisis precisely because it did not permit a satisfactory treatment of the individuals in the class struggle and because the inner experiences carried the reader not into the class struggle but right out of it.[29]

7   LET THE PEOPLE SPEAK FOR THEMSELVES: ON THE DOCUMENTARISM OF THE 1930s AND 1940s (in collaboration with Jürgen Enkemann)

I Principal features of the genre

One of the first preconditions of the striking international growth and consolidation of the documentary genre in the twenties and thirties is without doubt the invention and development of the new media of photography, film and radio. Yet the very length of the time-lag between the first massive expansion of film and its use in documentary indicates that little may be gained by simply pointing to the level of development reached by the technological forces of production. A whole range of further explanatory factors must be taken into account, some of which (political developments; changes in the moods, needs and desires of wide sections of the working population) will be listed below.

When we turn to the documentaries themselves, it becomes clear that a use of the genre implies not only a particular stance but also a very conscious choice of subject matter. The documentarist focuses quite deliberately on those who are the principal consumers of the new media: the broad mass of the working (not to mention the unemployed) population. In this sense, documentary answers 'modern man's legitimate claim to being reproduced.' Walter Benjamin, from whom this quotation is taken, invested other hopes, too, in the new media. He saw the 'distinction between author and public' as 'about to lose its basic character'.[1] For British documentarism, this was admittedly only true in individual cases. Authors and the public here

remained divided as before, and by far the greatest number
of documentarists on the British scene were intellectuals.
Such being the case, it seems logical to conclude that the
expansion of this genre in Britain must also be bound up
with a change in the consciousness of the (literary and artistic) intelligentsia. This change manifests itself in the well-
known shift towards the left of intellectuals in the Thirties
Movement, a shift which has only recently begun to be submitted to detailed sociological analysis. The economic and
political factors spelt out in previous studies of the period,
such as the world economic crisis, or the rise of fascism
and the threat of war, certainly had a role to play in this
development. Yet the decisive determinants must be sought
on a deeper level, in fundamental changes in the composition and social position of the intelligentsia. These changes
included an increase in forms of state-waged labour, such as
a gradual expansion of the educational system in the 1920s
(involving the establishment of four new universities) and
the foundation of the BBC, and they were accompanied by a
loss of privilege and prestige resulting, for example, from the
growth of student numbers after the First World War and
teacher unemployment in the 1930s.[2]

These and similar material conditions for the constitution
of the genre can only be touched upon in passing. However,
the answer to the question of why documentarism did not
develop fully in Britain until relatively late, in the second
half of the 1930s, is likely to be found in the factors outlined
above.

Documentarism did of course have its early precursors.
Documentary film in particular anticipated developments in
other forms by almost a decade. Indeed the 'premature' and
pre-eminent significance of this medium finds expression in
the very terminology by which it is described; the noun
'documentary' refers in English to documentary *film*, the
term itself having been coined by John Grierson, the 'father
of the British school of documentary film'.

Yet it is important to differentiate between the antece-
dents of a genre and its high point. As far as the period of its
mass appeal and representativeness is concerned, film differs
only marginally from social documentary photography, from

literary reportage, or the work of the Mass-Observation movement, to name but the major forms.

The fact that documentarists became active in so many different areas, and that the genre itself spread and became rooted in such diverse cultural forms, is founded not only in a particular historical situation, but also in a kind of basic documentary impetus binding these separate forms. This has implications for our approach here, in so far as, in contrast to existing monographs, we do not confine ourselves to one generic form, but look rather at a series of several different forms, each of which is subject to its own specific rules and conventions. From the point of view of cultural studies, too, this kind of broad-based approach is all the more fruitful, in that the tracing and parallel documentation of a common basic impetus across this multiplicity of forms might possibly reveal one aspect of the structure of feeling of the period.

Where, then, do the similarities touched on above actually lie? An answer to this question—at this stage necessarily a purely provisional one—can be given on five levels; the points listed here are offered as working hypotheses, to be examined in greater detail in the course of this study.

1. The level of the (democratised) object

At the heart of documentarism stand 'the poor, the damaged, the inconspicuous and the ordinary';[13] not, then, the destinies of heroes or other extraordinary individuals, but rather the fate of the masses. Thus documentarism stands in stark opposition to the dominant conception of art, which on principle refuses to see aesthetic value in these sections of the population, condemning them instead to a shadowy existence as part of the 'local colour'. The documentarists, meanwhile, are not interested in the living conditions of the masses *sub specie aeternitatis*; their motto is the here and now. The principle of immediacy (both of representation and effect), which is intrinsic to documentarism, applies firstly to the immediacy and urgency of the object represented, while at the same time referring to geographical proximity. Grierson speaks correspondingly of 'our insistence on the drama of the doorstep'.[4] As has already been noted, documentary film only reaches maturity when it turns its attention to social problems at home (and thus indirectly abandons the penchant for aestheticism which had occasionally characterised early exotic films, or film strips on British industrial landscapes). A similar shift of interest is apparent in Tom Harrisson's abandonment of South Seas anthropology in favour of his Worktown study (Mass-Observation), as well as in the road taken by George Orwell from the clochards and tramps of *Down and Out in Paris and London* to miners and the unemployed in the north-west of England.

2. The level of thematisation (of the social)

The most important themes of British documentarism are unemployment, housing and sanitary conditions in the slums, the labour process, forms of leisure activity and the behaviour of the civilian population in times of war (not only its reaction to the blitz, but also to general mobilisation and rationing measures, as well as to the moves towards greater equality which these initiated). This catalogue of themes is more strongly biased in a social than in a political direction. Weaknesses, injustices and shortcomings in the system are brought into focus by film-makers, reporters and social observers, in the hope that public exposure of these issues will pave the way for processes of improvement. In this sense, documentarists understand themselves as propagandists who, admittedly, generally confine themselves to tracing and spotlighting social evils. The causes of these problems are seldom documented, solutions rarely proposed. The leading mass-observers, for example, did hope to collect the material necessary to bring about a change in society; yet they practised political restraint in other areas. One thing alone was clear: 'Whatever the political methods called upon to effect the transformation, the knowledge of what has to be transformed is indispensable'.[5] Solutions to large-scale social problems can only be political in nature; yet it was precisely the treatment of unmistakably political themes which was avoided by most documentarists.

3. The level of (non-fictional) form

One evident similarity between the various branches of British documentarism is to be found in their common emphasis on factual rather than fictional representation. This basic characteristic was accompanied by a more or less explicit opposition to aesthetic theories in which non-fictional forms were dismissed as 'mere' journalism, or as culturally inferior. In the sphere of film, some documentarists went so far as to embrace openly anti-aesthetic positions. Grierson, for example, quite consciously set up an opposition in his writings between 'propaganda' and 'education' on the one hand, and 'art' on the other. Adopting this position did not necessarily imply the complete absence of aesthetic construction; it constituted instead a historical contribution to the undermining of a bourgeois aesthetic which was fixated on the concept of artistic autonomy. The validation of the—often spontaneous—documentary report, as opposed to a professional command of artistic technique, was a potential means of democratising creative and artistic activity (as is illustrated, for example, by the shop-floor reportage in *Left Review*). At the same time, however, the renunciation of fictional form carried with it the problem of a narrowing-down of the field of possibilities for realistic representation.

4. The level of (collective) methods of work
One feature of documentarism is its capacity to overcome the 'cottage industry individualism' of the traditional artist. Transcending the individualism of the artist's profession does not only mean breaking it down into a range of different functions in the film (or illustrated newspaper) production process—producer, director, scriptwriter, cutter (or, respectively, photographer, editor, typographer, etc.)— which one individual is as a rule unable to fulfil. It means above all working in a team governed by the principle of co-operation and not of competition. 'Documentary, like story-film', wrote Paul Rotha in 1936, 'should be the result of collective working but . . ., unlike story-film, co-operation should be directed to a common end and not riddled with rivalry born of personal advancement.'[6] In Grierson's Unit—the name itself is worthy of note—this aim was partially realised; the group drew its strength from a pool of different talents, whose bearers furthermore took turns in performing the functions listed above.

Yet the notion of 'overcoming cottage-industry individualism' contains an additional stipulation; there can be no documentarism without fieldwork, without 'on-the-spot' observation. Tom Harrisson reports that his team of mass-observers lived in Worktown (Bolton) for almost two years, observing, collecting, recording, before the first interviews were conducted.[7] The duration of the study may make this a special case, yet the principle remains generally applicable.

Writers of fiction, too, from whom the most stubborn resistance of all could be anticipated, were called upon to shed their individualist 'home-worker' role. Tretyakov, the most determined of champions of a 'literature of fact', had issued the following admonition to authors some time before:

The individual writer does not go in search of material wherever and whenever necessary. He writes inaccurately and attempts to find merit in the subjectivism of his scribblings. The individual writer takes infinitely long over his work, limping along far behind life itself. The individual writer works uneconomically; he does not even practise the most minimal division of productive functions. He is composer, collector of material, reviser and compiler all rolled into one.[8]

In Britain, it was left to Storm Jameson to deliver the following challenge to her contemporaries. 'We must be field workers in a field no smaller than England'; and, with one eye fixed on the example of film, 'The isolation of writers from each other is almost as deadly as their isolation from the life of farmers, labourers, miners and the other men on whom the life of the nation depends.'[9]

5. The level of the (historical) conjuncture

The years 1937–8 mark the breakthrough of British documentarism to the level of a cultural form influential amongst and representative of the masses. *The Road to Wigan Pier* appears in March 1937; the first number of *Fact* comes out in April; in May, Allen Lane begins his 'Penguin Specials' series (especially commissioned contemporary non-fiction) and, in the same month, on the occasion of the coronation, Mass-Observation goes into action for the first time. In 1938 the Unity Theatre in London and the Theatre

of Action in Manchester produce the first British Living
Newspapers; in the autumn of that same year, *Picture Post*
appears on the market.

Up to this point, much emphasis has been placed on the
position of the producers of the genre as a condition for its
constitution. Clearly it is now important to clarify the question of why attention was suddenly directed at social problems which—with the exception of those arising from the
war—had after all already existed in the twenties; the question, then, of the conditions which gave rise to a sharpening
of social perceptions amongst the literary and artistic intelligentsia, whilst at the same time pushing them towards the
use of non-fictional methods. It is, however, equally important to bear in mind the audience for the genre, as well as the
sensitivity of documentarism towards, and identification
with, explicitly articulated and latent moods and attitudes
'from below'. In his study of reasons for the success of the
weekly *Picture Post*, Stuart Hall describes as a characteristic
trait of a popular form of communication, 'that it *both*
responds to authentic trends, moods and attitudes articulated among people, and, in shaping up those moods and
attitudes within the limits established by the media at its
disposal, and the commercial context in which it is set, it
alters and transforms those sentiments perceptibly.'[10]

In short, then, British documentarism rode on the crest of
a populist wave, whose speed and direction it in turn partially determined. Although many periods of recent English
history have had their share of populism, in the second half
of the 1930s it clearly acquired sharper contours: in increasingly vehement grass-roots opposition to the National Government, for example, following its failure to overcome
social deprivation despite economic stabilisation since its
coming to power in 1931: in an increasingly apparent readiness amongst the rank and file of the labour movement to
adopt the policy of an anti-fascist popular front: and finally
in a collective struggle for survival against external fascist
influences. This populism is well illustrated by the images
and impressions of the dominant class current throughout
this phase: 'Colonel Blimp', the 'Cliveden set', 'guilty men'.
(The need for such picturesque clarity could itself be con-

sidered a populist element here.) In these images which, though initially created by individual journalists, subsequently passed into the general political and social vocabulary, and were reproduced a million times over in caricatures, articles and films, a radical distrust of the dominant élite comes to light. It should be noted here that this radical undercurrent was not, as might be supposed, quelled by the outbreak of war. On the contrary, it gained tremendous impetus, swelling for the first time to a high tide of populism—a development due to the initially catastrophic course of the war for Britain, which in turn clearly exposed the incapacity of the establishment to deal with the situation.

Similarly, the documentary genre numbered amongst the few significant cultural projects of the thirties to survive the end of the decade not only unscathed, but actually with a gathered momentum. 'In World War II the prevailing assumption was that the war was being fought for the benefit of the common people.'[11] The conviction that what was being fought was a 'people's war'—the coining of which term can be traced to Tom Wintringham, a contributor to *Picture Post*[12]—was persistently promoted and propagated by documentarism. The genre thus only became obsolete when the abuses which it denounced had been purposefully countered, or when the demolition of the five pillars of the old order, 'Want, Disease, Ignorance, Squalor, Idleness', demanded by the Beveridge Report, had been accorded the official status of a government programme; in other words, after the overwhelming election victory of the Labour Party in 1945. The position of the Labour Party as the political home of documentarism, and the notion of the Welfare State as its ideological one, mark out the limitations of British documentarism in the 1930s and 1940s.

This preliminary sketch of our object of study, although it characterises by far the most important manifestations of the genre, nonetheless does not encompass all its forms. Alongside the dominant strand of documentarism traced here, there was another which moved in a more political dimension, and to which, despite its purely marginal significance, attention should be drawn. Only thus can over-hasty conclusions be avoided on the limited possibilities of the genre

itself, made on the basis of the specific features of its principal strands. Examples of this 'other' documentarism will
be briefly mentioned in each of the following sections.

II The individual forms

Film

A historical survey of the documentary film movement in
England must begin by indicating the international influences to which it was subject. Certainly, British film-makers
developed their own documentary style; this was a goal
towards which Grierson had striven from the start. Yet there
were also decisive influences from outside. Early American
models were Robert Flaherty's Eskimo film *Nanook of the
North* (1920) and his South Seas film *Moana* (1926). Grierson was fascinated by Flaherty's insistence on intensive
observation, by his willingness to continue studying for years
on end the ethnic groups he had chosen to film, and by his
concentration on the characteristics which made them
unique. Nonetheless, he expressed reservations about
Flaherty's hostility to the civilised world. For him, in contrast to Flaherty, the object of greatest topical interest was
the industrial area of contemporary England.

Grierson looked to other models for his orientation
towards actuality and the industrial environment. 'I think in
this other matter one may turn to the Russians for guidance
rather than to Flaherty.'[13] Grierson was above all impressed by the Russians' new film-making techniques—other
aspects, such as the revolutionary pathos of Eisenstein, did
not interest him to the same extent. He himself collaborated
on the production of the English versions of Eisenstein's
Potemkin and Victor Turin's *Turksib*. Of this latter film,
which told of the building of the Turkestan-Siberian railway,
Paul Rotha writes that it both impressed and influenced
all of the British documentary film-makers.[14]

If, then, the English movement was able to look for inspiration to a whole range of pioneering works,[15] it was
nonetheless in Britain that the documentary method was, for
the first time in the history of film, programmatically defined

as a separate and distinct genre. As early as 1920 (or thereabouts) in Russia, Dziga Vertov had given a theoretical foundation to his 'Kino' programme; England in the early 1930s was the first to follow in his footsteps with a theoretical discussion of documentary film. From 1930 onwards, Grierson published numerous articles in various journals and magazines; documentary films were discussed in the press (with particularly detailed critiques in the *Observer*) and in film magazines; in 1936, Rotha, with his book *Documentary Film*, became the first person to publish a comprehensive survey, together with a theoretical analysis of the genre. His work included attempted definitions, such as Grierson's characterisation of documentary as 'the creative treatment of actuality'. Rotha's decidedly more precise formulation, 'the use of the film medium to interpret creatively and in social terms the life of the people as it exists in reality' was, however, not to appear until the publication of the second edition of his book in 1939.[16]

The English school of documentary film first came into being with the establishment of a film department at the Empire Marketing Board (EMB) under the directorship of Grierson, who returned from the USA in 1927. The principal function of the EMB, founded the previous year, was to provide an information and public relations service which could combat the crisis in the British market and revitalise trade within the Empire. The films to be made for the EMB were to offer as lively and as informative a portrait as possible of life in the areas from which they came—both in Britain and abroad—as well as of production processes in various industries. Even during this period, Grierson was already able to call upon an enviable number of assistants, some of whom, such as Basil Wright, Harry Watt, Arthur Elton, Edgar Anstey and Stuart Legg, later numbered amongst the most significant of documentary film-makers. Paul Rotha, too, worked for a time with the EMB Unit. Before the unit was closed down, a considerable number of films were thus produced, although only a few of these (such as *Aero-Engine* and *Industrial Britain*) are deserving of detailed consideration. This period should instead be considered as an initial phase which gave the group a thorough introduction to the tools of their trade.

Following the dissolution of the EMB, the group was taken over by the General Post Office (GPO) and annexed to its public relations service. From then on the main theme of its films, with titles such as *Telephone Workers* and *Weather Forecast*, was the vivid and graphic representation of modern communications techniques. The GPO-financed productions included two excellent films, *Coal Face* (1935) and *Night Mail* (1936). Benjamin Britten supplied the music for both of these, and W. H. Auden the accompanying poems. *Coal Face* was directed by Alberto Cavalcanti, who had joined the GPO Unit in 1934, and under whose influence the group acquired an increasingly distinctive and more strongly poetic documentary style.

The remaining significant documentary films of this period—made almost exclusively by Grierson's co-workers and produced in part by Grierson himself—were not financed by the GPO, but by large state and/or private concerns; Rotha's *Shipyard* (1934–5), for example, by a shipping company, and Wright's *Song of Ceylon* (1934) by the Ceylon Tea Marketing Board.

Documentary film entered a new phase with the beginning of the Second World War. The renaming of the GPO Film Unit as the Crown Film Unit and its attachment to the Ministry of Information in 1940 indicate the direction it took from this point onward; documentary film production was from now on to be harnessed for the general war effort. 'Most war documentaries were made to fulfil very precise functions: to advise or reassure people or explain events.'[17] Now for the first time documentary film became the medium of mass enlightenment which Grierson, who by this time had emigrated to Canada, had always understood it to be. The most interesting and technically most brilliant films of this period stem, however, from a director whose work lies outside this particular scheme of things. Humphrey Jennings, prominent in the thirties as a surrealist poet and co-founder of Mass-Observation, but hardly ever as a film-maker, certainly also emphasized the keenness and determination of people on the 'home front', in films like *London Can Take It!* (1940) and *Fires Were Started* (1943). To this extent, they do possess a basic element of didacticism; yet far more significant in his films is one aspect of war which is continually evoked and at the same time glorified: the image of the united nation, bending together to a mortally perilous task. One element remains, admittedly, unspoken: the fact that a nation welded together by external necessity alone still carries within it latent social contradictions, which can only temporarily be concealed under the wartime veil of social harmony.[18]

As observed above, the first common feature of the documentarism of the Thirties Movement was the level of the democratised object. In the film movement, this level (as opposed to the thematisation of the social) was important right from the very beginning. As early as *Drifters*, working people stand at the centre of the action; everyday labour takes on dramatic form—though not without a tendency towards romanticisation which, for example, disguises the social dependency and alienation which affect these workers as they do any others. Yet contradictions are not entirely excluded: thus Grierson, for example, contrasts the dignity of labour with a market in which only financial gain—and never the labour on which it is based—becomes visible. Grierson always held this weighting of emphasis within the film to be important—as the pathos of the following quote from his 1929 article on *Drifters* illustrates: 'men at their labours are the salt of the earth.'[19] As late as 1970, two years before his death, he wrote a letter to Paul Rotha, in which he stressed, 'It was among the first of my intentions that we should get the British workman on the screen.'[20]

One could justifiably object here that the portrayal of the worker took place within an apolitical and, in its initial phase, uncritically affirmative framework. Yet it remains the case that the sphere of the filmed object underwent a—historically not insignificant—process of democratisation in these films, both as a result of detailed, precise observation and through convincing filming, which are not achieved in a number of more strongly political and radical films. Time and time again, comments of the following kind can be found in the film notes: 'Concentration was not only on the machines but on the men whose skill made them possible' (on *Aero-Engine*), or 'In *Night Mail*, the constant focus is on

the men working in the train, on their dedication and efficiency.'[21] The progressive element in this kind of representation lies in its attempt to give palpable form to the technical
world around us, to show it to be created by the labour of
individuals. Grierson may not be wrong in seeing this as a
reason for the lasting influence his films have had in the
socialist countries of Eastern Europe.

On the level of social theme, and in contrast to the Russian directors of the twenties, as well as documentary film-
makers like Joris Ivens, the fundamentally reformist position
of the English films is striking. Particularly opportunist are
the films made before 1935. They show an almost total lack
of any social criticism; the positive side of 'industrial society'
is highlighted, the economic and social crisis in Britain
ignored. At this point, the particular standard of objectivity
frequently set by documentarists loses its legitimation.
Behind the faithful reproduction of factual detail lies the
distortion of broader relations; a society floundering in deep
crisis—the year 1931 was experienced by the English
bourgeoisie itself as one of the great shocks of the century—becomes the smoothly functioning industrial society
of *Industrial Britain*.

Rotha, who was already making explicit reference to the
exclusion of these wider social relations by 1936, named
the following reasons:

The real economic issues underlying the North Sea herring catch,
the social problems inherent in any film dealing seriously with the
Industrial Midlands, lay outside the scope of a Unit organised
under a Government department and having as its aim 'the bringing alive of the Empire'. The directors concerned knew this, and
wisely, I think, avoided any economic or important social
analysis.[22]

This institutional dependency must be taken into consideration in any evaluation of the social and political
intentions of the school of documentary film-makers
—notwithstanding the generous amount of leeway enjoyed by Grierson and his team at the EMB and the GPO.
Alan Lovell, who, in his *Studies in Documentary*, seems to
equate the ideology of documentary films entirely with

Grierson's personal views, paints a false picture in this respect.[23] The left-wing tendencies of various documentarists, as well as the continual allegations and political suspicions of the authorities, are evidenced in a whole series of reports. On the other hand—and this applies particularly to Grierson himself—it would be false to assume a radical conflict between film-makers and those by whom their work was commissioned. Although in his writings Grierson criticises the exploitation of the workers and the 'bankruptcy of our national management',[24] neither of these phenomena was being portrayed at this time (1931) in his films. And his statements (and indirectly, his films as well) basically reflected the crisis-management consciousness which determined the course of political events in the period following the world economic crisis.

Around the middle of the thirties, socially critical elements began to appear more frequently in the films, after Paul Rotha had set an early precedent in 1934 with his film *Shipyard*. In films such as *Housing Problems, Enough to Eat?* and *Today We Live*, urgent social problems—desolate housing conditions, undernourishment, unemployment —were taken up. In a period during which the Labour Party was gaining new ground with its programme of social reform, in a time, too, of the building of a broad front against the forces of the right in Europe, the bodies which provided financial support granted the film-makers this critical latitude. Just how limited it generally was is illustrated by *Housing Problems*: its devastating portrayal of inhumane living conditions is followed by an optimistic summary of the urban renewal plans then about to be implemented. Seldom is the direction indicated towards a critique of the system as a whole, neither are there any pointers towards the historical conditions of any given development. The notable exception, in a medium where these elements are so rare, is *Today We Live* (1937); yet even here, political alternatives are not brought sharply into focus. Dependence on financing bodies made documentaries on workers' demonstrations and hunger marches impossible.

These and similar events were covered in the thirties almost exclusively by socialist film clubs—the Federation of

Workers' Film Societies, the Socialist Film Council and the (Workers') Film and Photo League—in the context of workers' newsreels and short agitational films[25]. The limited sphere of influence of these groups can, however, be read off the following figures: until the year 1936, a total of eight workers' newsreels and an estimated two dozen films of different kinds (short documentaries and feature films, almost without exception silent) made primarily with the support of the Communist Party, the Independent Labour Party and the London Co-operative Society, stood against 300 completed documentary films.[26] Moreover, the modest opportunities for distribution open to these small organisations left them in no real position to restore this imbalance, though the situation improved in the latter half of the decade owing to the developing network of Kino, the main distributor of Soviet films.[27]

The connections binding the British documentary film movement to a social democratic politics of reform (and, in its initial phase, to a policy of reforms in the structure of monopoly capital) were apparent above all on the level of the explicit statement, in particular in film notes. Yet beyond this level, and as a result of the tendencies towards democratisation already noted, as well as its honest, unromantic way of taking the worker seriously, documentary film nonetheless developed a form of visual realism (which also ran in part through the accompanying spoken text), which cannot be captured by the concept of reformism.

As far as the phases of its development are concerned, film differs from other documentary forms in the early date of its birth. Amongst the various reasons for its early inception (which included, for example, the influence of international film), one that was decisive was the particularly rapid recognition of the prime importance of film as a medium of mass information in certain circles of the establishment during the period of world economic crisis. Grierson's statements from the year 1931 illustrate particularly well the original connections between the beginnings of documentary film and the deepening economic crisis. Following a number of observations on the devastating effects of the crisis, he writes:

Our confidence is sapped, our beliefs are troubled, our eye for beauty is most plainly disturbed: and the more so in cinema than in any other art. For we have to build on the actual. Our capital comes from those whose only interest is the actual. The medium itself insists on the actual.[28]

In this time of great catastrophe, then, a reorientation towards that which was immediately to hand, towards the actual, took first place; there was no time left for romantic fictions. The providers of capital were the first to perceive this clearly. In an interview later on in his life, Stuart Legg reduced the connections touched upon here to the following simple formula: 'Documentary has always flourished in times of trouble and not when things are going smoothly.' In the same interview, he roots the documentary film movement in the quasi 'pre-revolutionary situation' which had arisen during the depression. 'There was need on the part of the government for communication, and a little later, industries too.'[29] However, although the early documentaries, which were predominantly shown in film societies, schools, and exhibitions, met with considerable public response, widespread public distribution in cinemas only started in the second half of the thirties and reached its climax in the forties.[30]

The preference mentioned in the first section for factually-oriented documentation as opposed to fictional representation meant, as far as film was concerned, a simultaneous assault on the commercialised 'cinema of illusion', the dream factories of Hollywood imperialism, which absolutely dominated cinema in Britain during this period. Grierson had, it is true, always called for the 'creative' treatment of factual material, a demand which opened up new opportunities for aestheticisation which some directors (notably Cavalcanti and Jennings) did not hesitate to exploit. Yet renouncing fictionality could and still can build a foundation for the development of a new kind of realism in opposition to antiquated fictional models which can only reproduce reality in distorted form (a potentiality which is commonly overlooked by rigorous critics of the documentary genre). This recognition does not entail a new blindness to the weaknesses of the genre, which have quite rightly been stressed in a number of theoretical analyses. Its close links with the factual limit opportunities for generalisation and make it difficult to delineate perspectives for action. The documentary film-maker certainly has access to a number of different means of overcoming these limitations—montage techniques, for example—yet certain shortcomings (whose general tendency is towards an opportunist acknowledgement of the status quo) remain in the long term difficult to avoid. One such limitation is the difficulty, if not the impossibility of producing credible portraits of individuals in the private sphere. It is significant that one of the more critical documentary films of the thirties, *Today We Live*, should operate on the outer limits of the documentary form, by working mainly with scripted re-enactments and studio sets.

Wildenhahn's postulate that documentary film can fulfil an important historical function as a prefigurative stage in the development towards what he calls a 'synthetic' realistic fictional film seems to be verified here.[31] The English documentary film tradition has indeed continued to be influential on this level. Traces of it resurface in feature films of the sixties (*Saturday Night and Sunday Morning* for example) and in a whole series of more strongly committed social and political films of the seventies (such as *The Big Flame, After a Lifetime, Days of Hope*).

Photography
The photography of the 1930s also bore the vivid hallmark of social documentary interests. The trend towards documentary was accelerated by technological developments. Following the rise of the conveniently portable and less conspicuous miniature camera, photography revealed itself to be an ideal medium for the documentation of the social environment. The photographer was rarely confronted with a number of the problems which dogged the documentary film-maker: with the opposition, for example, between documentation and fictional representation. Doubtless there was some opposition between the artificial studio photo, which remained popular right up into the thir-

ties, and the spontaneous snapshot. In contrast to the visual artist, however, who, before the advent of photography, had been alone in fulfilling the function of visual representation, the photographer was more or less obliged from the start, by virtue of the technical nature of the medium, to produce precise and exact documents of the outside world.

Documentary photography as a socially critical cultural practice developed relatively late in Britain, and was not able to match the extent or the significance of its counterpart in the USA. In one sense this is astonishing, as the country could look back to a long tradition of photography of street-life and the slums.[32] Yet the threshold of partisanship, for the common people depicted and against oppression, injustice and inhumanity, which is the essential precondition for a social documentary use of the medium, was hardly ever crossed before the 1930s. More often than not, the guiding spirit of earlier 'social' photographers was that of the industrial archeologist who purely wants to preserve the traces of a vanishing past.

Thus it was not from a native source but from the Weimar Republic that the most decisive impulses came. Within the German labour movement, photography had already been recognised as a potentially democratic medium since the mid-1920s. Willi Münzenberg's *Arbeiter Illustrierte Zeitung (AIZ)* encouraged the participation of its readers in large-scale photo competitions. Outside the working-class movement, impulses came from the Bauhaus, from the photography of 'Neue Sachlichkeit' ('new objectivity' or 'new sobriety')[33] and from Franz Roh's internationally acclaimed collection of experimental work *Foto-Auge* (1929). In 1931 *Close Up* published some of Helmar Lerski's 'Köpfe des Alltags', portraits of nobodies (cleaners, beggars, stall-holders, typists, coachmen, etc.). Prominent English photographers, amongst them John H. Ahern and German-born E. O. Hoppé, travelled to Germany during these years to take photographs[34] and to gain first-hand experience of a scene which in turn was in touch with the latest Soviet and other montage developments (El Lissitzky and others). As a result, numerous photos marked by the 'new objectivist' style were produced in England in the early thirties, idealising modern technology in images of bridge constructions, power stations and machines. These pictures, hailed as 'ambassadors of industry' on the occasion of the Modern Industrial Photography Exhibition of 1933, recall some of the traits of the early films of the documentary movement. Yet in documentary photography as a whole during these years, a gradual movement away from posed portraits and reconstructed scenes which took their orientation from the closed work of art, and towards spontaneous photography, encapsulated in concepts such as 'open style' and 'candid photography', should be noted as a precondition for the later development of documentary photography.

Around the middle of the thirties, a number of decisive transformations paved the way for the development of documentary photography. Increasingly, the social world became the object of the photographic gaze; documentary film became a model for photography, not only in terms of theme, but also on a formal level, as the closed individual image declined in popularity in relation to the sequential narrative chain of images in the photo essay and social reportage.

The Listener published its first 'photo-newsreels', which took their orientation from film, in 1935. Humphrey Spender, as 'lensman' for the *Daily Mirror* from 1934, captured images of daily life amongst the British people, though much of his early social documentary from Stepney and Tyneside was never published by that paper.[35] In 1936 he took a sequence of photographs of the Jarrow Hunger March for *Left Review*. The photo-journalist Bert Hardy was now also giving priority to scenes from 'popular life', thus moving in the direction of *Picture Post*, which he was later to join and shape with his style. Bill Brandt, another who had resided on the Continent, and had been influenced in his early photography by surrealism, now undertook what amounted to a 'voyage of discovery' into the industrial north, in order to include in his panorama of English social life the everyday activities of the working class. Though Brandt in his celebrated collection *The English at Home* (1936) does not resort to photo montage, the juxtaposition of two photographs like 'East End Playground' and 'Kensington Children's Party' clearly carries a social message, and the contrast could not be starker than in his two shots from 1937, 'Coal-miner's Bath, Chester-le-Street, Durham' and 'Parlourmaid Preparing a Bath'.[36] *The English at Home* anticipated motifs later taken up by Mass-Observation, which made use of photography as one of its media and which recruited Humphrey Spender for that purpose. The fact that Gisèle Freund made a similar journey to the north of England in 1935, on which she shot a remarkable series of photographs in the depressed areas, goes incidentally to show that the traffic in these years was not entirely one-way to the Continent.

Indeed, important impulses came to English documentary photography in the second half of the thirties from emigrés from fascist Germany, who were already familiar with politically and socially critical photo-newsreels and reports, and particularly the use of photo-montage. One impressive piece of evidence for this is the illustated weekly, *Picture Post*, launched in October 1938, on which early photo-journalists from the *AIZ* collaborated.[37] This newspaper represented the culmination of the developments outlined above. Here the expertise of continental photo-journalism could be combined with elements of an English documentarism still in the bloom of youth. In editorial work, the non-hierarchical collective method of working which had already proved its worth amongst documentary film-makers since the early thirties played an important role. Immediately after its launching, *Picture Post* proved itself to be a huge success, reaching a circulation (in terms of copies printed) of one million within two months. This figure, astoundingly high for a socially critical magazine, was made possible by the general trend towards the left since the end of the thirties, and by the wave of populism mentioned above. The diverse and wide-ranging interrelationships of these trends, and the history of *Picture Post*, have been examined in detail by Stuart Hall;[38] further discussion of the subject would thus be superfluous here. The magazine was at its most influential during the war, when it became arguably the most important mouthpiece of the home front, documenting not only events at the front, but above all the solidarity and raw courage of

the mass of the civilian population. While it was not produced by 'the people' in the literal sense—not by its readers,
in other words—but rather by highly experienced professional journalists, it nonetheless uniquely embodied the
fundamental principle of documentarism, 'let the people
speak for themselves', by reflecting the experiences, views
and hopes of the mass of the population. At the same time,
however, as Hall has shown, it failed for the most part to
give expression to more profound social contradictions.

Again, to a limited extent, expressly political documentary
photography can also be said to have existed at the time. It
originated in the Workers' Camera Club, which merged with
the Kino organisation in 1934 to form the already mentioned Workers' Film and Photo League. Just what role it
effectively played in the furthering of an oppositional cultural practice, and in how far it succeeded in its aim to provide and popularise film and photos of working-class interest, 'giving a true picture of life today, recording the industrial and living conditions of the British workers and the
struggle of the employed and unemployed to improve these
conditions',[39] is extremely difficult to establish today. The
case of Edith Tudor-Hart, recently rediscovered, who was a
member of the League, is in many ways a unique one in that
she was Austrian-born, of middle-class origin and equipped
with an acute sense of women's issues.[40] Yet the commitment which radiates from her photographs of working-class
children or backyard scenes may after all be representative
of the League and is certainly of a different calibre than that
of the photographic work of Mass-Observation.

Literature
Amongst the earliest examples of documentary literature in
the thirties are two studies of unemployment: E. Wight
Bakke's *The Unemployed Man*, and a series of twenty-five
interviews with the unemployed in the magazine *The Listener*. Both appeared in 1933, both are motivated by a
primarily sociological interest, and both arose out of decisive
influences from similar studies overseas.

Bakke was a young American economist, whose goal in
coming to Britain in 1931 was to research into the extent to

which the financial support of the unemployed could be seen
to exercise a negative influence on their morale and will to
work—hardly a favourable starting point from the point of
view of the unemployed themselves, in a year in which
weekly maintenance payments were reduced from 17s. to
15s. 3d. Once confronted, however, with the concrete situation in Britain, with inadequate statistics and a lack of
'objective data', the author began a process of reorientation
which eventually led him to produce a study quite different
in method and results from the one originally planned.
Bakke made contact with social workers, interviewed the
unemployed, planned and carried out case studies. Most
importantly, however, he determined 'to take lodgings with
a working-class family, to share their life insofar as it was
possible to do so, to join in their activities or loaf on the
streets or at factory gates as the occasion might require'.[41]
By means of this approach, which sociology already knew as
'participant observation', the author anticipated George
Orwell's road to Wigan by a full four years.

The method of 'participant observation' had been initiated in the twenties by the Chicago School of Sociology as an
alternative to the dominant school of positivist sociology,
and had already led in the USA to a whole series of studies
of marginal groups and ethnic minorities. Motivated by a
fundamentally humanist belief in the value of human contact, the participant observers, not unlike the turn-of-the-
century Muckrakers, sought the company of tramps, drop-
outs, or, in this case, the unemployed, with the aim of sharing their situation, reconstructing particular experiences,
researching into the way of life which the observers thus
experienced 'from the inside', as it were. The manifest
danger of romanticising their object was countered by some
participant observers by a certain 'hard-boiled' approach to
the outside world. Both this romanticism and the attendant
'hard-edged' tone can be detected in parts of *The Road to
Wigan Pier*. One of the advantages of the method used here
is its credible mediation of a view 'from below', from the
perspective of 'us' (as opposed to 'them')—a credibility
which can in part be attributed to the detailed reproduction
of actual speech. Bakke reproduces a number of original

statements, distressing not only for the hopelessness they
express, but also for the knowledge of their authenticity, to
which a multitude of different examples bear witness. An
electrician on his situation:

You get so finally you leave the last thing that gives you pride in
yourself, your job as a skilled man, and you take up something
else. No one who hasn't gone through it knows how that tears you
up in here. I haven't gone through it completely yet; but I see it
coming. And I lay awake at nights, and it's a nightmare. But you
have to work you see, even if it's at something else, to keep your
self-respect.[42]

The same procedure was adopted by H. L. Beales and
R. S. Lambert when, with the help of a group of social workers, they put together a collection of interviews, originally for
The Listener, but reappearing a year later in book form
under the title *Memoirs of the Unemployed*. A representative cross-section of twenty-five unemployed, chosen according to age, gender, type of employment and place of
residence, were given the opportunity to produce written
accounts of their situation. In order to attain a certain level
of uniformity and comparability in these statements, the
interviewees were provided with a set of 'guidelines', a list
of topics which, besides personal questions—on their individual and family background, the date of their dismissal and
the present state of their debts or income—also took into
account the psychological, social and in some cases political
consequences of unemployment.

For these twenty-five statements, then, Beales and Lambert could claim with some justification that 'the *Memoirs*
represent the authentic voice of the unemployed authors
—the first occasion on which this voice has been heard
in the long discussion of unemployment that has dragged
on for so many years.'[43] As for representing the *voices* of
the unemployed, the question of course arises of why, when
they were first published in the house journal of the BBC,
they were printed in Standard English, instead of being
broadcast in the unadulterated idiom of the people.

This question touches upon an ideological barrier of the
first order. As a medium with the potential of reaching all

sections of the population, radio aspires to the reduction of educational and other privileges. Yet the same privileges were artificially maintained by the BBC's proscription on anything other than 'correct' English, which effectively deprived the mass of the population of their right to opportunities for public expression. Whole areas of experience which are more or less impossible to capture in BBC English thus remain dependent upon forms of communication that pre-date the mass media. (Herein lies, incidentally, one of the reasons for the failure of radio broadcasting to establish itself amongst the central documentary forms of the period.)

There seems to have been only one major exception to the rule, and that is another series about unemployment in which eleven unemployed were actually brought to the microphone. Though *Time to Spare*, which was broadcast in 1934, was far from striking a radical chord, and though it is by no means clear whether the producers did not in some way edit the talks, the mere fact of allowing the people concerned to speak for themselves, for the first time, over the national radio, giving them an opportunity to describe their plight in full detail, led to a public controversy. The National Government attempted, unsuccessfully, to stop the series, but in due time the relatively progressive Talks Department was dismantled.[44]

George Orwell, commenting upon a quite different form of documentary literature, the 1938 collection of shop-floor reportage, *Seven Shifts*, recognised the possibilities of broadcasting when he remarked, 'I think the first prole novel that comes along will be spoken over the radio.'[45] Though Orwell, as so often, inclines here towards hyperbole, he nonetheless correctly assesses the structural relationships between content, medium and recipient of a text.[46] To what public *The Listener*, as opposed to the radio, was addressing itself becomes clear from the reaction to the first printing of the interviews:

certain of the *Memoirs* aroused the humanitarian feelings of their readers much more strongly than others. The cases of the unemployed business man and the ex-Army officer made a stronger impression than, shall we say those of the elderly South Wales miner or the young man in search of a career.[47]

There was at this time a general consensus that the proletariat was to carry the main burden of unemployment. But
when sections of the middle classes also found themselves
drawn into the whirlpool of economic crisis, the shock
moved many of them to solidarity with their fellow-sufferers.
At one point in his 'diary' sketch, 'Hop Picking' (1931),
which records his adventures amongst English tramps,
Orwell notes the same experience. On one of his rambles
across Kent, he begs money from a 'gentleman', and forgets
for a moment to speak Cockney. At this, 'he looked closely
at me and said how painful it must be for a man of my stamp
etc. Then he said, "I say, you won't be offended, will you?
Do you mind taking this?" "This" was a shilling, with which
we bought some tobacco and had our first smoke that day.'[48]

Like the sketches 'The Spike' and 'Clink', both of which
derive from the same period, though both are more substan-
tially reworked, 'Hop Picking' already exhibits many of
the features which can be taken as characteristic of the
documentary style developed by Orwell:

—lively, picturesque and deliberately transparent descriptions which, should it be thought necessary, take in even the
smallest of 'damning details'.

—a direct, candid language, which presents itself as un-
affected, non-intellectual, non-'literary'.

—a deliberately utilised hardness of expression, which
engages the reader's attention, while at the same time avoid-
ing the mere arousal of sympathy or pity for the figures
portrayed.

—a tendency towards over-hasty generalisations on the basis
of isolated observations (this is what makes some of Orwell's
claims so contentious).

—the occasional snatch of comedy, lightening the tone with
a humour which arises less from the situations themselves
than from comments on the events portrayed.[49]

On the other hand, the themes of these early documentary sketches by Orwell do not yet coincide with those areas
later given priority by British documentarists. Gathered
rather from the sphere of the *lumpenproletariat* than from
the proletariat itself, the material shows similarities with the
works of American pioneers in participant observation,

recalling the early classic of the genre, *The Hobo*, which had focused on the way of life of homeless tramps and casual labourers.

Orwell's documentary work first gains a clearer sense of social (and political) purpose under the economic conditions, specified in section I, which led to the rise of British documentarism as a whole. Between 1931–2, the years in which the early sketches were published or reworked and *Down and Out in Paris and London* was written, and 1936, when Orwell was commissioned to carry out his research for *The Road to Wigan Pier*, lie the four years in which three novels—*Burmese Days, A Clergyman's Daughter* and *Keep the Aspidistra Flying*—but no reportage, were written. Mindful of Raymond Williams's warning against a schematic separation of Orwell's 'documentary' and 'imaginative' works,[50] we do not wish to claim two unconnected, completely distinct forms, but the date of Orwell's 'return' to the documentary form does not seem to us to be a matter of chance alone. *The Road to Wigan Pier* is a product (and agent) of the second half of the decade—not because poverty or unemployment had not existed before, but because these were now for the first time regarded as relevant topics for an intelligentsia newly sensitised to political issues.

Orwell's reportage, which remains today the most widely read work in the Left Book Club selection, was the subject of political controversy when it first appeared.[51] Criticism from the left was kindled by the polemicism of the second, autobiographical and self-reflexive section of the book, in which the author developed his ideas on socialism and a potentially successful socialist strategy for Britain. Later critics have also pointed to the exclusion of details of relations of ownership and dependency in the coalmines, as well as the inadequacy of Orwell's sociological categories. Yet the persistently harsh, if not vituperatively hostile tendency of these critiques all too easily obscures the positive aspects of the book, the points at which it questions prevailing ideologies—aspects which emerge most clearly from a comparison with other documentary forms, as well as with other examples of literary reportage.

The issue of urban redevelopment is one case in point.

Orwell can certainly never be accused of glorifying living conditions in the slums. 'But the trouble is that in destroying the slums you destroy other things as well.'[52] Moving onto new suburban estates, the workers leave behind them not only cramped and unhygienic housing conditions. As the street, the local pub and the corner shop lose their importance as sites of communication, the whole tightly-knit network of working-class culture, with its community and kinship relations, is threatened with extinction.

In contrast, the documentary film *Housing Problems* —despite some clearly relatively critical elements—completely ignores this aspect of urban renewal. A number of explanations come to mind, of course, for the silence of the occupants of new council houses on this subject when placed in front of the camera or microphone by Elton and Anstey. The reason does not necessarily lie in any rigid belief in technological progress on the part of the film-makers, a belief which would have blinded them to such problems. Their dependence on financial support from such bodies as the British Gas Association may equally have had a role to play, as may also the difficulty of finding the right perspective from which to project the problem onto the screen in the course of a fifteen-minute film (without settling for one of two false alternatives, slum versus corporation estate).

For whatever reason, the film undeniably conceals one significant side-effect of slum clearance which Orwell's critique of the unquestioning equation of technological with social progress, and socialism with the ideology of growth, grasps in all its centrality. One further point highlighted by an Orwell 'stumbling towards a study of ideology'[53] appears in the chapter which describes working conditions underground. Although the author occasionally tends here towards an exaggerated emphasis on the workers' physique, he refuses to consider the labour process in isolation as 'intrinsically interesting'—as did a whole number of documentary film-makers. Orwell rather pursues the work process right up to its end product, coal fuel, and is thus able to reveal the character and form of the commodity.

Here am I, sitting in front of my comfortable coal fire. It is April but I still need a fire. Once a fortnight the coal cart drives up to the door and men in leather jerkins carry the coal indoors in stout sacks smelling of tar and shoot it clanking into the coal-hole under the stairs. It is only very rarely, when I make a definite mental effort, that I connect this coal with that far-off labour in the mines. It is just 'coal'—something that I have got to have; black stuff that arrives mysteriously from nowhere in particular. . . .[54]

There is not an immediate connection between the coal glowing in the grate and the human labour involved in producing it; neither are members of the middle classes, in their distance from the production sphere, aware of it: it is to such an audience that Orwell's *The Road to Wigan Pier* is really addressed. It seems to him therefore all the more important to draw out the implications of this concrete example of miners' labour for the significance of material production in general.

It is so with all types of manual work; it keeps us alive and we are oblivious of its existence . . . it is so vitally necessary and yet so remote from our experience, so invisible, as it were, that we are capable of forgetting it as we forget the blood in our veins.[55]

One omission in *The Road to Wigan Pier* which has been the subject of justifiable criticism represents at the same time a point of difference from the diary;[56] it is the exclusion of any political activity on the part of the workers interviewed and observed by the author. The reason for the obliteration of such elements can be located in Orwell's excessive emphasis on the 'corporative' consciousness and behaviour of English workers, and their withdrawal into themselves as a class. Here the overall picture painted of the English working class tends towards an excessively passive description of 'the situation', giving the impression of an apathetic acceptance of given conditions, without devoting so much as a page to active efforts to change this situation.

One example of mining reportage which adopts precisely the opposite procedure is Montagu Slater's *Stay Down Miner* (1936). Here militancy steps into the foreground, at the expense of a description of the miners' situation. The subject of the work is the history and circumstances surrounding the spectacular pit occupations through which the organised miners of South Wales put up a fight against the introduction of non-union labour by the coal companies—willing workers brought in from outside, having themselves fallen prey to devastating unemployment in the South Wales mining area. The author himself was not able to follow the bitter and sometimes violent struggles which took place in the course of the occupations. By the time he arrived on the scene, the 'stay-down strikes' were already more or less over. His record of the events is therefore based on conversations with the protagonists, as well as on a study of the local press of the time.

Where Slater reports on the mood of the mining villages, his reportage gains special value as a document of the period. His observation of the wounds left unhealed after the General Strike, his account of the night-long vigils of almost the entire village population—these bear unique witness to the extraordinariness of this particular struggle.

Yet as soon as the author undertakes to enrich his portrayal of mood and atmosphere with more general information and details, his account becomes fragmentary and unstructured. With regard to the economic aspects of this branch of industry, to working conditions underground, the domestic circumstances, the eating habits, the everyday life of a mineworker in times of 'industrial peace', the reader is left in the dark. For this reason, the motives for the 'stay-down strikes', the miners' determination and the solidarity of the village community are neither adequately documented nor successfully portrayed.

Over and above this, Slater's uneconomical and unclear style lacks the necessary disruptive force.

As we watch them marching along, with a good swing to the band's rhythm (it is a good three-mile walk, mostly uphill, from Risca, and the men are just getting into their stride) as we watch them it is worth remembering that there is something especially pointed in the arrival of the Risca miners. Last week it was they who were the centre of the fight against these invaders, these locusts, these robbers of our men's jobs, politely called 'non-Federation men', or 'non-political Unionists'.[57]

The fussiness and indiscipline of such formulations gives rise to suspicions that the author, succumbing perhaps to the influence of tension in the atmosphere, failed to get to grips with his material. In the (eighty-page long) booklet, there is no real attempt, as there is in Orwell, to develop arguments, to dismantle ignorance and prejudice, and thus to shake the reader out of safe and comfortable assumptions. In the end, the audience primarily addressed appears to be the party members already committed to the cause. Thus the opportunities offered by the reportage form are never fully exploited in Slater's work.

Despite the author's enthusiastic attempts at its propagation,[58] the documentary genre clearly did not number amongst his strengths. Thus the most telling and convincing description in the entire work comes not from Slater, but from the pen of a local worker activist.

The madness of that Monday morning was unforgettable; in their extreme rage men were fit for anything. Yet, as the day went on and they returned to a more normal state of reasoning, there was no weakening of the fight, but rather a stronger desire to fight to the finish, and a keen wonder why we had not employed this weapon of non-violence before. The little food men had was sparingly eaten, and water was also taken care of, especially when we found that the tank in the stables (where we had made our headquarters) was covered with fat, ugly, dead and living black beetles, a sight to turn one's stomach![59]

The deliberate tone of this passage, the taken-for-grantedness of its representation of heroic endurance down the mine-shaft, show that those most directly affected can give more forcible and gripping descriptions of their situation than the reporter who comes in from outside. Indeed, the thirties saw a considerable increase in the volume of reports, records and correspondence in which, as in the *Memoirs of the Unemployed*, the workers themselves put pen to paper. Shop-floor reportage had already been produced, if sporadically, before then; the collection of lectures entitled *Workers on their Industries* (1893), for example, and the particularly noteworthy anthology, *Working Days (Being the Personal Records of Sixteen Men and Women Written by Themselves)* (1926).[60] Yet these had remained as a rule isolated publications, which did not seem to arise out of a wider context of discussion or programmatic aims.

In *Left Review*, on the other hand, and later also in *Fact*, non-fictional literary contributions and declarations of theoretical positions on the literature of reportage can be seen to increase to an extent where it is possible to talk of the deliberate promotion of documentarism. The first social-ist writing competitions in *Left Review*, for example, although the topics they set ('A Street Scene', 1934; 'An Hour or a Shift at Work', 1935) were certainly suitable for treatment in non-fictional forms, still registered a clear pre-dominance of texts with fictional scenes and plots. To a large extent, this was due to the exclusion from the competition announcement of any encouragement for, or instuctions on, documentary writing; on the contrary, it encouraged an orientation towards fiction by its inclusion of a literary pro-totype. In the first competition, Amabel Williams-Ellis, the organizer of the enterprise, simply presented a scene from one of her own novels, encouraging competitors to 'describe the same scene from another point of view'.[61] This restrictive and patronising attitude towards potential participants, as well as the orientation towards traditional principles of bourgeois aesthetics, were sharply criticised six months later by Alick West at the first public editorial meeting of *Left Review*.[62] This critique, combined with a plea for a documen-tary mode of writing, which was made in the January 1935 issue on the occasion of the second writing competition, may have brought about a gradual change of mind: 'What is wanted is the sort of "reporting" of the immediate scene that we see on the films when we are shown how an aero-engine is made or how a hat is trimmed. In such reporting comment is out of place'.[63]

Documentary film is explicitly drawn upon here as a model for literary documentary forms. Even more signifi-cant, however, is the fact that the anonymous author of this editorial announcement (Montagu Slater?) placed the writ-

ing competition in a more broadly-based programmatic
framework, whose aims were both to promote literary reportage through *Left Review*, and to 'publish first-hand accounts
of life and work in contemporary England'.[64]

Of the entries for the competition in March 1935, whose
title was 'Nine Workers describe a Shift at Work', hardly a
single one fails to include documentary elements, in the form
of detailed descriptive passages and observations drawn
from everyday working life. The majority nonetheless still
use the closed story form to give life and sequence to the
observations made.

The prizewinning contribution, 'Monday Morning in the
Machine Shop', by Kenneth Bradshaw, tends towards com-
pliance with Grierson's postulate of the dramatisation of
(non-fictionally represented) everyday events. One example
of this is the description of what might normally appear as
the unexciting start of a working day.

One by one the workers troop in, and take up their positions by
their machines. My boss, the toolsetter, stands beside me. We
await Zero hour. . . . Suddenly the 8 o'clock hooter screams. The
dynamo starts. Up go the lights. Out go hastily nicked cigarettes. A
hundred hands move a hundred overhead levers releasing power
into the machines.[65]

The author reveals his talent for pithy documentary representation at those points where he restricts his use of
metaphors and combines lively reporting with precise and
detailed descriptions. Where spontaneous reportage of
events in industrial production is concerned, the worker-
writer, familiar with this sphere, fulfils particular preconditions not met by the middle-class author. On the other hand,
the text from which the above quote is taken shows weaknesses and appears exaggerated at points where top-heavy
metaphors are used to give the impression of mechanical
hubbub and chaos.

Apart from a 'Criticism Competition', only one of the
competitions of subsequent years, with titles ranging from
'An Encounter' and 'Strike', to 'School Days', excluded fictional representations entirely: this was 'What Life means to
me.'[66] What was expected here was not the kind of reportage

which concentrated on individual events, but rather a different form of documentary literature: the autobiographical
report. One of the prizewinners of this competition was the
mineworker Bert Lewis Coombes, whose subsequently published autobiographical works, *These Poor Hands* (Left
Book Club, 1939), *These Clouded Hills* (1944) and *Miner's
Day* (1945), became the most well-known examples of this
literary genre.[67]

In general, there was a marked increase in the number of
workers' autobiographies published during this period. Between the twenties and the thirties, their number appears
to have more than doubled. Novels, too, were published in
increasing numbers.[68] Several reasons may be given for this
fresh impetus to working-class literature, and for its notable
rise from 1934 onwards:

a. From the point of view of the producers: the increase in
    'leisure time' brought about by unemployment, as well as
    the deliberate encouragement of political and cultural
    activities by socialist organisations within the framework
    of open discussion meetings, summer schools, writing
    competitions etc.
b. From the point of view of the audience: the discovery of
    the worker, particularly by large sections of the intel-
    ligentsia, as object and subject of literary creation.
c. From the point of view of the publishers: an increased
    readiness to publish, on the basis of this reawakening of
    interest.

It was not only the quantity, however, but clearly also the
political quality of worker autobiographies which increased.
Taking as a basis the typology drawn up by Wolfgang
Emmerich,[69] one can perceive an increase in militant self-
portraits, in which one individual life-history is portrayed as
an exemplary process of political development, as opposed
to autobiographical descriptions written by upwardly mobile
ex-members of the proletariat (such as John Hodge, *Workman's Cottage to Windsor Castle*, 1931) or works written
predominantly from the perspective of the victim, the object
of history (for example G. A. W. Tomlinson, *Coal Miner*,
1937). After all, the period with which we are dealing here
did produce such significant proletarian self-portraits as Jack

Hilton's *Caliban Shrieks* (1935), William Gallacher's *Revolt on the Clyde* (1936), William Holt's *I Haven't Unpacked* (1939) and Harry Pollitt's *Serving My Time* (1940).

The present survey of documentary literature of the period would be incomplete without some reference to the infiltration of documentary impulses into the novel itself. While it is certainly true that English literature did not produce anything comparable to Dos Passos' monumental trilogy, *USA* (1930–6), the wave of documentarism nonetheless did not fail to produce some ripples in the novel form. Evidence of this is to be found, for example, in John Sommerfield's *May Day* (1936) and Christopher Isherwood's *Goodbye to Berlin* (1939). Sommerfield's novel describes preparations for the 1st of May, and is at the same time a novel about the city of London, whose sights, sounds and smells the author records across a period of two-and-a-half days on all levels of society, at work and at leisure.

One contemporary critic made early reference to the photographic techniques employed in this novel,[70] with its succession of panoramic views, close-ups and snapshots of life in London. More recently, structural parallels have been seen between *May Day* and Walther Ruttmann's documentary film *Berlin–Symphonie einer Großstadt* (1927),[71] in which the passing of a working day in the city is similarly captured. Be that as it may, it is clear that the novel introduces newspaper headlines and political slogans from banners and the walls of houses; that it is concerned, not with the inner lives and destinies of a handful of characters, but with a cross-section of the London population (who admittedly pass a little too hastily in and out of its pages); that within this cross-section, attention is focused above all on the lower strata of society; and that within the working class itself, politically conscious groups are often brought into the limelight by Sommerfield. It is also known that the author participated in other documentary projects of the period, notably in Mass-Observation.[72]

The title of 'novel' seems at first hardly appropriate to Isherwood's loose sequence of six short narratives, some of which had previously been published separately elsewhere. The diary-like character of individual pieces, the presence of a first-person narrator bearing the name of the author and assuming the role of the camera, seem to align the work unmistakably with the documentary form. Yet this becomes less obvious on further reading when *Goodbye to Berlin*, in its style of narration, its characterisation and its description of milieu, is seen to be more broadly and more elaborately fictionalised than *May Day*. This remains a work of fiction, despite the use of the 'camera' as a gesture towards documentary. Photography, as Gisèle Freund reminds us, is in itself no guarantee of objectivity: 'Photography can never express more than what the photographer sees. . . . The sensibility of any given individual perceives the same object in unique ways characteristic of her or him alone.'[73]

In Isherwood's case, this sensibility takes on a strongly private character. While political powers are always felt as a presence waiting threateningly in the wings, they are only thematised in so far as they become a burden or a source of constraint on personal relationships. One is left with a sense that, in a different situation, where the grip of the political sphere on personal life was less pervasive, or where it took on less dramatic proportions, the author would have devoted himself entirely to the realm of the private.[74] Even the figures we meet here—a prostitute, a barman, a Jewish merchant, a cabaret singer—do not correspond to the usual 'inventory' of documentarism. They are, rather, bizarre characters, diminutive outsiders, 'damaged' certainly but not 'ordinary' or 'inconspicuous', nor necessarily 'poor'—to quote Stott's definition of documentarism once again.

Mass-Observation

From the point of view of the medium preferred (although not exclusively) by Mass-Observation, this project belongs under literature. And yet the extent of its cultural intervention as well as the uniqueness of its approach demand its classification *sui generis*.

The concept 'mass-observation' (M-O) implied three things:
1. That the object of observation was to be the everyday behaviour of the masses: 'actual behaviour under normal living conditions'.[75]

2. That this task was to be fulfilled, not by social scientists, but by the masses themselves, who were to be activated for this purpose: 'only mass observation can create mass science'.[76]

3. That insights into the deeper motives of human behaviour were to be gained from the mass and variety of observations and facts gathered by this method, above all from the spheres 'of custom and agreement', 'of unwritten laws and invisible pressures and forces'. Furthermore, 'the availability of facts will liberate certain tendencies in science, art and politics, because it will add to the social consciousness of the time.'[77]

The project, outlined here as a single set of aims, was initially divided between two geographically, politically and methodologically divergent groups, who worked independently, indeed without knowledge of each other, until they joined forces at the beginning of 1937. The northern axis of the movement had been founded by Tom Harrisson, an anthropologist who believed the time was ripe to abandon studies of South Sea cannibals for the industrial working class of northern England, and to whom the living conditions he encountered here as a member of the middle classes were hardly more familiar. A few months after Orwell had explored Wigan, Harrisson, faithful to the anthropological principle, 'penetrate, observe, be quiet yourself', settled barely ten miles away in Bolton, with the intention of carrying out anthropological fieldwork here. Bolton, whose identity was concealed in the first few publications under the names 'Northtown' and 'Worktown' in order to shield the project from excessive publicity, had been chosen for its representative position as a medium-sized industrial town, 'its shares in common with other principal working-class and industrial workplaces throughout Britain'.[78] Harrisson was initially supported in his enterprise by just under a dozen more-or-less voluntary assistants; later, as M-O began to enlist more widespread support and the study was extended to take in the neighbouring town of Blackpool, the traditional holiday resort of English workers, the number of assistants greatly increased, particularly during university vacations.

The individual steps which research was to take were precisely laid down beforehand, and included, as one study of pub culture indicates,[79] sending out observers into pubs in all the different districts of Worktown, as well as a process (in this case ten-month long) of 'observation without being observed', the evaluation of statistics and other source material, and the subsequent processing of all the material gathered by the team as a whole.

In contrast to this sober approach, with its claim to scientific objectivity, the southern centre, based in Blackheath, exhibits a somewhat more literary orientation which can in part be attributed to the working relations of the group. Charles Madge and Humphrey Jennings, its leading lights, had, like all their other colleagues—William Empson, David Gascoyne, Kathleen Raine and Ruthven Todd—previously made a name for themselves as poets or critics.[80] A further difference lies in the inclusion of the subjectivity of the observer into their work:

On February 12th, 1937, thirty people made an experiment. They had never met each other, they lived in widely scattered parts of the country and they differed greatly from each other in their surroundings, in their work and in their views about life. What they had agreed to do was to set down plainly all that happened to them on that day.[81]

No predetermined object of study, then, but rather details from the storehouse of everyday experience, selected according to the criteria of individual priorities; above all, however, the assimilation of personal experiences and thoughts, of individual judgements on particular experiences and observations. The representative and systematic recording of facts was here to arise more or less of its own accord, through the gradual collection of observations from all parts of the country and sections of the population.

In accordance with this principle, one solitary diary entry was seen to carry little weight as documentary evidence; the experiment had rather to be repeated throughout the year on the twelfth day of every month. Here 12 May 1937 was a particularly significant date. This was the day of the coronation and enthronement of the new King (George VI), a symbolic act whose preparations and circumstances are recorded in the first large-scale M-O publication, *May the Twelfth*, which moreover includes not only eye-witness reports from London, but also observations from the provinces, descriptions of preparations for the coronation as well as scenes from the everyday life against which this spectacular event—and this was an essential aim of the project—was constantly to be measured. The appearance of this work, with its partial similarity to fragments from a novel—and its reception by some critics as such—seemed indeed to mark out ways of overcoming the 'homeworker individualism' (Tretyakov) of the writer, while at the same time offering opportunities for public representation to underprivileged sections of the population.

In view of the heterogeneity of the approaches described here, it is not surprising that the coming together of the two groups at first amounted to no more than simply adding one approach to the other. This was evident not only in their differing reasons for the necessity of an 'anthropology at home', but also in the curious list of objects of study which accompanied their first joint public statement. The serious and the whimsical stood side by side, 'beards, armpits [and] eyebrows' with 'anti-semitism' and the 'distribution, diffusion and significance of the dirty joke'.[82] On the other hand, despite continual internal differences, it was precisely the fusion of subjective and objective approaches which contributed to a strengthening of the movement. Without the establishment of a network of observers and diary-writers, who kept in contact by letter, the Worktown enterprise would have remained the business of a small group of academics, outsiders in the last instance, whose work would have been characterised by the aridity and abstraction of questionnaire sociology and statistical tables. Without the corrective of a patient, systematic and previously planned process of research into carefully chosen (as opposed to eclectically added) behavioural forms, the Blackheath initiative would, on the other hand, also have been little more than a literary one-day wonder.

The future of M-O was finally assured when its initiators succeeded not only in securing the support of a number of prominent scholars and writers, including Bronislaw

Malinowski, Julian Huxley, John Hilton, J. B. Priestley and H. G. Wells, but also in achieving a publishing breakthrough with the appearance of the Penguin Special, *Britain*. With the various editions of this work, numbers printed must certainly have reached the hundred-thousand mark; within a month of its publication (January 1939) it had to be reprinted. The book marks the climax and at the same time the end of the collaboration of Madge and Harrisson. Jennings had already withdrawn not long after the coronation survey. Madge and Harrisson went their separate ways after the latter had suggested placing the work of M-O entirely in the service of the Ministry of Information, following Britain's entry into the war. As it turned out, the publications of M-O in the years 1940–5, with the exception of *The Pub and the People* (1943), which had already been completed and its publication announced before the outbreak of war, were entirely devoted to problems on the 'home front'. A selection of titles will serve as illustration: *War begins at Home* (1940), *Clothes Rationing* (1941), *War Factory* (1943), *The Journey Home* (1944).[83] In addition, the movement, which now operated on an increasingly grand scale, carried out hundreds of other projects not recorded in publications; similarly, the results of studies of fighting morale and the mood of the people, neither of which was encouraging or patriotic, were also not published. One work, which analyses diaries and recorded observations on the reactions of the civil population to city bombing, did not appear until 1976 (Tom Harrisson's *Living through the Blitz*).

Any critical assessment of the achievements of M-O should not underestimate its positive features. The movement was certainly the most ambitious, most far-reaching and most radically democratic of all documentary projects of the thirties and forties. All the basic features of the documentary genre named in section I, from the catalogue of social themes to its collective mode of work, can be found here in unadulterated form. M-O also showed imagination in its use of media; from literature through photography to painting and—in one case at least—to radio, M-O made use of all the media then at its disposal.[84] It was furthermore the only documentary form in which the separation of author and public was indeed in the process of losing 'its basic character' (Benjamin), and in which author, public and object of study were merged into one. No other cultural undertaking of the period was able to motivate so many people to participate in creative work over such a long period of time. M-O succeeded with the greatest of ease where the artists' organisations allied to the socialist movement (Writers' International, AIA, etc.) with their unique preoccupation with the fight against fascism, had failed; indeed it achieved a goal to which it had never seriously aspired, namely the establishment of a correspondents' movement—not amongst workers, as socialist programmes would have demanded, but amongst the middle classes.

The fact that the middle classes made up the majority of mass-observers with the lower middle class and the middle middle class taking equal shares, was the most significant conclusion reached through an analysis of the first five hundred participants, which was carried out at the end of the first year by the initiators of M-O.[85] Workers, as well as members of the upper middle class, each constituted only approximately twelve per cent of the participants. In simple terms, one might say that the 'typical' mass-observer was the unmarried male office-worker, aged around twenty and living in the provinces.

Any critique of M-O has to begin with one significant omission. Ironically enough, in a town with the pseudonym 'Worktown', every possible form of (in)activity was studied, from smoking and drinking habits through analyses of voting behaviour to church activities and tombstone inscriptions; yet the entire production sphere was consistently excluded. (Here Harrisson's approach is similar to that of Richard Hoggart, whose *The Uses of Literacy* he anticipates, in more ways than one, by twenty years.) Certainly studies of the workplace and the production process would have been somewhat difficult to execute, given that one of the principles of the mass-observer was not to appear as such. Nonetheless, this difficulty could have been at least partially overcome by having recourse to those mass-observers who were working-class as well as by making direct appeals to workers' organisations and individual factories.

Our purpose in drawing attention to this omission is not simply to add one more element to the list of activities worthy of observation, but rather to highlight a fundamental conceptual weakness of the movement. However promising the programme drawn up by Jennings, Madge and Harrisson in their first joint statement may have sounded, with its call for the tracing of unconscious and repressed fantasies, needs and desires amongst the masses; however rightly it had pointed out that the popular press exploited these needs and desires, the everyday reality of the masses quite plainly evades all attempts to grasp and understand it, if such an observation is not based on the close connections and functional links between the spheres of production and reproduction. That is if it fails to consider the masses within and in relation to the production process, and to separate out classes, strata etc., from the total population: in other words, if there is not simultaneously some kind of 'class observation' carried out.

More often than not, the questions asked of M-O's object of study prove to be correspondingly inadequate—a fact which becomes manifest around the second criticism of the M-O project, namely its lack of a successful synthesis of the data collected. It is simply not enough to base a whole survey on the observation that 'most people spend more time in public houses than they do in any other buildings except private houses and workplaces', and thus to observe when the pubs are most frequented, how much beer is consumed, how many times in the course of a certain space of time the glass is carried to the lips (!), and/or what the topics of conversation are. The crucial point of interest here should be the question of the meaning, purpose and possible ambivalence of this and other 'recreation patterns'. Should they be considered as expressions of a need for compensation for the discipline of workaday routines, or do they represent the grasping of an opportunity to combat isolation through forms of interaction outside the workplace? Yet both this kind of question, and questions round the distinction between dysfunctional/counterproductive and integrative/conformist factors in everyday, as well as in out-of-the-ordinary (in)activities and modes of behaviour, presuppose a political interest whose absence amongst the group under discussion may well be regretted, yet for which they cannot be reproached.

Formulated with more than forty years' hindsight, this critique by no means aims to question the value of many individual observations made by M-O. It has been possible to properly appreciate the extent to which its basic idea paved the way for other movements ever since social history extricated itself from a one-sided historiography of organisations and movements, and turned its attention to the way of life of historical individuals and groups. The barely categorised, let alone properly interpreted material in the M-O archive represents an unfathomable wealth of information on the late thirties and forties.

Minor forms (documentary theatre, radio documentary, the Fine Arts)

In addition to the four principal forms of British documentarism examined so far, documentary goals and approaches were also to be found to a lesser extent and with less widespread influence in a number of other spheres; in the theatre, in radio and in the Fine Arts. The following brief survey of these forms confirms the impression that the genre as a whole was of central cultural significance in this period.

The Living Newspaper can be taken as a typical example of small-scale open form in the theatre. As its name suggests, it took up issues of burning political and social interest, bringing them to life through a portrayal of their effects on the life of the average woman or man. The abandonment of traditional plot structure, as well as of a fixed inventory of characters, was complemented by total concentration on the chosen theme and the exploitation of all dramatic resources (music, megaphone, lighting effects, recitation, antiphony, pantomime, dance and acrobatic elements). Stage props on the other hand played no part in the English Living Newspaper, since they would have impaired the mobility of travelling troupes. As far as organisation was concerned, the Living Newspaper was based on the idea of 'self-made' theatre, whose precondition was an ensemble or collective which produced its own scripts, rather than relying on plays already

in print. This production principle was to be found wherever
Living Newspapers took to the stage, whether in the New
York Living Newspaper Unit of the Federal Theatre Project, at the London Unity Theatre, the Manchester Theatre
of Action, the Glasgow Workers' Theatre Group or the Play
Unit of the Army Bureau for Current Affairs (ABCA). This
form of theatre thus demands from the participants a high
level of spontaneity and flexibility, which enables them to
intervene whenever necessary in topical debates or to re-
adjust passages in currently running plays overtaken by more
recent events. So for example the Living Newspaper No. 2,
Crisis (1938), was put together and performed at the Unity
Theatre in the space of two days.[86] And Ewan MacColl
recalls *apropos* of the Theatre of Action that the play *Last
Edition* performed in 1938 was rewritten and extended from
week to week, in order to take into account the increasing
gravity of the political situation, as well as the reactions of
the audience.[87]

The outbreak of war interrupted efforts in Britain—which
had in any case begun relatively late in comparison with the
USA—to promote this documentary theatre form on a widespread scale, though there were other impediments as well
such as the control exercised over public theatres by the
Lord Chamberlain's Office which, for instance, ruled out the
explicit naming of public figures or companies. The wartime
situation did, on the other hand, effect a new and unex-
pected renaissance of the form, through performances by the
ABCA Play Unit to front-line troops. Through its use at the
front, admittedly in modified form, the Living Newspaper
reassumed responsibilities for information and education
which recalled its origins in the Red Army and Russian
workers' clubs.

At least half of the British soldiers on the field of battle
were unable to read a daily paper or listen to radio news
broadcasts. Those responsible for the running of the ABCA,
some of whom had already been active in the Worker's Educational Association, thus came to the conclusion that they
should provide regular news reports, as well as discussions of
world affairs and the front-line situation.

A true team spirit reigned amongst the members of the

ABCA Play Unit, five of whom were women. 'The company had to do the work of stage hands, electricians, carpenters and furniture removers, as well as act; each script gained from the contributions and suggestions offered by any member of the Play Unit.'[88] Nonetheless, the names of at least some of its members should be mentioned: André van Gyseghem, Jack Lindsay, Ted Willis, Stephen Murray and Michael MacOwan—a list which bridges the gap between ABCA and the Unity Theatre, as well as making visible the continuity of socialist theatre.

It seems, too, that the ABCA Play Unit succeeded in overcoming one of the difficulties inherent in the Living Newspaper whose essentially informational nature hardly favours audience participation; it tends rather to maintain the audience in the role of passive observer and consumer. The Play Unit on the other hand, following the principles of the initiators of ABCA, whose prime concern was to stimulate processes of discussion and reflection, adopted methods which aimed to provoke discussion after the end of the performance, while not neglecting the informational and entertainment features of theatre.

As early as six months after its foundation in June 1944, the Play Unit was able to boast fifty-eight performances to around 20,000 soldiers, conducted on the basis of a repertoire of five 'plays'.[89] The distinctly left-wing tendencies of ABCA work in general, and the even more strongly socialist profile of the Play Unit, following their involvement with the Unity Theatre, appeared so suspect to the Conservatives, Churchill above all, that various (unsuccessful) attempts were made to put an end to the entire project. Clearly there were feelings at the highest level that a change of mood was gathering momentum—a change from which the Labour Party was to profit in 1945. For one characteristic feature of the work carried out here was the fact that 'the topics suggested for discussion in "Current Affairs" began by ranging across the world, but from the end of 1942 they reflected the increasing preoccupation with domestic life at home after the War.'[90]

As with all other forms, the significance of documentary theatre waned following the end of the war and the euphoria over the Labour election victory. The ABCA Play Unit did, it is true, continue its work for a time in the British Zone of Germany; the Unity Theatre, having survived the thirties (to emerge admittedly much weaker than before), did manage to put on the occasional Living Newspaper performance (*Black Magic*, 1947); 'Theatre 46', initiated by Slater, Lindsay and Bernard Miles, did put on one play on the situation in the mines. Yet these represented the swan-song of a genre rather than signs of a new beginning

The insignificance of radio documentary relative to the possibilities of the medium as a whole is indicated amongst other things by the fact that the term itself did not become established until radio began to be used for propaganda purposes in the Second World War, and 'wartime documentary' was born. Up to this point, documentary broadcasts were found, if at all, either in the Talks Department (in the early thirties) or under the heading of 'Features'. The latter term gives rise to some confusion. While, in the language of film, 'feature film' refers to the story as opposed to the documentary film, the same term means precisely the opposite for radio. Although the boundary between feature and drama cannot be clearly drawn, the BBC adhered in practice to the principle, 'Features dealt with fact, drama with fiction.'[91] The feature can thus be characterised in somewhat simplified form as a radio play without a plot.

In the years 1927–30, features comprised only 1.04 per cent of the national weekly programme (1.27 per cent at the regional level). With 77–78 hours' broadcasting time per week, this meant around 50–60 minutes—hardly enough time to incorporate more than one or two broadcasts. Even then, it is not clear whether these features bore a documentary emphasis. Until 1935, the proportion of features actually continued to fall on the national level to a low of 0.5 per cent, although it rose on the regional level to 2.1 per cent. By 1938, the figures stood at 1.3 per cent and 2.1 per cent respectively.[92]

If radio documentary must be distinguished from the staged radio drama or literary radio play, then it must also be kept distinct from radio reportage, which transmits live (or recorded) events to the listener without substantial preliminary editing.[93] An integral part of documentary, on the other hand, is the shaping of material in artistic form: 'the creative treatment of actuality' (Grierson).

As long as the BBC held back from fulfilling the fundamental requirement of the genre—'let the people speak for themselves'—the central object of British documentarism, the day-to-day experience of ordinary people, could not become the topic of radio broadcasts. Whether social issues did or did not find their way on to the radio in anything other than watered-down form depended probably also on the producer. During the period in which John Pudney headed the features department of BBC North in Manchester, Ewan MacColl, for example (who was still known during these years by the name of Jimmie Miller), together with his lifelong companion Joan Littlewood, enjoyed considerable scope for independent work—a fact of which they took advantage on the occasion of the hundreth anniversary of a Chartist mass demonstration to put on a historical documentary play (*The Chartists March*).[94] The possibilities offered by the medium were fully exploited here by switching from studio to studio and thus following the march as it progressed across the length and breadth of the country. (The mind boggles at the prospect of a similar play on the hunger marches of the 1930s.)

This kind of programme was, however, a rarity, even during the time of the rise of wartime documentary. Harnessed entirely for the war effort, the function of war documentary was to highlight the necessity and circumstances of mass mobilisation on the home front, as well as to calm fears and anxieties, and to offer interpretations of potentially threatening developments. Wartime documentary thus rarely adopted the oppositional or critical stance which would have shaken the status quo. Here the form shows its affinity to the documentary films made during this period, as well as to the surveys of Mass-Observation.

In the field of the Fine Arts, isolated documentary tendencies can be detected, above all around the Artists' International Association (AIA).[95] Undeniably, the Artists' Association developed many more initiatives on the political and organisational level (solidarity campaigns for persecuted artists, activities in support of the Republicans in the Spanish Civil War, annual exhibitions) than on the level of theoretical clarification and the practical development of new art forms. Nonetheless, across the colourful spectrum of AIA members, whose interests ranged from naïve realism to constructivism and surrealism, at least one group can be seen to have opposed abstract and aestheticist positions, and to have worked instead towards clarity and concreteness in their art: the Euston Road School (1937–9), whose most important representatives included Graham Bell, William Coldstream, Victor Pasmore, Robert Medley and Claude Rogers. The work of the group's founder, Graham Bell, in particular, but also that of Coldstream, documented the lives of working people through their preference for motifs from everyday city life (small shops and cafés, buses and trams). Bell's picture, 'The Café' (1938), for instance, depicts not only the salon and its clients, but also the shop assistant, whose portrait fills the entire left-hand side of the canvas. Binding and simultaneously separating the two is the bar which, with cakes and crockery painted in the finest detail, dominates the centre of the picture.

Another artist also connected with the AIA was James Boswell, whose drawings captured the everyday reality of city dwellers. His sketches (and occasional lithographs) of London street life were for a long time overshadowed by his satirical cartoons for *Left Review*, and were not recalled to public attention until the Nottingham exhibition of 1976. These pub, street and market scenes from Soho and London's East End revealed a whole new facet of Boswell's creative work. Instead of a bitingly aggressive contemporary commentator ('Jubilee', 1935; 'The Press and Mass Hysteria', 1935), instead of the disturbingly provocative finger of accusation ('Means Test', 1934; 'Hunger Marchers', 1934), we meet here an affectionate observer and documenter of the pursuits of ordinary people ('Amusements', 1938; 'Hangover Square', 1939), who nonetheless did not fail to recognise their vulnerability ('The Dying Street', 1938).[96]

A further example of documentary influences in the Fine Arts is, finally, the work of a group of worker-painters, the Ashington Group, founded in 1934 far from the metropolis and its cultural and political scene, and named after a mining town in County Durham. Work began under the auspices of a WEA course. Under the guidance of an enthusiastic young artist, the participants achieved, through collective work and discussion, an unpretentious and (given their amateur status) astonishingly expressive representation of their working and living conditions. Typical motifs were, for example, miners at work, the fish-and-chip shop, families on their allotments complete with slag heaps in the background—and so on. The unequivocal precedence given to content, to the situation or idea portrayed (as opposed to the perfection of form), the concreteness and realism of representation originated here less in conscious decisions, as it had done for the great majority of documentarists, or in impulses towards social commitment. It was rooted rather in the concrete experience of the artists themselves, in their daily confrontation with the object world of labour.

The widespread recognition enjoyed by the group during the thirties can to a large extent be traced back to the newly-awakened interest of intellectuals in documentarism. Certain problems (which were similarly intrinsic to other sections of the documentary movement) arose in this context; on the one hand, important impulses were transmitted to the group through this widespread interest; on the other hand, however, there was a danger, both of this interest becoming patronising, and of introducing influences which would corrupt its original style. Thus John Feaver, who has documented the development of the Ashington Group, later gave the following somewhat ironical account of his personal recollections:

Inevitably, in the era of . . . the Federal Art Project under Roosevelt's New Deal, and documentary enthusiasms, the group became a magnet for well-meaning meddlers. They, the 'art-loving pit-men', were treated as flowers in a wilderness. Their paintings were often taken to represent the horrors of labour underground when, mostly, they were intended to show the dignity of their work and the skills involved. There were others who liked to point out that they weren't naive enough.[97]

The existence of the Ashington Group, as well as the reactions to it, once again remind us of the fact that, behind and alongside the principal strands of British documentarism, there were other, less middle-class, less professional, but nonetheless original documentary tendencies at work.

Translated by Erica Carter

NOTES

Chapter 1: Plebeian poets in eighteenth-century England

1. Quoted from the German edition, *Reisen eines Deutschen in England im Jahr 1782*, ed. Otto zur Linde (Berlin, 1903), pp. 24–5 (my translation—HGK).
2. *The Idler*, no. 7, 27 May 1758, *The Yale Edition of the Works of Samuel Johnson*, eds. John M. Bullitt and C. F. Powell, vol. 2 (New Haven, 1963), p. 23. See also the travelogues referred to by E. J. Hobsbawm in his *Industry and Empire* (Harmondsworth, 1969), ch. 1, *passim*.
   Even more striking for some Continental observers was the fact that artisans could be seen in coffee-houses reading newspapers during their morning breaks or might order a journal to be sent to their workplace; cf. Richard D. Altick, *The English Common Reader* (Chicago, 1957), p.40.
3. Rayner Unwin, *The Rural Muse. Studies in the Peasant Poetry of England* (London, 1954), *passim;* Phyllis Mary Ashraf, *Englische Arbeiterliteratur vom 18. Jahrhundert bis zum Ersten Weltkrieg* (Berlin, 1980), pp.46–54. But see Raymond Williams, *The Country and the City* (London, 1973), p.135, who speaks of 'labourer-poets'.
4. I would like to mention but two names for each country: Robert Tannahill and Robert Burns for Scotland; John Frizzle and Henry Jones for Ireland. The Scottish contribution is, of course, incomparably more significant.
5. In terms of availability Duck has always fared better than the other plebeian poets dealt with here, Bloomfield excepted. Individual works of the 'thresher-poet' were reprinted in 1830 (*The Shunammite*), 1930 (*The Thresher's Labour*), 1973 (a facsimile of the *Poems on Several Occasions*), 1974 and 1976 (excerpts from *The Thresher's Labour* in two anthologies: John Barrell and John Bull, eds., *The Penguin Book of English Pastoral Verse*; and David Wright, ed., *The Penguin Book of Everyday Verse*).
6. See, for example, Barrell and Bull, *op. cit.* pp.375–81; and to some extent also Williams, *op.cit.* pp. 87–95.

7. *The Weaver's Miscellany, or Poems on Several Subjects by John Banks, now a Poor Weaver in Spittle-Fields* (London, 1730); Mary Collier, *The Woman's Labour: An Epistle to Mr. Stephen Duck, in Answer to his Late Poem, called The Thresher's Labour* (London, 1739).
8. *Poems on Several Occasions by Mary Collier, Author of the Washerwoman's Labour with Some Remarks of her life* (Winchester, 1762), p.iv.
9. For a thoroughly researched biographical account see Rose Mary Davies, *Stephen Duck, The Thresher Poet* (Orono, Maine, 1926).
10. Elizabeth W. Gilboy, *Wages in Eighteenth-Century England* (Cambridge, Mass. 1934), pp.130–5.
11. *The Bricklayer's Miscellany, or Poems on Several Subjects: Written by Robert Tatersal, A Poor Country Bricklayer* (London, 1734).
12. The following distinction is based on G. D. H. Cole and Raymond Postgate, *The Common People 1746–1938* (London, 1939), pp.67–80.
13. Note that the Scottish Colliers were actually serfs until 1775/1796; see chapter four. On the other hand, miners were often better paid than some of the craftsmen in the second category. Hence status and income were not necessarily congruent.
14. Tatersal, *op. cit.* p.23.
15. 'An Irish Miller, to Mr. Stephen Duck', *The Gentleman's Magazine*, III (1733), p.95.
16. Cf. Davies, *op. cit.* p.66; Ivanka Kovačević, *Fact into Fiction. English Literature and the Industrial Scene 1750–1850* (Leicester, 1975), p.45.
17. Tatersal, *op. cit.* p.30.
18. *ibid.* p.32.
19. Ann Yearsley, *Earl Goodwin: an historical play* (London, 1791), and *The Royal Captives* (London, 1795); James Woodhouse, *The Life and Lucubrations of Crispinus Scriblerus: a novel in verse, Written in the last century* (London, 1814), first complete edition in *The Life and Poetical Works of James Woodhouse*, ed. Reginald I. Woodhouse, 2 vols. (Norbury, 1896).
20. A count of the entries under 'Poetry' in *The New Cambridge Bibliography of English Literature*, vol. 2 (London, 1971), produced a ratio of about one woman in ten poets.
21. cf. Lawrence Stone, 'Literacy and Education in England 1640–1900', *Past and Present*, 42 (1969), p.102.

22. G. M. Trevelyan refers to twenty master-printers for the whole of the kingdom in the second half of the seventeenth century, whereas he estimates the number of publishers and booksellers in the eighteenth century at around 150 in London and about as many in the provinces; see his *English Social History* (London, 1946), pp.263, 413.

23. Arnold Hauser, *Sozialgeschichte der Kunst und Literatur* (München, 1969), p.565 (my translation—HGK).

24. A. S. Collins, *Authorship in the Days of Johnson* (London, 1927), pp.118–22, 189–95.

25. Stone, *op. cit.* p.109. In Scotland, owing to its democratic education system, the figure was considerably higher, *ibid.* pp.120–1.

26. M. G. Jones, *The Charity School Movement* (Cambridge, 1938); Joan Simon, 'Was there a Charity School Movement? The Leicestershire Evidence', in Brian Simon, ed., *Education in Leicestershire 1540–1940* (Leicester, 1968), pp.88–100.

27. Joseph Spence. 'An account of the Author', in Stephen Duck, *Poems on Several Occasions* (London, 1736), pp.xvi–xvii; Woodhouse, *Crispinus Scriblerus, passim.*

28. *Poems on Several Occasions by Mary Collier,* p.iii; Joyce Marjorie Sanxter Tompkins, 'The Bristol Milkwoman', in her *The Polite Marriage, Eighteenth-Century Essays* (Cambridge, 1938), p.61.

29. Robert Raikes, letter of 25 November 1783 to *The Gentleman's Magazine,* LIV (1784), p.412.

30. Jones, *op. cit.* p.153.

31. See chapter four.

32. *The Thresher's Labour* is quoted from *Poems on Several Occasions* (1736), pp.11–12, 16.

33. *ibid.* pp.13–14.

34. *ibid.* p.24.

35. *ibid.* p.14.

36. *ibid.* p.25.

37. *The Complete Poetical Works of James Thomson,* Oxford Edition, ed. J. Logie Robertson (London, 1908), pp.66–7.

38. Tatersal, 'The Bricklayers Labours', *op.cit.* p.28.

39. Collier, 'The Woman's Labour: To Mr. Stephen Duck', quoted from *Poems on Several Occasions,* pp.9–10.

40. For a more extensive treatment of the dispute between the two poets see my article 'Stephen Duck and Mary Collier. Plebejische Kontro-Verse über Frauenarbeit vor 250 Jahren', *Gulliver,* 10 (1981), pp.115–23.

41. For Bloomfield see Williams, *op. cit.* pp.134–6.

42. See, for example, Bloomfield's letter to his brother George of 30 May 1802, in *Selections from the Correspondence of Robert Bloomfield*, ed. William H. Hart (London, 1870), pp.25–7, or his letter to Mr Pratt, not contained in this edition but quoted by Unwin, *op. cit.* p.105. Yearsley's letters have not been collected, but see Tompkins, *op. cit. passim.*

43. *Grub-Street Journal*, I, 21 January 1731; quoted from Davies, *op. cit.* p.61.

44. Letter of Richard West to Horace Walpole, 12 January 1737, *The Yale Edition of Horace Walpole's Correspondence*, ed. W. S. Lewis, vol. 13 (New Haven, 1948), p.123.

45. *The Monthly Review*, February 1778; quoted from Unwin, *op. cit.* p.69.

46. *Boswell's Life of Johnson*, ed. George Birkbeck, rev. edn. L. C. Powell, vol. 2 (London, 1934), p.127.

47. Letter to Lady Ossory of 1 December 1786, *The Yale Edition of Horace Walpole's Correspondence*, vol. 33 (New Haven, 1965), p.538.

48. 'A Dialogue, by Way of Apology', *Miscellanies in Verse and Prose by John Lucas, Cobler, A Pensioner in Trinity Hospital, Salisbury* (Salisbury, 1776), p.1.

49. *ibid.* p.3.

50. *ibid.* p.43.

51. See the poems 'Genius Unimproved', 'Addressed to Sensibility' and 'To Mr. . . . .' in her volume *A Second Book of Poems on Various Subjects* (London, 1787).

52. 'An Epistolary Answer to an Exciseman, who doubted her being the Author of the Washerwoman's Labour', *Poems on Several Occasions*, pp.30–2.

53. This is the motto prefixed to the edition of 1896.

54. Ashraf, *op. cit.* p.25 (my translation—HGK).

55. Robert Southey, *The Lives and Works of the Uneducated Poets*, ed. J. S. Childers (London, 1925), p.118.

56. Spence, *op. cit.* p.xxiv.

57. For Yearsley's quarrel with Hannah More see her 'Narrative', added to the fourth edition of her *Poems on Several Occasions* (1786), and Tompkins, *op. cit. passim.* For Woodhouse see *Crispinus Scriblerus, passim*, and Katherine G. Hornbreak, 'New Light on Mrs. Montagu', in Frederick W. Hillis, ed., *The Age of Johnson, Essays Presented to Chauncey Brewster Tinker* (New Haven, 1949), pp.349–61.

Chapter 2: Early socialist utopias in England 1792–1848

1. There is only one survey of utopian literature which makes any notable reference to the authors discussed here. A. L. Morton, *The English Utopia* (London, 1952), looks at Spence, Owen and Barmby (although not in the last case on the basis of a reading of his utopia which Morton believes lost). Ashraf in her *Englische Arbeiterliteratur,* mentions Spence, Morgan and Bray.
2. See for example Hans Ulrich Seeber, *Wandlungen der Form in der literarischen Utopie* (Göppingen, 1970), pp.27–8.
3. In the English title of this work, *Socialism: Utopian and Scientific*, this is somewhat less conspicuous. Engels's work came out in 1882, but see already the earlier *Manifesto of the Communist Party* (1848), written jointly with Marx. Only a few years before, in ' "Die Rheinischen Jahrbücher" oder Die Philosophie des wahren Sozialismus' (1846), they had expressed quite different views, defending 'English Communism' against the Germanic supporters of 'true socialism', and—an interesting point from our perspective—naming four of the authors mentioned in the present study. 'Thomas Morus, the Levellers, Owen, Thompson, Watts, Holyoake, Harney, Morgan, Southwell, Goodwyn Barmby, Greaves, Edmonds, Hobson, Spence will be much amazed, or may turn in their graves, if they hear how they are being declared not to be communists.' *Marx Engels Werke,* vol. 3 (Berlin, 1969), p.488 (my translation—HGK).
4. This approach is, moreover, highly problematic in relation to socialist utopias after 1848. For this point see E. P. Thompson, 'Postscript 1976' to his book *William Morris. Romantic to Revolutionary* (London, 1977) and Raymond Williams, 'Utopia and Science Fiction', in his *Problems in Materialism and Culture* (London, 1980).
5. Even the most recent bibliography of utopian works can be seen to perpetuate this ignorance. In Lyman Tower Sargent's *British and American Utopian Literature 1516–1975: an Annotated Bibliography* (Boston, 1979) there is a mistake in the title of Spence's *The Constitution of a Perfect Commonwealth. Being the French Constitution of 1793. Amended, and rendered entirely conformable to the Whole Rights of Man* (1798). John Minter Morgan's *Hampden in the Nineteenth Century* (1834) is wrongly dated, and the name of Goodwyn Barmby deformed beyond recognition.

6. In 1982, two small publishing houses produced new editions
   of his writings: G. I. Gallop ed., *Pig's Meat. The Selected
   Writings of Thomas Spence, Radical and Pioneer Land
   Reformer* (Nottingham: Spokesman, 1982); H. T. Dickinson,
   ed., *The Political Works of Thomas Spence,* (Newcastle:
   Avero, 1982). Both editions contain useful introductions to
   the life and work of the author. The Spokesman edition costs
   the tidy sum of £30, and is by no means complete, although
   the quality of its print is certainly high. The Avero edition is
   less costly and contains all the most significant political and
   utopian texts by the author, including above all a series of
   songs; its one drawback is its use of reduced typescript, which
   makes it difficult to read.

7. For a biographical account, see Olive D. Rudkin, *Thomas
   Spence and his Connections* (London, 1927) and T. M. Parssi-
   nen's entry in the *Biographical Dictionary of Modern British
   Radicals,* vol. 1, *1770–1830,* eds. Joseph O. Baylen and Nor-
   bert J. Gossman (Sussex, 1979), pp.454–8.

8. *Pig's Meat* was distributed as a weekly magazine between
   1793 and 1795. At the end of the year, individual issues were
   then bound and resold as annuals.

9. *Pig's Meat,* II (1794), pp.68–72; *ibid.* pp.205–18. In 1795,
   both texts reappeared together in a volume entitled *Description of Spensonia.* In 1814, Spence reprinted *The Marine
   Republic* in his last magazine, the short-lived *Giant-Killer, or
   Anti-Landlord.* This version contains some minor modifica-
   tions.

10. For a more detailed study of Spence's utopias see my essay
    'Thomas Spence: *Description of Spensonia* (1795)' in Hart-
    mut Heuermann and Bernd-Peter Lange, eds., *Die Utopie in
    der angloamerikanischen Literatur* (Düsseldorf, 1984),
    pp.60–79.

11. There is a striking discrepancy between the first and second
    versions of a perfectly structured state, which relates to the
    representation of women's participation in political life. In the
    1798 *Constitution,* women are granted access to employment
    as public officials. Article 8 of the section 'Declaration of
    Rights' reads as follows: 'All citizens are equally admissible to
    public employments. Free people know no other motives of
    preference in their elections than virtues and talents.' (Avero
    edition, p.59). In the 1803 plan, this statement is revoked: the
    paragraph now reads, 'All male citizens are equally admissible
    to public employments . . .' (Article 7, Avero edition,
    p.104).

Article 5 of the section entitled 'Of the State of Citizens' makes the same point more precisely: 'Female citizens have the same right of suffrage in their respective parishes as the men: because they have equal property in the country and are equally subject to the laws and, indeed, they are in every respect, as well as on their own account as on account of their children, as deeply interested in every public transaction. But in consideration of the delicacy of their sex, they are exempted from, and are ineligible to, all public employments.' (*ibid*. p.107) I know of no author who has yet commented on the difference between these two versions. It seems to me to be clear that it is not a case of Spence's first version being ambiguously formulated, but that he actually reversed his position in the later version. The reasons for this are unclear. Was the author subject to criticism from amongst the ranks of his own supporters? Or did his own private experiences cause him to retreat in this way?

12. *A Further Account of Spensonia* (1794), Avero edition, p.33; Spokesman edition, p.90.
13. *The Constitution of Spensonia* (1803), Article 155, Avero edition, p.17; Spokesman edition, p.184.
14. *Report to the County of Lanark* (1820), in Robert Owen, *A New View of Society and Other Writings*, ed. John Butt (London, 1972), p.295.
15. *A Catechism of the New View of Society and Three Addresses* (1817), *ibid*. p.222.
16. *Report to the County of Lanark*, *ibid*. p.267.
17. From Owen's Dedication to his *The Book of the New Moral World* (1842), (New York, 1970), p.xv.
18. *Letter published in the London Newspaper September 10th, 1817* (Fourth Letter of 6 September 1817), in *The Life of Robert Owen. Written by Himself*, vol. IA (London, 1857), pp.132–3.
19. For a biographical sketch see J. F. C. Harrison, *Robert Owen and the Owenites in Britain and America* (London, 1969), pp.32–5; cf. also John Saville's entry in *Dictionary of Labour Biography*, vol. 1 (1974), pp.247–9.
20. *The Revolt of the Bees* (1826), (London, 1830), p.25.
21. It is interesting that Spence, whose father had emigrated from Scotland to Newcastle, also quotes Ramsay. Does Morgan's interest in Scotland indicate a similar origin? Not only did he locate his utopia in Scotland, but he also supported the first Owenite community in Orbiston (Lanarkshire).
22. *The Revolt of the Bees*, pp.42–3.

23. *ibid.* p.106.
24. *ibid.* pp.52–3.
25. *ibid.* pp.156–7.
26. One fundamental difference between Owen and Morgan is the latter's view of religion, resulting in a lifelong attempt to reconcile Co-operative and Christian ideas. 'Minter Morgan's distinctive contribution to Owenism was that he confronted this difficulty as early as 1819 and established the precedent that a Church of England Philanthropist could also be an Owenite.' Harrison, *Robert Owen,* pp.34–5.
27. *The New Moral World,* VI (1839), p.52. From 1826 onward *The Revolt of the Bees* had also been serialised in *The Cooperative Magazine.*
28. In 1937 the manuscript was discovered in the United States, but it took another twenty years before it was published: John Francis Bray, *A Voyage from Utopia,* ed. M. F. Lloyd-Pritchard (London, 1957).
29. For an account of Bray's life see Lloyd-Pritchard's introduction and John Saville's entry in *Dictionary of Labour Biography,* vol. 3 (1976), pp.21–5.
30. For an assessment of this work see G. D. H. Cole, *A History of Socialist Thought,* vol. 1, *The Forerunners, 1789–1850* (London, 1953).
31. Handwritten note of the author on the title page of his manuscript, *A Voyage,* p.35.
32. *The Revolt of the Bees,* p.49.
33. *A Voyage,* p.74.
34. *ibid.* p.86.
35. *ibid.* p.140.
36. In 1842 Bray undertook a journey to France. Shortly after, he emigrated to the United States. According to his own testimony the manuscript had already been completed by this time.
37. *A Voyage,* pp.166–7.
38. *ibid.* p.160.
39. *ibid.* p.32.
40. cf. J. F. C. Harrison, *The Second Coming. Popular Millenarianism 1780–1850* (London, 1979). Sargent, *op. cit.,* lists a posthumously published work by Richard Brothers. *The New Covenant Between God and the People* (London, 1830).
41. For an account of the author's life and work see the article by A. L. Morton and John Saville in *Dictionary of Labour Biography,* vol. 6 (1982), pp.10–16.
42. There is reason to believe that Barmby is the anonymous

author of a series of articles in *The New Moral World* in which Shelley is enthusiastically celebrated. The first instalment of 'A Review of Modern Poets' appeared in vol. V, no. 6 of 1 December 1838, the last in no. 35 of 22 June 1839. The articles focus on *Prometheus Unbound* and *The Revolt of Islam*.

43. *The Warwick Guide to British Labour Periodicals 1790–1970*, eds. Royden Harrison *et al*. (Sussex, 1977), does not give any location for *The Communist Chronicle*. In fact, there is an almost complete run in the Dr Williams Library (London), lacking only no. 28 (1845). According to James H. Billington (*Fire in the Minds of Men. Origins of the Revolutionary Faith*, London, 1980, p. 589) there is yet another set in the New York Public Library. Dating the individual issues of the journal poses some problems, as it does not carry any publication dates, perhaps in order to disguise its rather erratic appearance. Nos. 5–14 came out as monthlies, and from no. 15 the journal was 'Published every Saturday', though this claim must be taken with caution. The numbering of the issues begins with no. 5, since Barmby saw *The Communist Chronicle* as continuing the work of *The Promethean*, nos. 1–4, which had stopped in June 1842. Various allusions to contemporary events as well as letters from correspondents allow one to assume that the journal commenced in January 1844 (no. 5) and faltered in April 1846 (no. 40). 'The Book of Platonopolis' was serialised in nos. 35 and 37 [1846].

44. 'The Book of Platonopolis', *The Communist Chronicle*, 35 [1846], p.233.

45. *ibid*.

46. Barmby's prospectus for this planned 'communitarian library' numbered fourteen works, amongst them, from antiquity Plato's *Republic*, Euhemeros' fragment of the island of Panchaia and Theopompos' fragment of the fabulous Meropis; from early modern times the works of More, Bacon, J. Hall, Campanella and Harrington; from the eighteenth century predominantly French authors such as Fénélon, Morelly and Rétif de la Bretonne.

It is not evident that Barmby knew that the name Platonopolis had already been used in the ancient world. Porphyrios, the biographer of Plotin, reports that his hero intended to build a city of that name in Campania, in which the inhabitants were supposed to live in conformity with Plato's philosophy.

Another use of the term occurred in 1779 when Josephe-

Alexandre-Victor Hupay de Fuvea published his plan for a *Maison de réunion pour la communauté philosophe dans la terre de l'auteur de ce projet,* which was to be called Platonopolis. See Billington, *op. cit.* pp.79–81. This, if at all is a more likely source of inspiration for Barmby who may have come across the author by reading Rétif de la Bretonne.

47. See his article 'Past, Present and Future Chronology. An Historic Introduction to the Communist Calendar', *The Promethean,* 2 (February 1842), pp.30–2, and 3 (March 1842), pp. 53–4.

48. See Barmby's account of the history and collapse of his own community experiment which, characteristically, he refused to regard as a failure; 'A Brief Account of the Moreville Communitorium', *The Communist Chronicle,* 6 [1844], pp.83–4.

    In a later article about model communities (Orbiston, Ralahine, Motherwell, Tytherley) he shows fewer inhibitions in this respect and admits quite openly, 'it now fully appears that such efforts, when contemplating self-support, are, in the present unprepared state of public opinion, ineligible as to means; and, therefore, futile and injurious to the cause which they would endeavour to serve.' *The Communist Chronicle,* 15 [1845], p.153.

49. *The Promethean,* 3 (March 1842).

50. 'An Essay Towards Philanthropic Philology', *The Promethean,* 1 (January 1842), pp.15–18.

51. See 'Declaration in Favour of Electoral Reform' which is signed, among others, by the two Barmbys, *The Promethean,* 1 (January 1842), p. 14; and Catherine Barmby, 'The Demand for the Emancipation of Woman. Politically and Socially', in *New Tracts for the Times,* vol. I, no. 3 (London, n. d. [1842]), of which there is also a facsimile in Barbara Taylor, *Eve and the New Jerusalem. Socialism and Feminism in the Nineteenth Century* (London, 1983).

52. R. G. Garnett, *Co-operation and the Owenite Socialist Communities in Britain, 1825–1845* (Manchester, 1972), pp. 218, 236.

53. Hubertus Schulte Herbrüggen, *Utopie und Anti-Utopie. Von der Strukturanalyse zur Strukturtypologie* (Bochum, 1960), *passim.*

54. Sargent, *op. cit.,* quotes another work from the 1820s which is set into the future: [John Baines], *Revelations of the Dead-Alive* (London, 1824).

55. The relevant passage is contained not in one of the utopian sketches but in *The End of Oppression* (1795), Avero edition, pp.36–7; Spokesman edition, p. 95.

56. *A Voyage*, p.190.
57. *The Life of Robert Owen*, vol. 1, p. 227. The incident which Owen relates here—having taken part in a discussion during a coach journey he is at first mistaken for Spence—occurred around 1819.
58. *Hampden in the Nineteenth century* (London, 1834), vol. 1.
59. *The Communist Chronicle*, 12 [1844], p.134.
60. Werner Hofmann, *Ideengeschichte der sozialen Bewegungen des 19. und 20. Jahrhunderts* (West Berlin, 1971), p.75 (my translation—HGK).
61. *The Coming Race, The Novels and Romances of Edward Bulwer Lytton* (New York, 1897), vol. 23, p.435.

Chapter 3: The historical bent of the Chartist novel

1. J. F. C. Harrison and Dorothy Thompson, *Bibliography of the Chartist Movement* (Sussex, 1978), p.xi (my emphasis—HGK). I would like to acknowledge the help of Michael McColgan in preparing the English version of this chapter.
2. Martha Vicinus, *The Industrial Muse: A Study of Nineteenth-Century British Working-Class Literature* (London, 1974), p.94.
3. Of the works discussed below only *Political Pilgrim's Progress* was reprinted in book form (Newcastle, 1839). Ernest Jones had his *Woman's Wrongs*, first serialised in *Notes to the People* (1851–2), republished as *Women's Wrongs. A Series of Tales* (London, 1855), and an altered version of his *The Romance of a People*, from *The Labourer* (1847–8), saw the light again as *The Maid of Warsaw, or the Tyrant Czar* (London, 1854).
4. 'A People's Paper', *Notes to the People*, II (1852), p.753.
5. 'Preface', *The Labourer*, I (1847), no page numbers. This probably comes from the pen of Ernest Jones, the editor. 'Our Last Circular', *The Chartist Circular*, II, no. 146, 9 July 1842 (editor: William Thomson).
6. I have consulted *The Northern Star, The Chartist Circular, The English Chartist Circular, Reynolds Political Instructor, The National, The Northern Liberator, The Labourer, Notes to the People, The Democratic Review, MacDoualls Chartist Journal and Trades Advocate, The Red Republican, The Friend of the People*, and *The Northern Tribune*. Details about these papers and journals in Harrison and Thompson, *op. cit.*

188 *Notes to pages 50 to 56*

7. Dedication to Feargus O'Connor prefacing ch. I, *The Northern Star*, 31 March 1849.
8. Louis James, *Fiction for the Working Man* (Harmondsworth, 1974), p.86.
9. See Horst Rößler, 'Literatur und politische Agitation im Chartismus. Eine Studie zu Thomas Doubledays *Political Pilgrim's Progress', Englisch Amerikanische Studien*, III (1981), pp. 108–21. The work was serialised in *The Northern Liberator* from 19 January to 30 March 1839.
10. *The Pioneers* was serialised in *The Chartist Circular*, II, from 21 May (no. 139) to 9 July 1842 (no. 146). The quotation is from 28 May 1842 (no. 140).
11. *ibid*. 9 July 1842 (no. 146).
12. See Elizabeth Gaskell, *Mary Barton. A Tale of Manchester Life* (London, 1848), esp. chs. I–X.
13. 'Preface', *Notes to the People*, I (1851), p.20; ch. XXXVII, *The Northern Star*, 5 January 1850 (my emphasis—HGK).
14. Martha Vicinus, 'Chartist fiction and the development of a class-based literature', in H. Gustav Klaus, ed., *The Socialist Novel in Britain* (Brighton, 1982), pp.9–10; Jack Mitchell, 'Aesthetic Problems of the Development of the Proletarian-Revolutionary Novel in Nineteenth-Century Britain', in David Craig ed., *Marxists on Literature* (Harmondsworth, 1975),
    p. 257.
15. R. G. Gammage, *History of the Chartist Movement* (London, 1969 [1854]) pp.361–6; Vicinus, 'Chartist fiction', pp.19, 25. But see John Saville, *Ernest Jones: Chartist* (London, 1952), pp.251–5 who categorically denies any such claim and argues in my view convincingly that 'by no stretch of imagination can O'Connor be identified with the character of Simon de Brassier' (p.253). Peculiarly enough, if there are any parallels to be drawn between De Brassier and a real-life Chartist leader, then Jones himself comes nearest. Descending from an aristocratic family, he was initially a thoroughgoing conservative and joined the Chartist movement only after a financial disaster in 1845–6. cf. *Diary of Ernest Jones, 1839–47, Our History*, Pamphlet 21 (1961).
16. Mitchell, *op. cit.* p.256.
17. Ch. XXXVII, *The Northern Star*, 5 January 1850.
18. Kingsley started writing his novel at about the same time as Wheeler, early in 1849. Jones was then still in prison.
19. cf. the opening lines of Jones's poem 'We Are Silent':

We are dead, and we are buried!

Revolution's soul is tame!
They are merry o'er our ashes,
And our tyrants rule the same!

The following verses 'But the Resurrection's coming/As the Resurrection came', with their religious overtones, seem to affirm an unshakeable belief rather than actually refute the prevalent note of dejection. (*Notes to the People*, I, 1851, p. 92.)

20. See, for instance, his *The Rise, Progress and Phases of Human Slavery*, serialised in *Reynolds Political Instructor*, I (1850), later reprinted in book form (London, 1885).
21. Ch. XXXVII, *The Northern Star*, 5 January 1850.
22. Ernest Jones, *The Romance of a People, The Labourer*, II (1847), p.12. However, this work is still very much a blend of romance and older historical novel. Its theme is not English history, but scenes from the Polish freedom struggles.
23. Ch. VIII, *The Northern Star*, 26 May 1849; see also ch. XXVII, 6 October 1849.
24. Raymond Williams, 'Forms of English Fiction', in Francis Barker *et al.* eds., *1848: The Sociology of Literature* (Essex, 1978), p.279.
25. See note 7.
26. The following arguments are summed up and criticised by Mitchell, *op. cit.* pp.245–6.
27. *ibid.* p.265.
28. Ashraf, *Englische Arbeiterliteratur*, p.23 (my translation—HGK).
29. Until some publisher undertakes to bring out these Chartist novels, there remains for study in class the problem of inaccessibility, though it is not really insurmountable. Most university libraries will have a copy of the 1968 reprint of Ernest Jones's *Notes to the People*. And it is always possible to order individual photostats from the British Museum Newspaper Library in Colindale, which has a file of *The Northern Star* (in the case of Wheeler's novel).

Chapter 4: Forms of miners' literature in the nineteenth century

1. Mention must be made of the pioneering chapter on the literature of the early nineteenth-century coalminers' unions in

Martha Vicinus, *The Industrial Muse: A Study of Nineteenth-
Century British Working-Class Literature* (London, 1974),
pp.60–93. And to this has lately been added John Field, 'The
Archetypal Proletarian as Author. The literature of the British Coalfields, 1919–1939', typescript (1981). However, both
studies cover only a period of some twenty years. There is also
a wealth of scattered information, if not always accurate in
detail, in Phyllis Mary Ashraf's *Englische Arbeiterliteratur
vom 18. Jahrhundert bis zum Ersten Weltkrieg* (Berlin, 1980)
which has as yet hardly been used in the English-speaking
world. An English stencilled version of this book is circulated
and used for study courses in the German Democratic
Republic.

2. Edward Chicken, *The Collier's Wedding. A Poem* (Newcastle,
    1778), p.18. This is from the fifth edition. To my knowledge,
    no copy of the first edition of 1730 is extant, but the British
    Library has a copy of the second edition of 1764. A modern-
    ised and badly mutilated version of the poem has been
    included in *The Penguin Book of Everyday Verse. Social and
    Documentary Poetry 1250–1916*, ed. David Wright (Har-
    mondsworth, 1983, pp.309–20.
3. *The Collier's Wedding*, pp.23–9.
4. *ibid*. p.3.
5. A life of the author is provided by William Cail in a new
    edition of 1829. The actual edition is next to worthless as a
    result of the many omissions and emendations through which
    Cail hoped to make the text palatable to the prudish
    nineteenth-century reader.
6. *The Collier's Wedding*, p.5.
7. (London, 1755), p.6.
8. Other eighteenth-century poems with allusions to coalmines
    include Thomas Yalden, *To Sir Humphry Mackworth on the
    Mines, late of Sir Carbery Price* (1710) and Richard Jago,
    Edge-Hill (1767). For a discussion of the poems of industry
    see Francis D. Klingender, *Art and the Industrial Revolution*,
    rev. edn. (London, 1968 [1947]), pp.16–21.
9. See above, chapter one.
10. Printed in *British Parliamentary Papers: Children's Employ-
    ment Commission (Mines)*, vol. 7 (London, 1842), p.385.
11. The *Letter* is mentioned in 'Observations on the Laws Relat-
    ing to the Colliers in Scotland' (for the full title see below,
    section 'Pamphlets'), which was first published in the *Glasgow
    Courier* for April 1799, according to a pamphlet of 1825
    which reprints the 'Observations' and adds 'a few reflections

on the present relative state of the colliers & coal-masters' (Glasgow, 1825), pp.19,44. The latter pamphlet is also available as a reprint in *Repeal of the Combination Acts. Five Pamphlets and One Broadside* (New York, 1972).

12. E. P. Thompson, 'The Crime of Anonymity' in Douglas Hay *et al.*, *Albion's Fatal Tree* (Harmondsworth, 1977), p.255.
13. Quoted from *ibid*.
14. Quoted from Richard Fynes, *The Miners of Northumberland and Durham* (Menston, 1971 [1873]), p.21.
15. Ashraf, *op. cit.* p.88.
16. A number of Chartist speeches have been analysed by Martha Vicinus in her article ' "To Live Free or Die": the Relationship Between Strategy and Style in Chartist Speeches, 1838–1839', *Style*, 10 (1976), pp.481–503.
17. In his research on the South Wales strike of 1816 David J. V. Jones does not seem to have come across reproductions of speeches (*Before Rebecca,* London, 1973). But Alan B. Campbell mentions in his *The Lanarkshire Miners* (Edinburgh, 1979), p.55, the existence of an incomplete draft of address by the Ayrshire Colliers' Committee, found in the possession of a union organiser who was arrested in 1817. The best documented struggle of the first half of the nineteenth century, from the point of view of access to speeches and resolutions, is the great strike in the north-eastern coalfield of 1844. See *The Miners' Advocate* and Fynes, *op. cit. passim*. The latter paraphrases also some of Thomas Hepburn's speeches of 1831–2.
18. I have not seen the Scottish *Colliers' and Miners' Journal* (founded 1842), which can lay a claim to being the first miners' paper in Britain. In fact, it is doubtful whether any of the half-a-dozen issues apparently produced have survived. See Campbell, *op. cit.* pp.250–1.
19. See Robert Colls, 'In Memoriam of Ben Embleton', *New Edinburgh Review*, 32 (1976), pp.17–18.
20. Thomas Cooper, *The Purgatory of Suicides. A Prison Rhyme* (London, 1845), pp.1–3.
21. Thomas Wright, *Grainger's Thorn* (London, 1872), pp.88–92 for Harrison's, the strike-leader's, speech; pp. 97–101 for Grainger's address.
22. Published (Glasgow, 1825) and (Newcastle, 1825) respectively. Both are reprinted in *Repeal of the Combination Acts.*
23. *A Voice from the Coal Mines* (South Shields, 1825), pp.6–7. Reprinted in *Repeal of the Combination Acts.*
24. *Observations on the Laws Relating to the Colliers in Scotland,*

quoted from the 1825 reprint mentioned in note 11, pp.32–3, 39, 41.

25. cf. R. Page Arnot, *A History of the Scottish Miners from the Earliest Times* (London, 1955), p.12.

26. *Brief Observations in Reply to 'A Voice from the Coal Mines'* (Newcastle, 1825) and *A Defence of 'A Voice from the Coal Mines'* (Newcastle, 1825).

27. *An Appeal to the Public, from the Pitmen of the Tyne and Wear* (Newcastle, n.d. [1832]), p.7. Reprinted in *Labour Disputes in the Mines. Eight Pamphlets 1831–1844* (New York, 1972).

28. 'The Miners' Catechism', quoted from Vicinus, *The Industrial Muse,* pp.76–7.

29. For a biographical account see the anonymously written 'Thomas Wilson, Author of the "Pitman's Pay" ', *The Northern Tribune.* II (1855), pp.52–4. The posthumous edition of *The Pitman's Pay* (London, 1872) also contains a memoir of the author, pp.xv–xxiii.

30. Thomas Wilson, *The Pitman's Pay and Other Poems* (Gateshead, 1843), part second, p.36.

31. *ibid.* part first, p.9.

32. David Wingate, *Annie Weir and Other Poems* (Edinburgh, 1866), p.9.

33. *ibid.* p.16.

34. Ashraf, *op. cit.* p.141 (my translation—HGK). See also the author's discussion of Wingate's verse tales, pp.136–9.

35. For a biographical account see Robert Spence Watson, *Joseph Skipsey. His Life and Work* (London, 1909).

36. Joseph Skipsey, *Songs and Lyrics. Collected and Revised* (London, 1892), p.8.

37. cf., for example, James C. Welsh's introduction to his *Songs of a Miner* (London, 1917), p.12; Frederick C. Boden, *Pit-Head Poems* (London, 1927), p.xi (a note on the author by Guy N. Pocock).

38. Two modern discussions of Skipsey's poetry are Vicinus, *The Industrial Muse,* pp.155–8; and Basil Bunting's preface to his choice of the author's verse: Joseph Skipsey, *Selected Poems* (Sunderland, 1976), pp.7–14.

39. *Children's Employment Commission (Mines),* vol. 7, pp.675–6 (no. 508).

40. *ibid.* p.250 (no. 107).

41. *ibid.* p.58 (no. 116).

42. 'Report of J. R. Leifchild', *ibid.* pp.514–15.

43. Reprinted 1856 and London, 1968.

44. Fynes, *op. cit.* p.v.
45. For Mayhew see E. P. Thompson and Eileen Yeo, eds., *The Unknown Mayhew. Selections from the* Morning Chronicle *1849–50* (London, 1971).
46. Miners' songs, though of much older currency, first found their way into print towards the end of the eighteenth century, starting with Joseph Ritson's *The Northumberland Garland, or Newcastle Nightingale* (1793), which contains a version of 'The Collier's Rant'.
47. Edited by A. L. Lloyd.
48. For a list of records see Ian Watson, *Song and Democratic Culture in Britain* (London, 1983), pp.239–43.
49. A L. Lloyd, Introduction to the Second Edition, *Come All Ye Bold Miners* (London, 1978), p.18.
50. David Harker, *One for the Money. Politics and Popular Song* (London, 1980), pp.159–77.
51. Robert Colls, *The Collier's Rant. Song and Culture in the Industrial Village* (London, 1977), p.18.
52. I am grateful to David Vincent for making photostats of these two works available. They were published in Barnsley and Radstock respectively.
53. Published in Rochdale, undated.
54. Rymer's autobiography was first published in Middlesbrough, 1898. A facsimile reprint was made available, complete with an introduction and notes by Robert G. Neville, by *History Workshop Journal*, nos. 1 and 2 (1976). The two quotations are from p.1.
55. cf. David Vincent, *Bread, Knowledge and Freedom. A Study of Nineteenth-Century Working Class Autobiography* (London, 1981), pp.40–6.
56. Vincent has had access to two unpublished manuscripts, one by Anthony Errington, a waggonway-wright, from the early nineteenth century, the other by Emanuel Lovekin from *c.* 1895; *ibid. passim.*
57. Raymond Challinor and Brian Ripley, *The Miner's Association. A Trade Union in the Age of the Chartists* (London, 1968), p.17.
58. Campbell, *op. cit.* p.251.
59. 'The Medical Student', 'The Miners: A Story of the Old Combination Laws', *The New Monthly Magazine* (1844), part three, pp.25–52. See also the collected stories of the author: Robert Douglas, *Adventures of a Medical Student* (London, 1848). This edition carries a 'Sketch of the Author'.
60. G. Wharton Simpson, 'Colliers and Coal Mining', *The Work-*

ing Man's Friend and Family Instructor, VI, no. 74 (31 May 1851); no. 75 (7 June 1851); no. 76 (14 June 1851). The appendix follows in no. 77 (21 June 1851). Kovačević lists this work in the bibliography of her *Fact into Fiction*, (Leicester, 1975), but gives an incorrect date and author.

61. For a biographical account of the author, see the 'Memoir' by Hall Caine added to the posthumously published novel *'Twixt God and Mammon* (London, 1903), pp. v-xxiv.

62. P. J. Keating, *The Working Classes in Victorian Fiction* (London, 1971), p.235. Keating has an interesting discussion of the novel, but his assertion that Tirebuck exaggerated the extent of the coalowners' attack on the miners' wages by speaking of twenty-five per cent is unfounded and needs to be refuted. This was the amount at stake.

63. For Heslop see below, chapter five.

Chapter 5: Harold Heslop: miner novelist

1. Alick West, *Crisis and Criticism* (London, 1937), pp.181–99. The chapter on Heslop is not included in the 1975 reprint of this book.

2. It is disheartening to see that Heslop does not even get as much as a mention in Dave Douglass's otherwise well-informed article 'The Durham Miners', in Raphael Samuel, ed., *Miners, Quarrymen and Saltworkers* (London, 1977), pp.207–95. Nor does he figure in the official history of the Durham Miners' Association by W. R. Garside, *The Durham Miners, 1919–1960* (London, 1971), nor, except for a footnote in R. Colls, *The Collier's Rant. Song and Culture in the Industrial Village* (London, 1977).

3. Letters to the present writer, 17 January 1980, 12 February 1980, and 10 April 1980. Interview with Heslop in March 1980. Since the first separate publication of this chapter an autobiography entitled 'From Tyne to Tone. A Journey', put to paper in the early 1970s, has come to light, which the author, then already suffering from bouts of amnesia, did not mention during our conversation. This work provides a very detailed account of his family background and initiation into work underground, but remains fairly reticent about his early trade-union and political affiliations. Other remarkable parts cover the days at the Central Labour College and the journey to the Soviet Union in 1930. I have used the autobiography to

correct a few factual details. Thanks to Phyllis Heslop for giving me access and to Andy Croft for making it available.

4. *Goaf* (London, 1934), p.7.
5. An exception is *The Earth Beneath*, Heslop's last novel, in which Auckland, South Shields, Durham and Hartley Colliery are explicitly named and the historical figures of O'Connor and Harney (the Chartists), Thomas Hepburn and William Crawford (the miners' leaders) and James Mather (the north-eastern mining expert) introduced.
6. Heslop's review appeared in *The Worker*, 26 September 1930; Colls, *op. cit.* pp.184–91, surveys the contemporary response to Grant's novel.
7. See e.g. his *Troubled Seams* (Seaham, 1955) and *A Wearside Mining Story* (Seaham, 1960), both non-fictional works.
8. Stuart Macintyre, *A Proletarian Science. Marxism in Britain, 1917–1933* (London, 1980), p.85.
9. *The Communist*, III (1928), pp.228–31.
10. *Plebs*, XXI (1929), p.214.
11. *The Gate of a Strange Field* (London, 1929), p.113.
12. *ibid*. pp.231–2, 233.
13. H. G. Wells, *Meanwhile* (London, 1927), p.189.
14. West, *op. cit.* p.197.
15. *The Sunday Worker*, 8 May 1927.
16. *Isvestya*, 14 September 1926; *International Literature*, I (1932), p.99.
17. *Goaf*, pp.124–5.
18. Gore Graham in *The Communist Review*, I (1929), pp. 380–2. This magazine succeeded *The Communist* quoted in note 9. It ran under the original title *The Communist Review* from 1921–6, and was then renamed *The Communist* (1927–8) before continuing under its former name.
19. *International Literature*, I (1932), p.100.
20. *The Worker*, 28 March 1930, 2 May 1930.
21. The idea of a novel removed from the coalpits had been suggested to Heslop by Harold Shaylor, originally an editor for Brentano, but after the failure of this firm a publisher in his own right.
22. *The Worker*, 17 October 1930.
23. cf. for this section Karl Eimermacher, ed., *Dokumente zur sowjetischen Literaturpolitik 1917–1932* (Stuttgart, 1972).
24. *Literature of the World Revolution*, special number (1931), p. 226. This was the forerunner of *International Literature*.
25. Both Rhys Davies and Liam O'Flaherty had earlier published short stories in the avant-garde quarterly *The New Coterie*

(1925–7) which Heslop may well have come across during his stay at the Labour College, for its promoters David Archer and Charles Lahr had a name for selling avant-garde, socialist and anarchist literature in their bookshops in or near Red Lion Square, Holborn.

26. *Literature of the World Revolution* (1931) pp.226–7. cf. the similar treatment of these writers in Heslop's article 'The Working Class and the Novel' in *The Labour Monthly*, XII (1930), pp.689–92, and again in *International Literature*, II (1933), pp.130–1.

27. 'Statement of the English Delegation', *Literature of the World Revolution*, p.122.

28. *Istorija anglijskoj literatury*, vol. III (Moscow, 1958), p.390; quoted from Karl Klaus Walther, 'Zur Entstehung und Geschichte der britishchen Sektion der Internationalen Vereinigung Revolutionärer Schriftsteller (IVRS)', *Zeitschrift für Anglistik und Amerikanistik*, XXII (1974), pp. 7, 16.

29. Letters from Douglas Jefferies to Sergej Dinamov, quoted in 'Iz istorii mezdunarodnogo obedinenija revoljucionnych pisatelej (MORP)', *Literaturnoe nasledstvo*, LXXXI (1969); quoted from Walther, *op. cit.* pp.8, 16.

30. The adoration of Dostoevsky is already apparent in the enthusiastic review of *Crime and Punishment* in *The Worker*, 4 October 1929. In Leningrad Heslop had tried in vain to pay a tribute to the author by visiting his grave. Nobody would help him in his search for it, as Dostoevsky was then regarded as the epitome of an obnoxious pessimistic individualism preaching the acceptance of suffering. Another defamed writer, whom he actually managed to visit in Leningrad, was Zamyatin, author of the influential utopian novel *We*.

31. Dorothy L. Sayers, review of *The Crime of Peter Ropner*, newspaper clip in Heslop's papers; source unidentifiable, though presumably from *The Sunday Times* in which Sayers had a weekly column of detective-story reviews from 1933 to 1935. See Ralph E. Hone, *Dorothy L. Sayers. A Literary Biography* (Kent, Ohio, 1979), pp.78–9.

32. Heslop, whose father was a Primitive Methodist preacher, is another example of the tradition of nonconformity channelled into left-wing socialism, a lineage traced by Raphael Samuel in 'British Marxist Historians, 1880–1980 I', *New Left Review*, 120 (1980).

33. *The Abdication of Edward VII* (London, 1937), p.164.

34. See below, chapter seven.

Chapter 6: Socialist novels of 1936

1. Martha Vicinus in the United States; Mary Ashraf (died 1983), Jack Mitchell and Hanna Behrend in East Germany; Jessie Kocmanová in Czechoslovakia; Ramón López Ortega in Spain; David Smith (not the Welsh historian) in Australia; Ingrid von Rosenberg and myself in West Germany. References to some of their publications *passim* in the notes of this book.

2. Quoted from Andy Croft's introduction to the reprint of Walter Brierley's *Means-Test Man* (Nottingham, 1983), p.vii. This is also the source for the earlier mentioned evidence for Brierley; for Heslop consult chapter five.

3. cf. my introduction to *The Socialist Novel in Britain*, (Brighton, 1982), pp.1–4.

4. cf. H. Gustav Klaus, *Caudwell im Kontext. Zu einigen repräsentativen Literaturformen der dreißiger Jahre* (Frankfurt, 1978), pp.38–55.

5. Some of these historical novels are discussed by David Smith in his *Socialist Propaganda in the Twentieth-Century Novel* (London, 1978), pp.102–10.

6. Three novels of 1936, which look back to the General Strike, constitute another interesting family of works: Storm Jameson, *None Turn Back;* Gwyn Jones, *Times like These*; Leslie Paul, *Men in May.*

7. cf. H. Gustav Klaus, 'Socialist Fiction in the 1930s: Some preliminary observations', in John Lucas, ed., *The 1930s. A Challenge to Orthodoxy* (Hassocks, 1978), pp.13–41, esp. pp.38–41. See also Andy Croft's more recent and more exhaustive bibliographical essay 'Socialist Novels from the 1930's', *Marx Memorial Library Bulletin*, 101 (1982), pp.8–12.

8. Ralph Bates, 'My Friend, Ralph Fox', in John Lehmann *et al.*, eds., *Ralph Fox. A Writer in Arms* (London, 1937), pp.8–9. See also Fox's remarks about Bates's novels in *The Novel and the People* (London, 1937), pp.112, 114–15.

9. Further biographical information in Alan Young, *Seven Writers of the English Left. A Bibliography of Literature and Politics, 1916–1980* (New York, 1981), pp.83–5. See also the fictionalised but partly autobiographical 'Précis of a Bolshevik biography' of the protagonist in *Lean Men* (Harmondsworth, 1938), pp.12–15, and Bates's last autobiographical novel *The Dolphin in the Wood* (New York, 1950).

10. In reply to this criticism the author has made the following interesting comment: 'You speak of a certain ambiguity, at the close of The Olive Field expressed in Caro's return to Los Olivares. The ambiguity is, as the book stands, apparent, but there was none in my mind. As I drew near to the close I came to believe that a second volume was necessary. The second volume was planned and one chapter was written, but then came the Civil War and I had other things to do. When after the passage of the war years I began to write again I found that the second novel about Los Olivares was beyond my courage to write.' And he adds that the theme was later taken up in *The Fields of Paradise* (New York, 1940) which is, however, set in Mexico. Ralph Bates, letter to the present writer, 8 June 1979.

    That Bates was not quite happy with *The Olive Field* as it came from the press in March 1936 is understandable when one learns that owing to his deep involvement in the turmoil leading up to the Civil War he had neither seen the typescript (produced from his handwritten manuscript) from which it was set nor found the time to correct the proofs. Cf. Stanley Weintraub, *The Last Great Cause* (London, 1968), pp.291–2. Bates used the occasion of the 1966 New York reprint to revise and correct the novel.

11. Mulk Raj Anand, *The Coolie* (London, 1936), p.285.

12. A longer discussion of *The Coolie* and some critical comments about the revisions Anand made for the 1972 reprint of the novel can be found in H. Gustav Klaus, 'Zum Beispiel *Coolie*. Ein Vorschlag zur Einbeziehung indo-englischer Romane in die englische Literatur des 20. Jahrhunderts', *Germanisch-Romanische Monatsschrift*, 28 (1978), pp.453–67.

13. 'Mulk Raj Anand Comments', in James Vinson ed., *Contemporary Novelists* (London, 1972), p.50. Anand is the only one of the four writers considered here who has received a fair amount of critical attention. The best studies are by M. K. Naik, *Mulk Raj Anand* (New York, 1973), and Saros Cowasjee, *So Many Freedoms. A Study of the Major Fiction of Mulk Raj Anand* (Oxford, 1978).

14. Georg Lukács, 'Narrate or Describe?', in his *Writer and Critic* (London, 1978), pp.134–5 (transl. Arthur Kahn).

15. cf. chapter seven.

16. John Sommerfield, *May Day* (London, 1936), p.30.

17. *ibid.* p.79. In the novel the passage is set in italics.

18. *ibid.* p.133.

19. John Saville, 'May Day 1937', in Asa Briggs and John Saville,

eds., *Essays in Labour History, 1918–1939* (London, 1977), p.234.

20. For a biographical account see Andy Croft, 'Returned Volunteer. The Novels of John Sommerfield', *London Magazine*, April/May 1983, pp.61–70; and the author's semi-fictional memoir *The Imprinted* (London, 1978).
21. James Barke, *Major Operation* (London, 1936), pp.126–7.
22. *ibid*. p.128. For a discussion of Barke's style see Ramón López Ortega, 'The Language of the Working-Class Novel of the 1930s', in Klaus, ed., *The Socialist Novel in Britain*, pp.130–1.
23. Jack Mitchell, 'The Struggle for the Working-Class Novel in Scotland 1900–1939', *Zeitschrift für Anglistik und Amerikanistik*, XXI (1973), p.410.
24. Robert Bonnar, 'James Barke—A True Son of the Soil', in *Essays in honour of William Gallacher* (Berlin, 1966), p.189. See also the author's autobiography *The Green Hills Far Away* (London, 1940).
25. See Lucien Goldmann, *Towards a Sociology of the Novel* (London, 1975), *passim*.
26. 'Sunshine and Shadow', ch. XVIII, *The Northern Star*, 4 August 1849. cf. chapter three on the Chartist novel.
27. The three Marxist quotations are from the *Eighteenth Brumaire* (Sommerfield) and the *Anti-Dühring* (Barke and 'Freedom . . . necessity') respectively.
28. E. P. Thompson, *The Poverty of Theory* (London, 1978), p.264.
29. Bertolt Brecht, 'Übergang vom bürgerlichen zum sozialistischen Realismus', *Gesammelte Werke*, vol. 19 (Frankfurt, 1975), p.377 (my translation—HGK).

Chapter 7: Let the people speak for themselves: on the documentarism of the 1930s and 1940s

1. Walter Benjamin, 'The Work of Art in the Age of Mechanical Reproduction', in his *Illuminations*, ed. Hanna Arendt (London, 1973), p.234 (transl. Harry Zohn).
2. cf. for example Gary Werskey, *The Visible College* (London, 1978), *passim;* H. Gustav Klaus, *Caudwell im Kontext,*

(Frankfurt, 1978), pp.38–55; Francis Mulhern, *The Moment of 'Scrutiny'* (London, 1979), pp.7–10, 318–23.

3. William Stott, *Documentary Expression and Thirties America* (New York, 1973), p.x. No similar large-scale investigation exists as yet for Britain, but see the brief informative 'Descriptive Chronology' of the evolution of documentarism by David Mellor in Humphrey Spender, *Worktown. Photographs of Bolton and Blackpool Taken for Mass Observation 1937/38* (Brighton, 1977).

4. *Grierson on Documentary,* ed. Forsyth Hardy (London, 1966), p.18.

5. Tom Harrisson, Humphrey Jennings and Charles Madge, letter to *The New Statesman and Nation,* 30 January 1937.

6. Paul Rotha, *Documentary Film,* second edn. (London, 1939), p.146.

7. Tom Harrisson, *Britain Revisited* (London, 1961), p.26.

8. Sergej Tretjakow, 'Fortsetzung folgt', in his *Lyrik Dramatik Prosa* (Leipzig, 1972), pp.209–10 (my translation—HGK).

9. Storm Jameson, 'Documents', *Fact* 4: *Writing in Revolt* (1937), pp.17–18.

10. Stuart Hall, 'The Social Eye of Picture Post', *Working Papers in Cultural Studies,* 2 (1972), pp.95–6.

11. cf. Paul Addison, *The Road to 1945* (London, 1977), p.131.

12. cf. Tom Wintringham, *New Ways of War* (Harmondsworth, 1940), pp.122–8.

13. *Grierson on Documentary,* ed. Forsyth Hardy, p.143.

14. Paul Rotha, *Documentary Diary* (London, 1973), p.38.

15. Two modern-city films were also of considerable influence: Alberto Cavalcanti's *Rien que les heures* (1926, about Paris) and Walther Ruttmann's *Berlin. Symphonie einer Großstadt* (1927), though the latter came under attack from Grierson.

16. *Grierson on Documentary,* p.13; Rotha, *Documentary Film,* motto of the book.

17. Alan Lovell and Jim Hillier, *Studies in Documentary* (London, 1972), p.78.

18. Stuart Hood rightly points out that Jennings 'has no place in his picture [*A Diary for Timothy*] for the strikes which in 1944 brought out a hundred thousand miners in Wales and more in Yorkshire; nothing to say about the regulations penalising "unofficial" strikers with heavy fines or prison sentences'. 'A Cool Look at the Legend', in Eva Orbanz, ed., *Journey to a Legend and Back* (West Berlin, 1977), p.149. For a different view see the critical statements contained in Anthony W. Hodgkinson and Rodney E. Sheratsky, *Hump-*

hrey Jennings—More than a Maker of Films (Hanover, USA, 1982), pp.75–6.

19. *Grierson on Documentary,* p.135.
20. Quoted from Rotha, *Documentary Diary,* p.48.
21. Rotha, *ibid.* p.61; Richard M. Barsam, *Non-Fiction Film. A Critical History* (New York, 1973), p.51.
22. Rotha, *Documentary Film,* p.122.
23. Lovell in Lovell and Hillier, *op. cit.* pp.9–36.
24. *Grierson on Documentary,* p.140. For more information on Grierson see Forsyth Hardy, *John Grierson. A Documentary Biography* (London, 1981).
25. cf. for this oppositional tradition Bert Hogenkamp, *Workers' Newsreels in the 1920's and 1930's, Our History,* Pamphlet 68 (n.d.); Victoria Wegg-Prosser, 'The Archive of the Film and Photo League', *Sight and Sound,* 46 (1977), pp.245–7; Trevor Ryan, 'Film and Political Organisations in Britain 1929–39', in Don Macpherson, ed., *Traditions of Independence. British Cinema in the Thirties* (London, 1980), pp.51–69.
26. Figures based on the filmography contained in Macpherson, ed., *op. cit.* pp.213–24; and on John Grierson, 'Censorship and the Documentary', *World Film News,* III (1938), p.304.
27. In 1936 Kino claimed to have provided screenings of its films for over a quarter of a million people within the preceeding twelve months. Ralph Bond, 'Cinema in the Thirties: Documentary Film and the Labour Movement', in Jon Clark *et al.,* eds., *Culture and Crisis in the Thirties* (London, 1979), p.249. By contrast, the documentaries on loan from the EMB Film Library reached 4.7 million people the same year. Cf. Rolf Reemtsen, 'Die englische Dokumentarfilmschule in den dreißiger Jahren', unpubl. Ph.D. dissertation (Cologne, 1976), p.54.
28. *Grierson on Documentary,* p.140.
29. Interview with Stuart Legg in Elizabeth Sussex, *The Rise and Fall of the British Documentary* (London, 1975), pp.80–1.
30. During the War some of the publicly screened documentaries had an audience of as many as twenty million people, *ibid.* p.160.
31. Klaus Wildenhahn, *Über synthetischen und dokumentarischen Film* (Frankfurt, 1975), pp.98, 121.
32. See the catalogue of the exhibition *The Real Thing* (London, 1975) and the brief survey in Roland Günter, *Fotografie als Waffe. Zur Geschichte und Ästhetik der Sozialfotografie* (Reinbek, 1982), pp.108–11.

33. cf. John Willett's informative account *The New Sobriety. Art and Politics in the Weimar Period, 1917–33* (London, 1978).
34. While in Germany, Hoppé produced the volume *Deutsche Arbeit. Bilder vom Wiederaufstieg Deutschlands* (Berlin, 1930). This work focuses not on working men and women but celebrates in a quasi-reified way the achievements of modern industrial technology. The people who built the constructions or work the machines are either absent (in the majority of cases) or remain in the background, vague figures with little individuality.
35. See the interview with Humphrey Spender in *Camerawork*, 11 (1978), pp.6–7, and the modest catalogue of his 1981–2 touring exhibition *The Thirties and After*.
36. Bill Brandt, *The English at Home* (London, 1936), pp.57–8. The anthropological note and the social message of the book were further emphasised by Raymond Mortimer's introduction. It is interesting to note that the rightly famous 'Miners Returning to Daylight', which is included in the volume (*ibid*. p.15), dates from as early as 1933. See the exhibition catalogue *Bill Brandt. Early Photographs 1930–1942* (London, 1975).
37. For the history of *Picture Post* cf. Tom Hopkinson, ed., *Picture Post 1938–50* (Harmondsworth, 1970), and his autobiography *Of This Our time. A Journalist's Story, 1905–50* (London, 1982).
38. Hall, *op. cit.*
39. 'Manifesto of the Workers' Film and Photo League' (1934), quoted from Ryan, *op. cit.* p.56.
40. *Camerawork*, 19 (1980), pp.2–4. See also Tudor-Hart's photographs in Margery Rice, *Working-Class Wives* (Harmondsworth, 1939, repr. 1981).
41. E. Wight Bakke, *The Unemployed Man* (London, 1933), p.xiv. Despite his sympathies for those hit by unemployment it is striking how much time the author spends in demonstrating that they remain immune to radical and, especially, Communist propaganda.
42. *ibid*. pp.69–70.
43. H. L. Beales and.R. S. Lambert, eds., *Memoirs of the Unemployed* (London, 1934), p.13.
44. Paddy Scannell, who documents the controversy, reports the producer Felix Greene as emphasising that nothing was deleted or altered that the speakers wished to say, 'Broadcasting and the politics of unemployment 1930–1935', *Media, Culture and Society*, II (1980), p.20. We had no access to the original broadcasts, but the printed versions, *Time to Spare,*

ed. Felix Greene (London, 1935), retain nothing of whatever working-class accent or dialect the talks might have had.

45. Letter to Jack Common, 20 April 1938, in *The Collected Essays, Journalism and Letters of George Orwell*, eds. Sonia Orwell and Ian Angus (Harmondsworth, 1970), vol. I, p.349. *Seven Shifts* was edited by Common.

46. There is of course another side of the coin. In assuming that the printed word cannot convey a proletarian consciousness, Orwell underrates the possibilities of a socialist literature. One may ask whether this assumption is behind a striking silence in *The Road to Wigan Pier*: the miners are never allowed to speak for themselves.

47. Beales and Lambert, *Memoirs of the Unemployed*, pp.50–1.

48. *Collected Essays, Journalism and Letters*, vol. I, p.83.

49. *ibid*. pp.87, 77, 85, 93, 77. These pages contain examples of the characteristics of Orwell's documentary style given above, in the same order. See also the analysis of Orwell's style in Richard Hoggart, 'George Orwell and *The Road to Wigan Pier*', in his *Speaking to Each Other* (London, 1970), vol. II.

50. cf. Raymond Williams, *Orwell* (London, 1971), p.42.

51. See the comments by Victor Gollancz and Harold Laski reprinted in Jeffrey Meyers, ed., *George Orwell. The Critical Heritage* (London, 1975), but also the reviews by Harry Pollitt ('Mr Orwell Will have to Try Again') in *The Daily Worker*, 17 March 1937, and by Derek Kahn in *Left Review*, III, 3 (1937), pp.186–7.

52. George Orwell, *The Road to Wigan Pier* (London, 1937), p.71. Reference must be made to the first edition, as the current Penguin edition omits the thirty-two photographs of the distressed areas which were obviously an integral part of the documentary appeal of the book.

53. Chris Pawling, 'George Orwell and the Documentary in the Thirties', *Literature and History*, 4 (1976), p.92.

54. *The Road to Wigan Pier, op. cit.* pp.33–4.

55. *ibid*, p.34.

56. cf. '*The Road to Wigan Pier* Diary', in *Collected Essays, Journalism and Letters*, vol. I, pp.194–243.

57. Montagu Slater, *Stay Down Miner* (London, 1936), p.18.

58. See his article 'The Purpose of a *Left Review*', *Left Review*, I, 9 (1935), pp.359–65. Slater's dramatic version of the events, performed and published under the title of *New Way Wins* (London, 1936), is an altogether more successful effort. The play has been reprinted as 'Stay Down Miner' in John Lucas, ed., *The 1930s* (Hassocks, 1978), pp.201–64.

59. *Stay Down Miner*, pp.75–6.

60. Edited by Frank Galton (1893) and Margaret A. Pollock (1926) respectively.
61. *Left Review*, I, 1 (1934), p.40.
62. 'Contributors' Conference', *Left Review*, I, 9 (1935), pp.367–8.
63. *Left Review*, I, 4 (1935), p.129.
64. *ibid*.
65. *ibid*.
66. Other documentary sketches, outside the writing competitions, include Brian O'Neill's 'Dublin Strike Episode', *Left Review*, I, 9 (1935), pp.339–40, and a number of pieces about Spain.
67. Coombes published also in *New Writing* and *Picture Post* and could be heard on the wireless. On this author see Jenni Calder, *Chronicles of Conscience* (London, 1968), and David Smith, 'Underground Man: The Work of B. L. Coombes, "Miner Writer" ', *The Anglo-Welsh Review*, 24 (1974), pp.10–25.
68. See above, chapter six, and the two bibliographies of socialist novel-writing in the 1930s quoted in note 7 of that chapter.
69. Wolfgang Emmerich, ed., *Proletarische Lebensläufe* (Reinbek, 1974), vol. I, pp.23–4.
70. *The New Statesman and Nation*, 16 May 1936.
71. Stuart Laing, 'Presenting "Things as They Are": John Sommerfield's *May Day* and Mass-Observation", in Frank Gloversmith, ed., *Class, Culture and Social Change. A New View of the 1930s* (Sussex, 1980), p.149.
72. For a more extended treatment of *May Day* see above, chapter six.
73. Gisèle Freund, *Memoiren des Auges* (Frankfurt, 1977), p.19 (my translation—HGK).
74. See also the interpretation of *Goodbye to Berlin* in Samuel Hynes, *The Auden Generation* (London, 1976), pp.355–9.
75. Harrisson, *Britain Revisited*, p.17.
76. Charles Madge, letter to *The New Statesman and Nation*, 2 January 1937.
77. Charles Madge and Tom Harrisson, *Mass-Observation* (London, 1937), p.48.
78. The last two quotations are from Harrisson, *Britain Revisited*, pp.26, 25.
79. *The Pub and the People. A Worktown Study by Mass-Observation* (London, 1943), p.11.
80. Moreover, Madge, Jennings and Empson had been pupils of I. A. Richards at Cambridge.

81. Charles Madge and Tom Harrisson eds., *First Year's Work by Mass-Observation* (London, 1938), p.7.
82. Tom Harrisson, Humphrey Jennings and Charles Madge, letter to *The New Statesman and Nation,* 30 January 1937.
83. Harrisson, *Britain Revisited,* contains an extensive list of M-O publications and reports files. For the further development of M-O see Tom Jeffrey, *Mass-Observation—A Short History,* stencilled occasional paper 55 (1978), Centre for Contemporary Cultural Studies, Birmingham.
84. Photographs by Humphrey Spender and Michael Wickham, and drawings by Julian Trevelyan, can be found in *The Pub and the People* and *Britain Revisited.* |See also Spender, *Worktown,* and *Camerawork,* 11 (1978).
85. Madge and Harrison, *First Year's Work,* pp.63–79.
86. The two Living Newspapers performed by London Unity Theatre, *Busmen* and *Crisis,* are discussed by Reiner Lehberger, *Das sozialistische Theater in England 1934 bis zum Ausbruch des Zweiten Weltkriegs* (Frankfurt, 1977), pp.147–58. See also Don Watson, '*Busmen*: Documentary and British political theatre in the 1930s', *Media, Culture and Society,* IV (1981), pp.339–50.
87. Ewan MacColl, 'Grass Roots of Theatre Workshop', *Theatre Quarterly,* III (1973), pp.65–6.
88. T. H. Hawkins and L. J. F. Brimble, *Adult Education. The Record of the British Army* (London, 1947), p.171.
89. *ibid.* p.172. For ABCA see also Robert Hewison, *Under Siege. Literary Life in London 1939–1945* (London, 1977), pp.162–3; Andrew Davies, 'A Theatre for the People's Army? The Story of the ABCA Play Unit', *Red Letters,* 13 (1982), pp.35–8.
90. Addison, *op. cit.* p.148.
91. Asa Briggs, *The History of Broadcasting in the United Kingdom* (London, 1970), vol. II, p.168.
92. *ibid.* pp.35, 51, 54.
93. At this point we contradict William Stott who counts the radio reports of Ed Murrow, London correspondent of CBS, as a documentary form. Cf. *Documentary Expression and Thirties America,* pp.84–6.
94. MacColl, *op. cit.* p.67; John Pudney, *Home and Away, An Autobiographical Gambit* (London, 1960), p.96.
95. For the AIA and the Euston Road School see Donald Drew Egbert, *Social Radicalism and the Arts. Western Europe* (New York, 1970), pp.506–8.
96. See the catalogue of the Nottingham exhibition *James Boswell*

1906–71. Drawings, Illustrations and Paintings (Nottingham, 1976), and the photographs of Boswell's work in Lucas, *The 1930s.*

97. William Feaver, 'Die Bergarbeiter von Ashington', in the exhibition catalogue *Englische Arbeiterkunst* (West Berlin, 1977), pp.61–2 (my translation—HGK). Feaver also mentions the visit of Tom Harrisson to Ashington in 1938.

INDEX

From the notes only those names have been indexed which were previously referred to in the text. Page numbers in **bold type** indicate substantial discussion.